ƒIELD oƒ BONES
AN IRISH DIVISION AT GALLIPOLI

for Jon, Elly, Tim and Simon

FIELD OF BONES

AN IRISH DIVISION AT GALLIPOLI

PHILIP ORR

And he said unto me, Son of Man,
can these bones live? And I answered,
O Lord God, thou knowest

EZEKIEL 37:3

Forgetting … is a crucial factor in the
creation of a nation

ERNEST RENAN

THE LILLIPUT PRESS

First published 2006 by
The Lilliput Press
62–63 Sitric Road, Arbour Hill
Dublin 7, Ireland
www.lilliputpress.ie

Copyright © Philip Orr, 2006

ISBNS 1 84351 065 0 and (after Jan. 2007) 978 1 85431 065 9

A CIP record for this title is available
from The British Library.

10 9 8 7 6 5 4 3 2 1

Set in pt Minion. Cover design, text design and typesetting
by Graham Thew Design.

Printed in England by MPG Books, Bodmin, Cornwall

CONTENTS

PREFACE: A NOTE ON FORM AND METHODOLOGY   vii

ACKNOWLEDGMENTS   xi

1 THE QUEST 1915–2006   1

2 VOLUNTEERS . . . . .AUGUST 1914–APRIL 1915   8

3 VOYAGERS . . . . .APRIL–AUGUST 1915   36

4 INVADERS . . . . AUGUST 1915   66

5 WARRIORS . . . . AUGUST 1915   110

6 CASUALTIES . . . . AUGUST–OCTOBER 1915   138

7 VICTIMS . . . . AUGUST 1915–NOVEMBER 1918   180

8 GHOSTS . . . . .NOVEMBER 1918–AUGUST 2006   208

NOTES   247

BIBLIOGRAPHY AND SOURCES   259

INDEX   263

PREFACE: A NOTE ON FORM AND METHODOLOGY

As I tried to understand the 10th Irish Division's experience of the Great War of 1914–1918, and the subsequent neglect of this significant piece of modern Irish history, I set myself four main objectives.

Firstly, I wanted to uncover those historical sources in which the story of Irish volunteer soldiers at Gallipoli might once more come to light. This meant searching for official military accounts of the campaigns fought by the division, especially within the British National Archive. There were plentiful newspaper archives to examine, both in Ireland and Britain and also unofficial diaries, photographs, maps, letters, scrapbooks and journals, in archives within Irish regimental museums and the Imperial War Museum in London. I aspired to find the few short personal accounts by veterans – or their friends – printed in limited editions, during or just after the war years. In due course I hoped to interview some of those Irishmen and women whose fathers and grandfathers fought with the 10th Division and who might still recall the impact on their families of the Dardanelles tragedy.

Second, I decided to focus not so much on intricate details of army strategy or the military 'hardware' of the battle as on the experiences of the men themselves. I sought the telling anecdotes and the honest, vivid descriptions to convey the psychological intensity of soldiering and the excruciating physical hardship and damage of the battlefield. If at all possible, I wished to discover what Irishness meant, as inspiration and consolation, to these men who found themselves as beleaguered Great War volunteers on the other side of Europe from their island home. I knew that this would assist with the power and focus of the emerging narrative.

Thirdly, it seemed important to indicate why the 10th Irish Division was so swiftly forgotten. Two chapters are devoted to the 'afterlife' of the Gallipoli story: one devoted to the experience of the survivors of Gallipoli throughout the rest of the Great War, particularly in light of revolutionary developments in Ireland during the war years; the other to study the way in which this battle disappeared from Irish national memory after 1918 while, by contrast, surviving and indeed thriving in the cultural life of two other Gallipoli combatant nations, Turkey and Australia.

Finally, it was important to choose the right literary form. The picture that sprang to mind was of the British Graves Registration Unit making its first search of the Gallipoli battlefields after the Armistice. The workers were confronted with the chaotic fragments of a battle fought three years earlier: broken bones and personal possessions scattered across a scarred landscape. Their task was to gather these remains, make sense of the human 'debris' and begin to assemble a dignified memorial story in the new military cemeteries of the peninsula. It was a job that foreshadowed my own, as I put together a heart-breaking bricolage of human detail, gathered from far and wide throughout the archives. To that end, I decided that the sub-headings in my chapters should be phrases 'gathered' from the nearby 'landscape' of the text, each one a fragment lifted from its narrative context and placed as a marker for further understanding of that part of an unfolding story of military chaos and confusion.

All effective historical narratives need a unifying form, despite an attempt to acknowledge the fragmentation of original material. In *Field of Bones*, I employed the time-honoured form of the quest, for two reasons: primarily to refer to my own search for the hidden story of the 10th Division, but also because the Irish volunteer soldiers of 1915 saw themselves as embarking on a significant journey of discovery and challenge. Some sought to prove their manhood on the field of battle, others to rediscover the martial glory spoken of by Homer and by Virgil. All were saturated in the regimental ethos of the period, which paid its homage to the legendary prowess of the Irishman at war. To understand that quest became my own.

Terminology

By 1915, the British Army consisted of several *corps*, which were divided into four or five *divisions*. A division contained approximately 17,000 men and was dominated by its three infantry *brigades*, each one containing four *battalions*.

Within each battalion, four or five *companies* existed and each company was made up of a number of *platoons*. The smallest unit of all was the *section*, containing merely eight to ten men.

At the top of officer hierarchy, the army was commanded by the *field marshal*. In charge of corps and divisions and brigades were various species of *general*, whilst a battalion was headed by a *lieutenant colonel*, and a company was headed by a *major*, with a *captain* as his second in command . In charge of the platoons were the most junior officers – the *lieutenants*.

Amongst the rank and file, an ambitious and able *private* might hope to rise to *lance-corporal* (one stripe), then *corporal* (two stripes) and then *sergeant* (three stripes). The much-feared *sergeant-majors* were the men in charge of military discipline amongst the rank and file and the *quarter master sergeants* had a key role in looking after their supplies and ammunition.

Infantry battalions within each brigade were recruited from a number of regional regiments, each with their own ethos, regalia and history, such as the Connaught Rangers or the Royal Dublin Fusiliers. Each unit within a division had an official war-diary – a record that the military historian often draws upon, in addition to the personal diaries kept by the men.

It is important to note that the word 'casualties' is not synonymous with 'fatalities' – an army's casualty list commonly included the injured, the sick and those who had 'gone missing' as well as the dead.

ACKNOWLEDGMENTS

To former colleagues and friends at Down High School, I offer my thanks for their support during the writing of this book. Brian Wilson was an invaluable companion and photographer during our research trip to Gallipoli, David Park offered creative suggestions about the way in which the text might be shaped, and Ken Dawson's rich historical insight was a constant source of help. Other academic staff who contributed in various ways included Ed Mitchell, David Donnan, Nigel Martin and Martin Coffey. A mention must also be given to James, Shane and Ross in the ICT department, who helped me complete several complicated tasks involving retrieval and the processing of visual material.

Staff at the Down County Museum deserve credit for their support of this project. Mike King, Madeleine Allen and Linda McKenna were of particular assistance. Elsewhere, Jane Leonard at the Ulster Museum and Craig Mc-Guckian at the Somme Heritage Centre offered valuable help. The staff at three regimental museums all contributed with archival material and expert insight – the Royal Inniskilling Fusilier Museum in Enniskillen, the Royal Irish Fusilier Museum in Armagh and the Royal Ulster Rifles Museum in Belfast. The Local Studies staff of the Linenhall Library in Belfast and the staff in the Public Record Office of Northern Ireland offered assistance. Staff at Killyleagh and Downpatrick libraries were also generously helpful. A particular word of thanks is due to Joe O'Leary junior and Paddy Hand, who assisted with my researches and who did so much to keep their fathers' Gallipoli memories alive long after other veterans had been forgotten.

Among the journalists whose help I wish to acknowledge are Paul Clarke of UTV, Stephen Walker of BBC Northern Ireland and Kevin Myers, formerly of *The Irish Times,* while among the academics who offered generous insight and advice, professors David Livingstone and Keith Jeffery of Queens University

Belfast, Dr Timothy Bowman of University College London and Professor Joe Lee of the University of New York merit particular mention.

Among the friends, acquaintances and interviewees who pointed me in the direction of some historical material or submitted occasional valuable critiques and intelligent support, I include Michael Longley, Jack Duffin, Roy Perry, Chris Clotworthy, John Fairleigh, Tom Egginton, Sam Neill, Charles Cooper, Anne McDermott, Martin Staunton and Sean and Hazel Armstrong. Not to be forgotten are the courteous staff at the Hotel Kum on the Gallipoli peninsula — including our superb taxi driver and guide, Annal, who made the trip to Turkey so very worthwhile.

The staff of the Irish National Museum, the Irish National Library, the Irish National Gallery, the Leopardstown Hospital Trust and The Royal British Legion all offered splendid assistance and I would particularly wish to acknowledge the help provided by Tom Burke of the Royal Dublin Fusiliers Association. Mike Lee was of great help to me during the latter stages of my research, and I was inspired by his work on the topic of the 10th Division at Gallipoli over many years. I would also like to acknowledge in particular the work of Sinead O'Hanlon who acted as my researcher and photographer during the latter stages of the project. Her meticulous and imaginative approach to the task was of infinite value.

In London, I have been indebted to the staff at the Imperial War Museum, the British Library, the National Army Museum and The National Archive. In Cumbria, the help of my sister Rosemary, my brother-in-law Paul and our mutual friend Phyllis Kelly were all of value in tracking down the story of John Hargrave.

It would be a failure in me not to acknowledge the men on whose experience I drew, the veterans who were actually 'there' at Suvla and at Anzac. Some of their names do not appear because their job was to write official diaries and documents or because they were the unofficial, often anonymous photographers of the Gallipoli campaign. Other key witnesses, combatants and scribes in the 10th Division regularly appear in the narrative and many of their personal details may be found within this text. However I must conclude by acknowledging all those who have done so much in recent years to open up the story of the Irish in the Great War. I see myself as part of a growing and dedicated team of people in Ireland who have been striving to recover these memories for the attention of future generations. I salute the tenacity, hard work, skill and devotion shown by all who have been in any way involved in this powerful project.

I
THE QUEST

1915–2006

When Turkish people were being resettled in the new, trouble-torn republic of the 1920s, some families came to the isolated and beautiful northern reaches of the peninsula in European Turkey, which had been known to British Great War soldiers as Gallipoli. They renamed these northern shores 'Kemikli Burnu', the bone-strewn headland. The pitiful pieces of debris that they found there were the partially buried remains of thousands of British and Turkish troops who had perished during the ill-fated military landings at Suvla Bay, which began in August 1915.[1]

Earlier in that summer, the gigantic Cunard passenger liner, the *Mauretania*, had made its way southwards through the Irish Sea, en route for the Straits of Gibraltar. Its sister-ship, the *Lusitania*, was tragically torpedoed in May, whereas the *Mauretania* had been converted for use as a troop carrier in the Great War. It was the winner of the Blue Riband prize for the fastest-ever crossing of the Atlantic Ocean, but now its hull had been painted in the colours of naval camouflage for a zig-zag voyage through the Mediterranean waters, beneath which German submarines were lurking. The *Mauretania* was heading towards Turkey, where a new phase of the campaign to gain possession of the Dardanelles Straits was about to open. Among the British troops on board were men of the 10th (Irish) Division.

In the wake of the *Mauretania* came many more Irish soldiers in smaller steamers, which had been converted from their peacetime roles to the task of ferrying infantry reinforcements towards the Gallipoli Peninsula on the northern shores of the Dardanelles. The 10th Division was 17,000 strong and thus one of the biggest bodies of soldiers ever to leave Irish shores, with men from every county in Ireland as well as every kind of political allegiance. It was in the vanguard of Lord Kitchener's famous New Army of volunteer soldiers and contained some of its earliest recruits. Among the many Irishmen who, down through history, have chosen the life of a soldier, the men of the 10th Division have claim to a special place.

The division left Irish shores buoyed up by a sense of patriotism and destiny. Although wartime Ireland was a volatile place where British rule was a contested issue, in the spring of 1915 the infantry battalions, which made up the biggest part of the division, had marched through the gates of their training camps and headed for Dublin. There, as a single unit, the troops had paraded from their barracks to the quayside through cheering crowds. Regimental bands played Irish airs, and the Union Jack and the flag of St Patrick fluttered from high windows. Three months later, after completing their training in the south of England, they packed their kitbags, put on the wide-brimmed helmets they would need for war in the East and marched to the docks once more.

Few people in the crowd who had watched them march through Dublin or who saw them walk up the gangway to the decks of the *Mauretania* in Liverpool dockyard that summer fully understood that the 10th Division was travelling to a war of brutality, ferocity and deep waste, where Lord Kitchener's young volunteer armies would be mown down by machine-gun fire on the Western Front and where, already, on the far-off beaches and cliff-paths of Gallipoli, troops from the empire had perished.

Even fewer observers in the crowd could have predicted that in leaving these shores, the 10th (Irish) Division would, in a sense, sail right out of history. Within the space of a few decades its name would be forgotten, its exploits publicly unacknowledged, and the motivations, experiences and final destiny of its soldiers enfolded in an enduring silence. Along with the millions of other men who returned from the battlefields of Europe in 1918, demobilized Irishmen came home to a world that had been irrevocably changed. The Irish now stood on the brink of a political revolution that would sweep away much of the structure of British governance on the island. As a result, Ireland's

British ex-servicemen, on returning from the trenches of Ypres and the Somme, found themselves in a difficult position. No less difficult would be the position of those who had travelled to the earlier and more distant battlefield of Gallipoli and who had, against all odds, managed to survive until the Armistice.

Within a few years a new Irish Free State existed, endeavouring to create a national identity without the emblems and traditions of Britishness. The long history of Irish service in the British army would be an unwanted story. The voyage of the 10th Division to the Dardanelles and the sufferings of the Irish at Gallipoli would appear in popular culture only as an occasional mention in the national folk-song repertoire, where its significance would be summed up in the lines from one later patriotic ballad –

> You fought for the wrong country
> you died for the wrong cause ...
> when the greatest war was at home.[2]

Years later a prosperous and self-confident Irish nation would feel able to reinvestigate the history of its bitter-sweet relationship with Britain and, as a result, to acknowledge the hundreds of thousands of Irish soldiers who fought in the British army throughout history. However, the story of the men who sailed for Gallipoli in the summer months of 1915 would, despite the appetite for rediscovery, remain profoundly buried. Even in an era when many Irish men and women recognized that it was no shame to have ancestors buried under the Union Jack on the Western Front, few made the long journey to the graveyards of Kemikli Burnu. Hundreds of Irish names remained unread in the Gallipoli cemeteries, on memorial stones inscribed with testimonies to what had once been an unquenched sorrow for dead fathers, brothers, husbands and sons.

The last resting place of the 10th Division's dead could not be in a more beautiful location nor in a part of the world more steeped in myth and history. From the southern tip of the Gallipoli peninsula, where in 1915, land-mines, bullets and artillery shells destroyed two rival armies, it is possible to look across the sea to the site of the ancient city of Troy where the heroes of that great Homeric epic, *The Iliad*, engaged in a war with spears, chariots, shields and swords. The northern stretch of Gallipoli is now a quiet place of isolated farmsteads, tomato-fields and neatly tended military cemeteries, many of which lie within earshot of a blue sea that rolls ashore onto deserted strands.

After ninety years of oblivion, a detailed history of the 10th Division might be thought of as irrecoverable. I wanted to find out whether, from a range of deeply neglected narratives, the story of the Irish volunteer soldiers of Suvla Bay and Anzac Cove could be retold in both military and human detail and to ask why, of all Ireland's Great War experiences, this should have been one of the most deeply buried.

There are difficulties for any storyteller who aims to reconstruct a battle fought so many years ago. This division that sailed to the eastern shores of the Mediterranean was made up of many units. From some parts of that division virtually no narratives survive, whilst the archives of others of its battalions offer the historian a rich array of poignant detail. The story of the Irish at Suvla and Anzac relies inevitably on those educated and confident enough to maintain a detailed written account of their experiences and, after the war, the cultural, economic or personal support needed to publish or place in archives their story of survival.

So, although any military history is partial – shaped not just by authorial intentions but by what old soldiers want to remember or what they decide to forget – the story of the 10th Division is, for cultural reasons, particularly so. It is dominated by the experiences of officers rather than the 'ordinary foot-soldiers' who filled the ranks, dependent on the testimonies of Irish Protestant and English members of the division rather than the many thousands of Irish Catholic troops and reliant on the voices of men who returned in 1918 to a unionist rather than a nationalist cultural environment. The reader's task is to discover within the story that does emerge, the lives of the thousands of men who were unable or unwilling to recount the Gallipoli memories that few in a post-war Irish Free State seemed to want to hear.

The army division that is my subject was not an entirely Irish body of men. Neither was the Irish experience of Gallipoli limited to this particular unit. Other Irish troops died at the Dardanelles, with Australasian units, with 'regular' battalions of the British army, and with naval units who were conducting operations in the eastern Mediterranean. The book does not presume to tell their story yet they too are part of a fractured national narrative.

Few nations deliver a rigorously honest and coherent narrative about their wars. The veterans of Suvla are merely a few in the global throng who, when wars end, are easily forgotten because they have fought 'for the wrong cause'.

As an author, the impulse to begin this story had its origins in a visit that I made one day to an empty, rain-soaked townland in the Irish midlands, when a local farmer referred to the road on which I stood as 'the Dardanelles'. For the first time, questions about Ireland and Gallipoli presented themselves to me for answering. Why was the name of a Great War battle – so often thought of as an Australian tragedy – inscribed upon this stretch of quiet Irish landscape? Did young men, born in places such as this, sail off to the farthest edge of Europe and find themselves an unremembered resting-place in a Turkish field of bones?

And if a story worth recovering should emerge, what way might it be told? The quest began.

A soldier's bones, Rhododendron Ridge, Gallipoli, 2005.
KEITH JEFFERY

Churchill's Gallipoli strategy, 1915.
JOHN BOYD

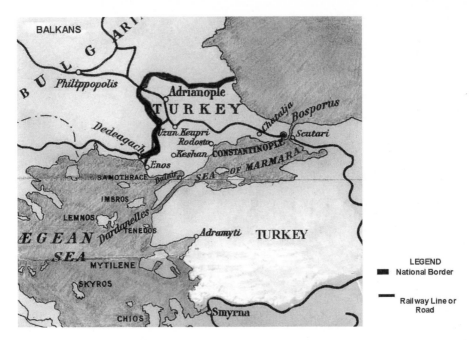

The Dardanelles Straits, the gateway to Constantinople.
BOYD

The Gallipoli Peninsula
MITCHELL

II
VOLUNTEERS

Recruitment area number 10

The relationship between the Irish people and the British army had always been a complicated one. Britain's dominance over its nearest neighbour had been achieved by military conquest and in 1914 Ireland was still garrisoned by thousands of British troops in camps and barracks across the island. Yet Ireland had also been a recruiting ground for Britain's armed forces as its power expanded across the globe. In the 1830s Ireland had provided over 40 per cent of Britain's fighting men, a figure much reduced by the turn of the twentieth century, although thirteen British soldiers in every hundred were still Irish. Famous generals such as the Duke of Wellington had had family origins in the ranks of the Anglo-Irish landed gentry, whilst numerous Irish regiments had played a role in recruiting foot-soldiers for the empire. The Royal Irish Regiment had been in existence since the seventeenth century, the famous 'Royal Inniskillings' had played a key role in the British victory at Waterloo, and some regiments, such as the Royal Dublin Fusiliers, had originated during the expansion of imperial power in India.

However, the military traditions of the Irish were many and varied. Ancient Irish mythology enshrined tales of flamboyant heroes such as Cuchulain and warrior bands such as the Red Branch Knights, their glory and prowess enthusiastically rediscovered by Ireland's Celtic Revival movement and by its band of conspiratorial separatists.

The Irish had not only fought for the British empire but against it. There was a strong tradition of Irish service in the national armies of Europe and in the seventeenth century Irish brigades known as 'the Wild Geese' had given the support of 30,000 Irish soldiers to the French. Service in the armies of Europe was not merely motivated by an Irish opposition to British hegemony. Opportunities for work, travel and adventure presented themselves to the young males of a poor island nation. Irishmen served in the armies of Russia, Bavaria, Spain, Portugal and Holland as well as France. Others travelled farther afield and fought in the national armies of the new states that were emerging in both North and South America.[1]

Now, in the second decade of the twentieth century, Britain's Liberal government had determined on a course that sought to meet the desire of most Irishmen for greater political independence. John Redmond's Irish Parliamentary Party had long been seeking Dublin-based 'Home Rule' within the Empire. However, such aims ran contrary to the aspirations of most of Ireland's Protestant minority. They deemed their power and prosperity to be dependent on full retention of the union with Britain. Old sectarian tensions, particularly in the north of the island, began to raise their head and rival paramilitary militias dedicated either to the union or to Home Rule, were arming themselves with smuggled rifles. The British army in Ireland found itself uneasily poised between rival factions, though with its own leadership innately sympathetic to the unionist cause. In this volatile context news of a looming European war came to Ireland in the summer of 1914.

Given Ireland's military history it is not then a surprise that 30,000 Irishmen in 1914 were already serving in the regular army and that many were sent towards the front line when war was declared, while thousands more were in the army reserve, eligible to be called up on the commencement of hostilities. Neither is it surprising that when the British realized they needed a vast volunteer army to take on the might of the German infantry, they planned for at least one division to be filled with Irish civilian volunteers.[2]

So in August 1914, as the British Secretary of State for war, Lord Kitchener, created a structure capable of holding this volunteer army, the new infantry divisions started to be numbered according to the traditional recruiting areas throughout the British Isles. The authorities hoped that recruitment area number 10, the island of Ireland, would provide Britain with some of the enthusiastic and able citizen soldiers so urgently needed. As a special honour, this new military unit would be given the full ceremonial title of the 10th (Irish) Division. It would be the first time that so substantial and well equipped a body of men had entered a war bearing the title 'Irish'.[3]

The train moved out amid cheers and fog-signals

The story of the the 10th (Irish) Division begins with men such as H.F.N. Jourdain. In 1914 he was already an officer with the Irish regiment the Connaught Rangers, in charge of its regimental barracks in Renvyle in County Galway on the rugged Atlantic coast. Like other officers, he had been alerted by his seniors to the likelihood of a European war as diplomatic relations between the great powers deteriorated throughout July in the aftermath of the assassination of the Austrian archduke, Franz Ferdinand. Jourdain, as he waited eagerly to hear of further developments, moved with his wife from their nearby lodgings into the spartan accommodation at Renvyle Barracks to be at hand for discussions with his staff and for immediate action if required. There, in early August, he received the news that would transform him from a 'peace-time' to a 'war-time' soldier. He would later recall:

> We all remained in barracks although the Galway races were on. After a cup of tea, I walked with two other officers and my wife outside the walls, down to Cromwell's Fort to get a breath of fresh air. It was a warm, calm evening, a veritable calm before the storm. I talked to one of them, saying that now after years of work we could get all the machinery in motion by one word, 'mobilize'. As I spoke, I looked at the barracks gate and there was an orderly running towards me with a telegram. I said 'And here it is!' It was exactly 6.53pm ...

Soon, Jourdain was touring the length and breadth of the western province of Connaught, in search of Irish recruits for Britain's war with Germany.[4]

Within hours of the outbreak of war, 'reserve' men such as John McIlwaine were rejoining their old Irish regiments. He had been a soldier as a younger man in Africa and India but he left the regular forces to work as a sorting clerk and telegraphist with the postal services in Newcastle-on-Tyne in the north-east of England. He had retained his place on the military reserve and was thus eligible to be 'called up' in event of war. When the declaration of hostilities eventually came on that warm day in early August, McIlwaine went at once to his local reserve army depot. Within hours he had said farewell to his wife and was on his way to Galway to rejoin the Connaught Rangers. Crossing England by train, he could see crowds of 'reserve men' like himself, thronging the station platforms. Then sailing across the Irish Sea to Dublin, he boarded a mail-train for Galway, meeting men he had last seen in far-flung parts of the British empire. On arrival he could still recognize, after years of absence, the smell of the turf smoke and the sound of noisy crowds, busy on a market day.[5]

Movement of regular, reserve and territorial troops along the railway lines and roads of Ireland was the most visible sign that war had arrived. Yet newspapers such as Belfast's *The Irish News* still advertised all the comfortable merchandise of peace-time holiday-making and summer travel, including leather suitcases, ladies' hat-cases, croquet goods and tennis racquets, while at Irish coastal resorts such as Newcastle, in the shadow of the Mourne Mountains, holidaymakers still walked on the strand or played summer sports, although, as a journalist in the local paper phrased it, 'the numbers on the links or playing tennis in the annual tournament are reduced and daily the papers are scanned'.[6]

By now, both local and national papers in Ireland began to carry recruiting notices and this would be followed before long by a government poster campaign. At Downpatrick, in County Down, posters invited men between the ages of eighteen and thirty to come to the barracks, situated in the former eighteenth century gaol in the Mall, if they were 'desirous of serving in His Majesty's Army'. They would then be welcomed into the very building where, days earlier, the reserve unit of the local regiment, the Royal Irish Rifles, had mobilized before marching through the crowded streets to the railway station. Then the train had moved out amidst cheers and the celebratory thunder of the locomotive's fog signals, en route to the city of Belfast where the men would become full-time soldiers.

While a miscellany of citizens from south-eastern County Down made its way through the barracks gates to join the infantry, the nearby Down Hunt Hotel welcomed recruits of a higher social status to join the North Irish Horse, a local cavalry regiment, the advertisements for which carefully warned that 'none but good horsemen need apply'.[7]

As the first County Down recruits into the New Army joined up, civil conflict brewed in the northern province of Ulster. Protestants there were in a narrow majority and felt wary of a prospective, Catholic-dominated Dublin parliament. Members of the self-styled 'Ulster Volunteer Force', led by Sir Edward Carson, and their nationalist rivals, the 'Irish National Volunteers', drilled and marched each night in the streets and country lanes where they had their respective pockets of support. Each organization wore uniforms emblazoned with the distinctive regalia of nationalism and unionism. Together, the rival volunteer bodies claimed a membership measured in hundreds of thousands. Until the conflict over Home Rule was resolved and a way cleared for thousands of these young men to enter the army without sacrificing their political principles and the quasi-military comradeship they already possessed, the first stream of Irish recruitment would never become a flood.[8]

In the metropolitan splendour of central Dublin, recruitment notices also filled the papers. This was the capital city that in 1914 was hosting a great summer 'Civic Exhibition' in the Linenhall buildings, an exhibition that proudly boasted a display of the latest in Irish architecture, town planning, commercial development, and agricultural modernization. Yet Dublin was also a city of poverty and political disaffection – poverty that, for some, was an incentive to join the army, with its regular wage and opportunity for adventure.

Within recent weeks, events on the streets of Dublin had not been conducive to support for the British military establishment. Men of the King's Own Scottish Borderer regiment, which currently acted as a garrison army in the city, had killed a number of civilians on the Dublin thoroughfare of Bachelor's Walk, firing on a crowd in the aftermath of the arrival of an arms shipment for the Irish National Volunteers. Elsewhere in Dublin the Marxist James Connolly and the radical educationalist and Gaelic scholar, Patrick Pearse, were already seeking to garner support for the militant, separatist cause by preaching a gospel of ardent opposition to the war.[9]

On 21 August 1914 the 10th (Irish) Division began its official life as a part of the famous 'first 100,000' of Kitchener's Army. At its head was General Bryan Mahon, a 52-year-old member of an Anglo-Irish family, described by those who knew him as a confirmed chain-smoker but an agile man with bronzed complexion and slim build. He had served at Khartoum in the Sudan with Gordon and was later responsible for the celebrated relief of Mafeking during the wars in South Africa. This Anglo-Irish military hero was to be seen, during the early days of the 10th Division's training, astride a magnificent chestnut steed with a cigarette in his mouth, gazing at his new soldiers.

The core of the division would be the three infantry brigades, numbered

29th, 30th and 31st in the British army's register. They came under the command of brigadiers R.J. Cooper, L.J. Nicholl and F.F. Hill. Cooper was a former Irish Guard, Nicholl had served on India's North-West Frontier, and more recently Hill had commanded troops in Belfast when a confrontation with the Ulster Volunteer Force loomed. Each brigade was, in customary infantry fashion, composed of four battalions, up to 1000 strong. Each battalion drew on the regimental mechanism that served to govern recruiting on a local basis throughout the British Isles, taking on a name and a number allotted to them by such historic Irish regiments as the Royal Inniskilling Fusiliers, the Royal Irish Fusiliers, the Royal Munster Fusiliers, the Royal Dublin Fusiliers, the Leinster Regiment, the Royal Irish Regiment, the Connaught Rangers and the Royal Irish Rifles. A number of the key men in each battalion were army veterans with experience of service throughout the empire, and it was their specific job to help train the new recruits.

Other elements in a typical infantry division were also assembled, including artillery, engineer, medical, veterinary and supply corps units. In due course the Royal Irish Regiment battalion became a 'pioneer' unit, charged with such back-breaking duties as digging trenches and building military roads. Their place as a group of infantrymen would be taken by a battalion of the Hampshire Regiment, who, although possessing an English name, had a long connection to Irish soldiering and already contained men from the Irish midlands. Pride in the regimental traditions of each battalion in the 10th would be much encouraged. New recruits to the Royal Dublin Fusiliers were quickly aware of their regiments' two enduring nicknames: 'the Blue-caps', recalling distinctive headgear worn marching across the sun-scorched landscape of India and 'the Toughs', due to the legendary resilience and assertiveness of Dublin's infantrymen.[10]

Patriotic commitment and a sense of adventure

Although an elegant building on the capital's western outskirts was the British army's centre of command, it was in other parts of the city that work was done to entice young men to support the war-effort. Frank Browning, President of the Irish Rugby Football Union, sent a circular to his players, just a few days after war was declared. Within a short space of time, he had established a 300-strong 'Volunteer Corps', which drilled at the Lansdowne Road rugby ground for several evenings each week. During these sessions Browning would encourage his men to enlist. Most of his volunteers came from a middle-class Protestant background and they included trainee doctors, barristers, clerks, stockbrokers, insurance agents and art students. Many of them lived in Dublin while pursuing their respective careers, and came originally from other parts of Ireland, including Donegal town or Londonderry in the north and Tralee or Kinsale in the south. At Lansdowne Road men from Portadown and Bally-mena, where unionism held sway, drilled alongside men from Castlebar, Skib-bereen and Limerick – where the Catholic majority endorsed the politics of John Redmond's Irish Parliamentary Party.

Among the rugby-playing volunteers was Charles Frederick Ball, from Loughborough in the English midlands, who had come to Ireland in order to be the assistant keeper at Dublin's Royal Botanic Gardens and the editor of a journal called *Irish Gardening*. Engaged to a local girl, he hoped to marry her in December but he could not let that stand in the way of his sense of patri-otic commitment.

Other Englishmen in the group included Reginald Ford, originally from Devon, now a Dublin schoolmaster. The rugby players also included some men from Irish nationalist families including Michael Fitzgibbon, son of John Fitzgibbon, the Redmondite MP for County Roscommon, who was a promis-ing law student. Several had been educated at well-known Irish Catholic schools such as Clongowes Wood College and Presentation College, Glasthule. They now expressed a desire to 'join up' alongside men of a very different religious background including sons of Protestant clerics such as Cecil Murray and Frank Laird. Within a few days the diverse, talented troupe of Lansdowne Road rugby footballers were able to enlist in the newly formed 10th Division of Kitchener's Army.[11]

However, these first weeks of the war also drew men towards the recruiting stations who possessed rather different social backgrounds. They came from the less prosperous streets of Dublin or of Ireland's provincial towns. Bartholomew Hand, a working-class Catholic boy from County Wicklow, had been a gardener on the famous and beautiful estate at Powerscourt, in Enniskerry. He joined up without his parents' knowledge or permission, searching for adventure. He was drafted into an Inniskilling Fusilier battalion of the 10th Division, which had so far suffered from poor recruitment figures in its rural Ulster hinterland.[12] Joe O'Leary, a young Catholic from the eastern seaside town of Skerries, joined the forces from similar motives, taking the train to Dublin city centre one evening and going straight to Grafton Street recruiting office. On the following day, after a medical, he received a payment of two shillings and ninepence and was asked to turn up at Amiens Street railway station. There he boarded a train to Armagh, where he joined a battalion of the Royal Irish Fusiliers, who recruited in yet another northern regimental area still having trouble filling its ranks.[13]

Prosperous, middle-class Catholic families also sent men into the division and often offered a deep family commitment to the war-effort. The Martin family of Monkstown, having built a timber-merchant business in recent years, were rich enough to own a house with five acres of gardens, including a summerhouse and tennis court. When the war came, brothers Charlie and Tommy joined up and were posted as trainee junior officers to the Royal Dublin Fusiliers. Their sister Marie became a volunteer nurse and eventually served on a hospital ship.

For some young men, the lure of a regular wage, a family tradition of soldiering or a flight from some personal problem rapidly overcame any possible distaste for a life in the British army. John and Philip Willis rushed to join the Royal Dublin Fusiliers, in the later words of one of John's sons, 'to get away from Dublin and get regular meals'. The Willis family had once been prosperous and had lived in a comfortable suburb, in a house next door to the dynamic Irish nationalist, Constance Markievicz. However, their father, a man of brutal temperament and dissolute habits, soon lost all the money that he had earned and the family sank deep into poverty. Now the brothers felt they had an opportunity to better themselves in the 10th Division, where John would soon train as a signaller.[14]

The tendency for siblings to join up was particularly strong among the commercial middle-class Protestant families of the greater Dublin area. The Findlaters owned a large food and drinks business in Dublin. The oldest, Alex, joined the Royal Army Medical Corps while two younger brothers, Herbert and Charles, were recruited to the Royal Dublin Fusiliers. The Lee family were also prosperous business-owners in the south County Dublin area. Once again, three males in a single family joined the forces on the outbreak of war. Ernest, a well-qualified surgeon, applied to join the Medical Corps and Joseph and Tennyson joined the 10th Division as trainee officers in a battalion of the Royal Munster Fusiliers. Joseph was a well-known lawyer and, despite his youth, a writer of sophisticated legal textbooks. Tennyson was a director in the family business, his name acquired because of his mother's deep love for the Victorian poet, Alfred, Lord Tennyson.[15]

Kitchener's Army particularly attracted men of sporting and athletic prowess. J.C. Parke from Clones, County Monaghan, joined a battalion of the Leinster Regiment. He had represented his country in America and Australia as a member of the British Davis Cup lawn-tennis team but he had also captained Ireland in rugby as a first class 'centre three quarter'.[16] Ernest Coldwell, who joined the Dublin Fusiliers, had won the British 'Graceful Diving' championship in London in pre-war years while Joseph Brady, who entered the same battalion, was a professional billiards player and undefeated Irish snooker champion since 1908.

The legal fraternity was well represented in the Dublin Fusiliers and included well-known barristers such as Poole Hickman and the young and gifted Reid Professor of Law at Trinity College, Ernest Julien.[17]

However, participation in a legally contentious labour dispute before the war certainly did not deter some men from a very different social background from also entering the division. A substantial number of unemployed dockers entered one particular company of the Dublin Fusiliers. They were known as the 'Larkinites' in reference to their involvement in the huge transport workers' strike organized by union leader James Larkin. Having struggled to regain employment after their dismissal from the docks, some had already gained work in the regular army, prior to August 1914. Others now followed and found themselves in the same battalion as young men from Dublin's sophisticated bourgeoisie.[18]

The British army stood between Ireland and an enemy

By mid-September the Lansdowne Road volunteer corps had entered over one hundred men into D Company of the 7th battalion, Royal Dublin Fusiliers. Others would join at a later date. They were known far and wide as 'the footballers' and aimed to model themselves on the units of 'Pals', popular in England because they brought in cohesive peer-groups of friends and colleagues from social classes that would not normally have considered soldiering.

On the other side of the country, H.F.N. Jourdain was now in charge of a newly formed battalion of the Connaught Rangers and was busy registering volunteer soldiers in County Galway. English by birth, he had spent many years in 'the Rangers' and as a widely travelled and knowledgeable soldier had acquired the nickname 'Savvy'. As he toured the county, he thought he could detect a degree of enthusiasm. Putting up green-coloured recruiting posters in country towns, he was often cheered by a small crowd. On returning to Renvyle he found himself busily dealing with a range of new recruits. One letter he received asked for the advance price of a fare to get to Renvyle. It concluded, 'Excuse the writing but I am in a hurry – God save the King, Yours John Cooney.' Another would-be recruit said, 'I deserted from the battalion five years ago; will you have me back now?' Among the old soldiers who tried to come back to the regiment in Renvyle was a sergeant who had marched to Khandahar with Lord Roberts in 1879. Thirty-five years later he wished to be back in uniform.[19]

Meanwhile, back in Dublin by 14 September, a young man called Noel Drury had joined Trinity College Officer Training Corps and had started drilling each afternoon and evening. Drury's family owned a local paper mill, in the running of which he might have been expected to play a future part. Now, despite his lack of military experience, he applied for a commission as an officer and before long was notified to join the 5th Connaught Rangers, which Jourdain had been assembling in County Galway. He put some rudimentary items of kit together, paid his remaining bills and before taking his train to the west, enjoyed what he would later describe in his diary as 'a nice little ceremony at home' when he was 'presented with a beautiful sword, suitably engraved, and a belt, by the work people'.[20]

Into a battalion of the Royal Inniskilling Fusiliers came a different kind of recruit. Francis Ledwidge, a 27-year-old from near the town of Slane in County Meath, was a Catholic from a background humbler than Noel Drury's. Alternately farm labourer, road worker and copper miner, in the months leading up to the war, he had become a member of the Irish National Volunteers, a trade union representative and an acquaintance of nationalist leaders Patrick Pearse and Professor Thomas McDonagh. As a young writer of some merit but little means, he had come under the patronage of the literary aristocrat, Lord Dunsany, who at the outbreak of hostilities had joined the new 5th Inniskilling battalion. Ledwidge decided that he too would join and 'test his mettle' as a soldier, despite his intensely nationalist sympathies. Ledwidge's reasons for 'joining up' included a mix of high-minded principles and romantic discontents. He would later say, 'I joined the British army because she stood between Ireland and an enemy common to our civilization.' He did not want Irish nationalists to be accused of accepting the protection of the British empire against German tyranny while doing nothing themselves to contribute to Germany's defeat.

Yet Ledwidge was also distressed by rejection from a local girl called Ellie, with whom he was in love. In June 1914 he had written a poem declaring his hunger for departure and adventure, now that she had spurned him:

> I'm wild for wandering to the far-off places
> Since one forsook me whom I held most dear … [21]

A future chronicler of the 10th Division, Captain Bryan Cooper, noted the great diversity among the men. He observed that many young subaltern officers were drawn from Trinity College, while experienced captains came from the district inspectorship of the Royal Irish Constabulary. Old colonial army officers had also returned to 'the colours' and youthful recruits had been drawn from both Protestant and Catholic working-class background, 'taking their tone' from some older soldiers in the ranks, to whom they were often related. Cooper estimated that by the time recruiting for the division was complete, 90 per cent of the officers and 70 per cent of the ordinary men in the ranks were either Irish or of Irish extraction.

Bryan Cooper himself came from a landed family in County Sligo, had been to Eton and was a sophisticated man who wrote poetry and enjoyed reading. Keeping up the military traditions of his family, he trained for the army in pre-war years, then became involved in politics and for a brief period was the Westminster MP for south County Dublin. Back at Markree in the winter of 1913–14 he played war-games on the floorboards of an empty room in the family mansion, its surface covered in white scrawls to indicate contours, railway lines and rivers, with tin soldiers representing rival armies. In 1914 came Cooper's chance to re-enlist and to play war-games for real.[22]

The Dublin 'Pals' were now a part the 7th Royal Dublin Fusiliers, and known to some of their less well-heeled fellow-soldiers as 'the Toffs in the Toughs'. On 16 September a substantial number marched off from the Trinity College Officer Training Corps H.Q. towards the railway station, en route for a barracks at the Curragh in County Kildare, a few miles to the west of the capital. As the men stepped down Dame Street and along the quays by the river Liffey, it seemed as if there were hands waving handkerchiefs at every window. A short time later, they were making a home out of a bare hut in an army barracks and learning to drill and route-march on long, sunny autumn mornings, looking forward all the while to their first military pay on 25 September.[23]

Among the other sections of the 10th Division assembling throughout the island during that autumn were three units of the field ambulance brigade. Among them was John Hargrave, a young man from a Quaker background who had spent much of his youth in the small village of Hawkshead on the southern edge of the scenic Lake District in England. On a clear day, from the nearby fells he would have seen the mountains of Mourne outlined beyond the Irish Sea on the western horizon.

However, late summer of 1914 found Hargrave in the Marylebone area of London, working as a journalist for a scouting magazine. There, among naked, unfit-looking men with tattoo-covered arms, he told the local recruiting officer of his Quaker pacifist background and of his suitability for the non-combatant medical corps. Within minutes he was enrolled and a few days later he was sent to Ireland on a foul-smelling cattle-boat bound for Waterford. From there he travelled on to the 10th Division's field ambulance brigade depot in Limerick, at the mouth of the Shannon. He considered the town dismal and disfigured by slum housing but soon the men of the field ambulance were performing extensive manoeuvres on the nearby mountains of Clare, despite the lack of a proper army uniform and genuine military or medical equipment.[24]

Another Englishman posted to Limerick, Private William Knott, a Londoner whose strong Salvation Army convictions had guided him towards field ambulance services, soon felt that Englishmen in an army uniform met with little favour in local eyes.[25]

The finest lot of fellows I have ever known

Despite Bryan Cooper's final statistics about the composition of the division and Jourdain's optimism about enlistment in Connaught, Irishmen were still not flocking to the doors of the recruiting stations in the late summer of 1914. Compared with most other parts of the British Isles, recruiting was proceeding badly. Reports in *The Irish Times* in mid-September indicated that the 10th Division was only 'half-full' and that it would have to seek English reinforcements. Towards the end of August, after three weeks of recruiting, only the Royal Irish Rifles battalion had come close to gathering in the 900 or more soldiers needed for a viable unit. It had had the advantage of recruiting in Belfast, where life in the army was of appeal to the many young men in that city who found themselves in dead-end, low-skill jobs. The Connaught Ranger battalion had been moderately successful, with half its ranks filled already. However, the two Irish Fusilier and two Inniskilling Fusilier battalions could scarcely muster more than 300 men in total, despite the energetic efforts of persuasive recruiting agents such as Bryan Cooper, who was reported to be talking each evening to the men in the marketplaces of County Sligo, accompanied by an eloquent priest, Father Doyle, who would soon become one of the 10th Division's Catholic chaplains. However, some officers were more wary than Cooper of trying to recruit for the British army in parts of a countryside made volatile by the recent Home Rule crisis.[26]

Recruitment officers thought they could discern factors that prevented men from 'joining up' and had nothing to do with the problems of contemporary politics. One of these factors was shared with another New Army division, the 12th. Out of all the six divisions that made up the ranks of the 'first 100,000' of the New Army, the 10th and 12th had the gravest recruiting problems. The 12th Division was endeavouring to recruit in East Anglia, a predominantly rural catchment area with a heavy involvement of young men in farm labour. What was more, this was the worst time of year to recruit in a rural region, given the busy autumnal focus on 'getting in the harvest'.

But in Ireland, since the catastrophic 'famine years' of the mid-nineteenth century, emigration had deprived rural communities of thousands of their best and fittest young men. Some of the potential volunteer Irish soldiers had long since emigrated to America, to find new lives for themselves in California and New Jersey.[27]

Reinforcements from England were soon drafted in. During September, the division's Leinster Regiment battalion was strengthened by 600 men from Bristol. Captain Godfrey Drage went in the same month from his Royal Munster Fusilier base in County Kerry to a depot in Yorkshire where he searched for men to help fill up the ranks of his own regiment. Drage was from an Anglo-Welsh family and on 5 August he drove in his 22-hp Ford motor car to Oxford's Cowley Barracks to offer himself for war service. With his own extensive pre-war army experience he found himself installed as an officer at the Royal Munster Fusiliers' depot on the southern Irish coastline at Tralee, in charge of what he would later describe as the 'finest lot of fellows I have ever known'.

However, it was clear that Munster would not yield the quota of at least 1800 recruits needed for two New Army battalions in the early weeks of the war, so he travelled to the depot at Pontefract in northern England to begin recruiting. There Drage confidently made a phonecall ordering two trains to carry troops from Pontefract to the Welsh port of Holyhead, then planned for a crossing on the ferry from Holyhead to Kingstown, just south of Dublin, and 'wired' Kingstown harbour to arrange for several hundred hot breakfasts for his men.

In Pontefract Barracks he made these men strip to the waist and then walked down the ranks, feeling each man's biceps. He took miners without further ado because of their wiry physique. The disgruntled adjutant of a local Yorkshire regiment soon curtailed Drage's recruitment drive but not before the Munster Fusiliers were enriched by a substantial number of fit and able Yorkshiremen. Sent by train to County Kildare, these men were marched to the Curragh camp from the railway station, across the bare, wet plain 'in shabby clothes and soaked to the skin … accompanied by eleven Dublin corner-boys' who had spontaneously joined the English soldiers as they had passed through Dublin.[28]

These English drafts were undoubtedly needed. Given the troubled political circumstances, men were a great deal more reluctant to commit themselves to a Kitchener division in Ireland than in Britain during the opening weeks of the war. On 3 September, the biggest single day for recruitment in 1914, when some 33,000 British citizens joined the army, 2151 men joined in Manchester but only 114 in Dublin. A set of figures published in early November showed that while recruitment in southern Scotland stood at a remarkable 237 per 10,000 of the population and the figures for London and the Home Counties showed a respectable 170 per 10,000, in Ireland 127 per 10,000 signed up in the area that comprised Ulster, Dublin, Wicklow and Kildare and a meagre 32 per 10,000 joined in what were referred to by the authorities as the 'agricultural' districts of Munster. Nonetheless, by the late autumn of 1914 a substantial wave of fresh Irish recruits was gained and certain influences had been at work allowing this to happen.

Political compromise had been reached on the 'Home Rule issue' whereby the legislation would be 'officially' placed on the statute books but not implemented until after the war was over, with the door still left open – as northern unionists understood it – for the exclusion of Ulster from the ultimate settlement. Sir Edward Carson and John Redmond now felt free to advocate the enlistment of their respective volunteer militias in Kitchener's Army. Indeed large-scale military service might well be a chance to gain Britain's favour and render a positive constitutional outcome more likely when the war was over.

As a result, on 3 September, the 36th (Ulster) Division had been formed, its battalion nomenclature reflecting the regional structure of the Ulster Volunteer Force, whilst on 11 September, a 16th Division had also been authorized as yet another body of men to be 'raised' in Ireland. On 20 September John Redmond spoke at Woodenbridge in County Wicklow stating it would be a disgrace if nationalist Irishmen 'shrunk from the duty of proving on the field of battle that gallantry and courage which has distinguished our race through its history'. Soon it became clear that the 16th Division might stand as equivalent to the 36th, and offer a military 'home' for young nationalists.

The 10th also benefited from these political and military developments throughout September, as numerous young men for whom Carson and Redmond were political mentors, now felt free to join. An analysis of the casualty figures from the first few months of engagement with the enemy shows that despite early difficulties with enlistment, Cooper's statistics were not far off the mark. Two-thirds of the men who died or were wounded with the division at Gallipoli were domiciled in Ireland.[29]

The motives for 'joining up' were undoubtedly mixed. Some men were anti-German, spurred by the British propaganda that characterized the German invasion of little, Catholic Belgium as a violation of the rights of small nations everywhere. Some simply thought that war would be an adventure. Others were glad of a new and different kind of 'work', whilst some were happy to follow their fellows, friends, neighbours or social betters into the army. Some, imbued with a vague sense of moral duty, thought that it was simply 'the right thing to do'.

Like ordinary soldiers everywhere, the men of the 10th Division could be confused about the war in which they fought: one old soldier in the Leinster Regiment was heard saying that he was off to fight the French! However, like all volunteer soldiers in the ranks of Kitchener's Army, the men in the 10th began their careers stark naked, stripped of all clothing in the recruiting station and inspected by a doctor for ailments such as varicose veins and bad eyesight. Like all the soldiers in the 'first 100,000' it took these men a long time to receive a full uniform and to be issued with their Lee Enfield rifles as opposed to the 'dummy' version.[30] And their first army pay would have given rise to a variety of feelings. Basic pay in the ranks was a shilling a day, not a lot in an era when a skilled tradesman could earn thirty shillings a week in civilian life. However, for many soldiers there were extra perks including separation allowances for families. A married soldier from an unskilled background might have received a weekly family allowance of twenty-two shillings if he had a wife at home with four children.

Many of the men who joined the British army in the autumn of 1914 could not read or write. With illiteracy rates for Ireland as high as 12 per cent in the pre-war years, and with recruitment procedure attracting many of the unskilled and poverty-stricken, it is likely that nearly a quarter of the men in some battalions were illiterate.[31]

Men followed the music down the winding roads

Within a short time of arriving in Galway to join the Connaught Rangers, Noel Drury was told to transfer to another battalion, the 6th battalion of the Royal Dublin Fusiliers. On arriving at his new billet, at the Curragh, he met a fellow-officer who was sent out to get him a suitable servant, who turned out to be a private called Costelloe from Cork whom Drury regarded as 'a decent chap'. Drury was placed in charge of No.10 platoon of C Company and soon he met the company's Sergeant Major, an old soldier called Murphy who had been lately in charge of gym and sports at a school near London. Murphy was particularly responsible for achieving the kind of discipline needed in this new and inexperienced band of soldiers. Drury was also delighted to find that the officer's mess at the Curragh was a reasonably comfortable place, with a piano on which some of the more musical among the men soon played a tune.

The 6th Dublin Fusiliers' sister battalion was encamped at the same barracks. Many of its former rugby players would later recall how they made their first route marches through the Irish countryside, encountering in November the first snows of the winter. The marches were a key part of training and toughening the men and also a means of encouraging military pride in regimental display. The troops were led by Irish pipers drawn from the ranks of Trinity College Officer Training Corps. The marchers were frequently accompanied by the regimental mascot, an Irish terrier called Jack. To help keep up their spirits on these marches, the rugby-playing Pals also organized a 'mouth-organ band'.[32]

For Bryan Cooper, memories of training at the Curragh were dominated by these 'field days' when the air was full of the vibrant sounds of drums, fifes and pipes as his men 'followed the music down the wet, winding roads around Kilcullen or the Chair of Kildare, with grey clouds hanging overhead'. The nationalistically minded men in the Connaught Rangers' band were not above provoking the well-known unionist, Bryan Cooper, with their choice of music when on the march, playing 'A Nation Once Again' repeatedly in his presence![33]

For many men, a highlight of the Curragh was the 'picture house' where films were shown in the evenings. Other favourite haunts were the denominationally affiliated Christian hostels, which provided extra food for the hungry soldier at a small price. The Methodist and Roman Catholic hostels were considered the best providers of 'nosh' including some fine 'bangers and mash'.[34] However, the men soon encountered the supreme and impersonal law of the army, which broke up the unity of friends and comrades who had enlisted together – a number of chosen individuals were sent to train elsewhere as machine gunners, in readiness for the demands of modern warfare.[35]

Meanwhile in Limerick John Hargrave was witnessing the toughening process whereby a bunch of inexperienced lads was 'put into shape' as they marched, day after day, through the streets of the town. Hargrave noted that 'a shirt-tail showed here and there, like the white scut of a rabbit', prompting one or two local women to shout out, 'Here comes my boy with his arse hanging out!' He still felt unhappy with life in the field ambulance brigade, upset by the way in which his commander punished small misdemeanours and placed his soldiers 'under close arrest for an undone button'.[36]

For Ivone Kirkpatrick, some of the best memories of his spell with the 5th Inniskillings in Ireland were of the weeks spent at Dublin's Richmond Barracks, not far from Phoenix Park, on whose broad expanse of grass the men would regularly train. Kirkpatrick's father was from County Kildare but the young boy was sent to the English Catholic public school Downside. After brief training at Camberley in the south of England he had been sent to Dublin as an Inniskilling Fusilier. He found his platoon to be full of Glasgow men with Irish family backgrounds.

Kirkpatrick's most painful memories of that early period in the 10th Division were of nights spent on the slopes of the Wicklow Mountains, several miles to the south of the Irish capital. The men had to survive the first snowstorms of the winter with no greatcoats to ward off the bitter cold.[37]

Francis Ledwidge, in the same Inniskilling battalion, was now working in the quartermaster's store as a clerk. In the evenings he was able to see his mentor, Lord Dunsany, and in the relatively relaxed circumstances of Richmond Barracks he spent time in Dunsany's room, discussing poetry. However, as the winter drew on, Ledwidge began to hanker for home and wrote to a friend in County Meath that he was 'drifting far away from Slane, very far'. Soon, Ledwidge would gain comfort from a new friendship with a fellow soldier called Robert Christie. His companion was a Belfast Protestant with ardently unionist convictions who had been planning to emigrate to Canada when war broke out but instead 'joined up' in search of adventure. Christie, like Ledwidge, was a keen writer who had recently had a one-act play performed at the Abbey Theatre in Dublin. When both men discovered that some of their recent poems had just been published in various literary magazines, they celebrated with cheese sandwiches and beer in the sergeants' room at the barracks. Political differences were no bar to friendship.[38]

For Godfrey Drage, in charge of C Company of the 7th Royal Munster Fusiliers, life was much better once he had been offered a bungalow near Kildare which he and his spouse could share as a married quarters with another officer and his young wife. Each morning he would drive to the barracks at the Curragh in his Ford motor car for early-morning parade at 7 am. Before long his chargers arrived – two steeds called 'Banbury' and 'Upton' from which he could survey his infantrymen on parade in traditional officer fashion. However, Drage was aware that the saddle of a thoroughbred was not always the best place from which to view the men of the New Army. He criticized his commanding officer, General Mahon, for 'spending too much of his time galloping daily across country and not nearly enough down on the ground with the Poor Bloody Infantry'.[39]

The men of that infantry had to spend time, like any other military unit, learning about the weapons and tactics of modern warfare and about the rules and systems of military command. On various training grounds, from Mullingar Barracks in the heart of the Irish midlands to the green sward of Dublin's Phoenix Park, the 10th Division learnt about the use of weaponry and the system of army hierarchy. They got to know the handful of hardened old sergeants and corporals who had been to India and South Africa in the course of their career. Exotic foreign words would flow off their tongue, such as 'bundook' for a rifle, 'koi hai' for 'come here', and 'juldi' for 'quickly!' The new troops became familiar with the pattern of the army day from the bugle call of Reveille in the morning to the sonorous notes of Last Post in the evening. They had to get used to sleeping in close proximity to one another each night and they had to become acquainted with the military obsession with tidy, clean army dress and the absolute veto on any kind of insubordination.[40]

A number of men now joined the division, having put off making the final decision. Frank Laird from Howth had first become vividly aware of the war when camping in County Kerry in August. He had seen the barbed wire defences being erected on Valentia Island to protect the installations that played a part in the cross-Atlantic telegraph cable system. Back in Howth he had seen Dublin Bay filled with a great fleet of steamers, which were there to take a batch of British soldiers from Irish garrisons to France. In Dublin he had also witnessed the men of the King's Own Borderer Regiment being given a hard time by a surging mob outside the railway station where they were preparing for departure. The crowd were hooting and spitting at them because of their conduct on Bachelor's Walk not many weeks before.

At first Laird was reluctant to volunteer, partly because he was thirty-five years of age with varicose veins but also because he was a self-styled 'man of peace'. Then he considered how a number of his friends who had already enlisted would regard him after the war was over: 'it seemed a poor affair to be peaceably pen-pushing while men were fighting and dying out yonder'. Given the mundane nature of his job as a civil servant it also seemed that 'here was a chance to get out of the groove with a vengeance'. So, after going into the Richmond hospital to have his varicose veins operated on, he enlisted and arrived at the Curragh with the Dublin Fusiliers by mid-December 1914.[41]

All through the winter of 1914/1915, the men of the 10th Division continued to train in small barracks across Ireland. The pioneer battalion trained in Longford, the Leinsters in Birr in County Offaly, and the signallers in Carlow. Because Irish regiments did not contain artillery units, the division's artillery-men came from England and were sent to Dundalk, Newbridge and Kildare for their first phase of training.[42]

A nation once again

By the winter of 1914, some sense of the war in far-off Europe had begun to manifest itself. Newspapers carried stories couched in the heroic language of the day. However, many articles still managed to convey the horrors of the new 'trench warfare' in France and Flanders. The edition of *The Irish News* for Christmas Day 1914 led with cheery stories of 'seasonable delicacies for men in the trenches' but on 28 December described how, in this new kind of warfare, 'our men have to jump from their own trenches and rush for the enemy's trench across a bare expanse 200 or 300 yards across'. The correspondent noted how after a short period 'the space between the trenches is heaped with the fallen.'

On New Year's Eve the same paper carried a story from an Irishman who had been in the trenches for several weeks and who condemned it as 'agonized living and agonized dying'. The soldier spoke of how the Germans are 'as brave as we are, they only obey orders, same as we do'. An Irish casualty list was also beginning to grow, its concise catalogue of sacrifice in the daily papers pointing towards a more complex story of grief, bereavement and ultimate resentment.[43]

As the enemy armies became bogged down in the mud of the trenches that so grimly characterized 'siege warfare', the idea of bypassing the Western Front developed in the minds of British High Command. Winston Churchill, First

Lord of the Admiralty, felt a campaign that focused on the eastern Mediterranean might knock Germany's Turkish ally out of the war and open up a route to relieve Britain's Russian ally, being hard-pressed in its campaign against the German army in eastern Europe. There was also the possibility of setting up a south-east European base for an infantry assault on Germany's other main ally, the Austro-Hungarian empire.

A Mediterranean Expeditionary Force was instigated, in the charge of Sir Ian Hamilton, a highly respected 62-year-old Scottish general. The initial naval attempt to breech the narrow and well-defended straits of the Dardanelles proved to be a failure. Soon, the operation to land thousands of infantrymen on the nearby coastline was being planned for April. Among these troops were 'regular' battalions of the Royal Dublin, Munster and Inniskilling Fusiliers, filled with Irish soldiers who had been in the army at the outbreak of war.[44]

Meanwhile, Noel Drury continued to enjoy his stay at the Curragh. By early 1915 he had gained a new servant, a 'taciturn, pallid-looking Welshman' called G.E. Thomas. There were frequent opportunities for a young officer to take leave of the barracks, so on several occasions Drury made his way to Jammet's restaurant in Dublin's Suffolk Street, in his 20.1-hp Talbot motor car, travelling from the Curragh in exactly forty-six minutes. On return to County Kildare he stored his precious vehicle in the courtyard of a house at the barracks and covered it up with a protective tarpaulin. Life became busier and such trips less frequent for Drury when he was appointed to the role of signals officer for the battalion and had to receive regular training in his new duties.

In the spring Drury was present at battalion sports days when the activities included such vigorous events as tug-of-war and relay races. Brigade field days, involving all four of the brigade's battalions were more elaborate and serious, involving lectures by brigade staff like Major Alexander, who gave 'wonderful accounts of the earlier movements in the war', illustrating his talks with models, charts and diagrams. Later, after the entire infantry had been told to move to barracks in Dublin, there was a full parade and inspection of the division by General Mahon and the British Viceroy, Lord Aberdeen, mounted proudly on horseback, in the Phoenix Park. While making individual inspections of the 6th Dublin Fusiliers, Mahon was often accompanied by another fine horseman, Drury's battalion commander Colonel Paddy Cox, one of the foremost steeplechase riders in Ireland.

On St Patrick's Day Drury experienced the Dublin Fusilier regimental custom whereby all the officers attended a Catholic service with the largely nationalist men in the ranks. Drury later remembered how, 'Good Presbyterians like myself paraded and marched off to the tunes of "The Boys from Wexford" and "A Nation Once Again" and went to the chapel for the first and probably the only time in our lives.' That night a 'grand concert' was held and Drury's fellow officer, 'Stuffer' Byrne, came out onto the stage to sing a few popular songs. He was dressed 'like a stage-Irishman gone mad' and Drury was amused by his 'pair of white hunting breeches which were so tight that it seemed as if he had been melted and poured into them', as well as his green tail-coat, large check waistcoat and shillelagh.

Drury worked hard throughout the month of March, learning how to signal with heliographs during the few sunlit days to be had. He also practised signalling with lamps at night. He made regular visits to see his friends the Figgis brothers, who were also serving with the division. He delighted in the company of Father Murphy, a Catholic chaplain who came across to Drury as a 'broad-minded kindly man … different from the priests I have met hitherto'. He also witnessed several inter-regimental practical jokes, including one when some sheep were 'driven into the mess and into the officers' rooms in the night'.[45]

However, despite such apparent fun and harmony, it was clear to politically perceptive officers such as Bryan Cooper that a number of local people did not approve of seeing Irish Catholic men in British army uniform and that a confrontation with a militant minority on the streets of Dublin was always a possibility. Bryan Cooper would later recall how his company of the Connaught Rangers was practising musketry one evening at the Dollymount rifle range on the shores of Dublin Bay. A disturbance erupted in Sackville Street in the city centre, protesting against the politically motivated dismissal of an employee from a government office.

His men had to make a detour, as it was felt, in the growing dusk, that the appearance of troops, especially Irish ones, might provoke a 'collision'. At one street corner on the route home, an old man stood with head bowed in the middle of the road, 'solemnly ejaculating from time to time: "God's curse on those who fight for England"'. Then at other turnings on the road, smartly dressed young men darted up to Cooper, crying, 'You are going wrong, that is the way to the barracks!' The road being indicated led in the direction of Sackville Street and Cooper felt that they were probably being 'set up' for a confrontation.[46]

Among the Connaught Rangers was one man for whom the last few months of wartime had been far from comfortable. John McIlwaine, who had, as an army reservist, joined his old regiment in Galway in August 1914, soon found himself shipped out to France with the first soldiers of the British Expeditionary Force and had therefore seen action with the regular army in offensives at the river Marne and at the Aisne canal. In early November he had been wounded and transported back by hospital ship to Southampton, then, via London's Waterloo station, he was sent to a military hospital in Camberwell, where he was visited by various well-meaning strangers profferring pieces of fruit.

McIlwaine noted in his diary:

> If the short November day permits, something of the rooftops and chimneys of South London can be seen. At Last Post, the nurses read prayers, then lights out and the last good nights and from nearby – some sister's or doctor's quarters – a gramophone grinds out a new tune: the sickly, sweet, lingering strains of 'Somewhere a voice is calling' before we sink into pleasant dreams …

On 27 November McIlwaine was discharged from Camberwell Hospital and by 8 December was back in Galway. By 20 March he was a member of the 5th battalion of his old Connaught Ranger regiment, preparing to do battle once more with the enemy, this time in the ranks of the 10th Division, with the responsibilities of being a platoon sergeant in charge of some of the rowdy, plain-spoken Yorkshiremen who had been drafted into the Connaughts.[47]

God will watch over you

By the last week in April it was time for the 10th to leave Ireland and pursue the final stage of training in the south of England. For Francis Ledwidge of the 5th Inniskillings, this would be a difficult departure. He had recently formed a relationship with a girl called Lizzie Healy whom he had met while on leave in County Meath. He wrote to her a few days before departure, telling her how he 'could see through the window across the soldiers' recreation ground, spire on spire of Dublin and hear the bells of its trams and the shout of all its worry and woe', reassuring her that his thoughts were often in 'the little kitchen where I first took you in my arms'. However, Ledwidge and Christie also found time to visit the Quinn family of Ellesmere Avenue, with whom they had developed a close friendship during their stay in the capital. Mrs Quinn hugged Christie on their last visit, insisting he take some holy amulets and ribbons with him on his journey: 'I know, Robert, you are not of our faith, but if you accept these, God will watch over you.'[48]

It had seemed to Noel Drury, on their earlier departure from the Curragh, that this significant experience was being reduced to 'a quiet folding of tents and a quiet stealing away without anyone to see us off', as the division 'sneaked off unsung in downpours of rain'. But the memory of this damp, un-celebrated departure from County Kildare was soon banished by marching for the last time through Dublin, where there was a real sense of occasion.

It was Dublin's own regiment of course, as *The Irish Times* would report, that received the warmest welcome. On that mild April afternoon the soldiers of the Royal Dublin Fusiliers marched along the banks of the river Liffey towards the centre of town, headed by a band of an Irish cavalry regiment, the 12th Lancers, and by the pipers of Trinity College Officer Training Corps. There were Union Jacks and the red and white flags of St Patrick in abundance, many affixed proudly to the soldiers' bayonets. Some men carried melodeons on their backs along with their kit. The crowd that greeted them included a number of lawyers who stood outside the elegant Four Courts, cheering the men in uniform. As the division passed by, journalists noted how 'fashionably dressed ladies walked beside their brothers and relatives', while 'immediately behind walked women in shawls'. From another vantage point they saw cigarettes distributed by the students of the Royal College of Surgeons to the men marching past on their way to the docks.

That night Drury boarded a ship waiting in the Alexandra Basin. The weather had changed to driving rain. Drury was feeling miserable. His men had just made their last slow train-ride through north Dublin to the harbour and he had been hard-pressed to prevent local women from handing bottles of whiskey to the soldiers, each time the train had pulled to a halt. Now, in the dark April night, accompanied by two destroyers, the troopships would soon leave the harbour and move across the Irish Sea towards the Welsh port of Holyhead, sailing in a zig-zag pattern to minimize risk from enemy submarines.[49]

For men of the Dublin Pals came a particularly moving moment. Having marched through dense crowds on the main Sackville Bridge over the river Liffey, they arrived at the dock to find Frank Browning of the Irish Rugby Football Union waiting for his 'footballers'. He boarded their troop-ship and just before its departure he was the last to leave it, shouting 'Goodbye and good-luck!' as it left the quayside.

For Private Knott of the field ambulance, departure from Dublin was a welcome development. He was, in his own words, 'keen to get to the war and do his duty'. He had noted how 'the streets were packed with people cheering and waving flags, some throwing chocolate and fruit', and picked out among the crowd a number of tear-stained faces. As his ship weighed anchor, while the bands on the quayside continued to play, he closed his eyes and prayed 'in gratitude to God for the wonderful way He proved Himself my refuge'.[50]

Other men in the field ambulance had tried to march on steadily to the sound of their regimental tune, 'Her Sweet Smile Haunts Me Still'. As they came on board their vessel, they heard all the ships in Dublin Bay sounding their sirens in a concerted but mournful salute. Here and there on the deck was to be seen 'a huddle of young Irish soldiers staring into the grey nothingness long after their homeland has disappeared beyond the horizon'.[51]

John Hargrave, as he crossed the Irish Sea, also reflected in amazement on the large and enthusiastic Dublin crowd: 'They swarmed after us, they broke our ranks, they jostled us, they linked arms with us, thrust rosaries, scapulas, packets of sweets into our hands.'

This final march of the 10th Division through Dublin on 29 April 1915 impressed many of those who witnessed it. Parnell Kerr, author of a book to be published in 1916, *What the Irish Regiments Have Done*, felt that, 'We have at last awakened to the ancient truth that the recognition of nationality is a source of strength and not of weakness to an Empire.' However, the march of the 10th through Dublin was one of the last great 'hurrahs' of the British empire in Ireland's capital. The war would be the context for a bloody armed insurrection on the streets of Dublin in the months ahead, led by Irish republicans such as Patrick Pearse, James Connolly, Thomas McDonagh and Constance Markievicz, while the European conflict would prove to be an experience of unanticipated brutality for the men of the 10th Division now disembarking in the darkness at Holyhead.[52]

John Hargrave, scout and field ambulance man.
SINEAD O'HANLON/ KIBBOKIFT.ORG

The 'Dublin Pals' line up to join at Lansdowne Road rugby ground.
O'HANLON/HENRY HANNA

Irish officers outside a Dublin chapel.
Q33205 IMPERIAL WAR MUSEUM

'The Long and the Short' of the 6th Royal Munster Fusiliers – Lieutenants J.B. Lee and J.L.G Fashum.
MICHAEL LEE

A group of 'pals' at the Royal Barracks, 29 April 1915. On the right is Joseph Brady, Irish snooker champion.
ARTHUR J.ENGLAND COLLECTION

Boyhood heroes – Royal Barracks, 29 April 1915.
ENGLAND

Eleven officers from 7th Royal Dublin Fusiliers, 29 April 1915.
Third from left, Michael Fitzgibbon; third from right, Poole Hickman; centre, Ernest Hamilton.
ENGLAND

Leaving Royal Barracks for the last time- 7th Royal Dublin Fusiliers, 29 April 1915.
ENGLAND

General Bryan Mahon, Boer
war hero and commander of
'the 10th'.
FERGUS D'ARCY

Ireland 1915 – men from every county joined the 10th Division.
BOYD

III
VOYAGERS

APRIL—AUGUST 1915

The birds sing here too

For Bryan Cooper the change to new divisional quarters at 'the Commons' in the Hampshire town of Basingstoke was welcome, even though shortages of important equipment still hindered him. Propelling a jam-tin, weighted with stones, across an imaginary no-man's-land was not a useful preparation for throwing real grenades on a real battlefield. Practice trenches were dug in the grounds of Lord Curzon's spacious park at Hackwood and the men were sent out daily to familiarize themselves with trench combat or go on long, hot marches along the stony Hampshire lanes, from which they would return footsore and thirsty, several hours later.

Sometimes during their journey, they would open a gate into a meadow and lie down for a midday rest or hide from the sun in the shadow of a beech tree. Cooper relished the local countryside, whose white, chalky soil showed through the grass, especially where a network of dummy trenches had been dug. This was a landscape untouched for centuries by the hand of war.[1]

For the Dublin Pals, the endless route marches, trench-digging and amateurish grenade practices stood out as negative aspects of life as a soldier at Basingstoke. However, they were impressed by the grandeur of the divisional inspection by King George and Queen Mary on 28 May, an event followed a few days later by another inspection conducted by the elegant Lord Kitchener, mounted on an imposing charger. After the inspection, the ranks of the division were altered when high command decided it would be best to transfer some 1200 men to the 10th from the 16th Division. The details of this transfer are unclear but it seems that the new arrivals replaced a number of 10th Division troops who were not physically fit, an important issue now that the prospect of front line action for the 'first 100,000' of Kitchener's Army was drawing closer. The men would seem to have been northern nationalists to a man and their arrival prompted fresh interest in the division by John Redmond.

Despite its problems, life in Basingstoke was reasonably comfortable for the Pals. They would later fondly reminisce about the division's mock battles in the Hampshire countryside when simulated warfare would combine with other less onerous and more profitable country activities, recalling how 'we sucked pheasants' eggs in the woods while we fought and cooked our captured rabbits afterwards'. The Pals also enjoyed jugs of home-made ginger beer, which were given to them by ladies who stood at the roadside as the route marches went by. On one occasion a woman came out of a small cottage with fresh bread, a pound of cheese and a jug of gooseberry vinegar, all for a shilling.[2]

For Frank Laird, six-inch deep mud caused by the rain did not spoil the thrill and mystique of being part of a large army under canvas: 'to turn on a clear summer night from the streets of little Basingstoke, crowded with Kitchener's men in search of spiritous refreshment or bacon and eggs, and wend one's way to the tented field glimmering with scores of lights, was to feel oneself very near to Fairyland'.

However, he thought the training process was sometimes unnecessarily gruelling, especially the practice of giving iron weights to the men to hang from their belts to simulate the full load of ammunition they would eventually carry at the front. Another dubious ritual was the military haircut carried out by one of the sergeants who used his clippers with zeal, leaving the men with the closely shaven 'hunnish head' deemed suitable for such hot spots as the Dardanelles.[3]

John Hargrave, as a field ambulance-man, had less route-marching to undertake. He would look out from the Basingstoke camp at the long, thin lines of infantry parading down the Hampshire roadways like a giant khaki centipede moving across the earth. He sometimes saw the infantry return to camp with wild roses tucked into the tops of their puttees or pinned to their caps and reflected on how verdant, leafy, and quaintly English the local area must have appeared to those Irish soldiers from the more rugged landscapes of west Munster and Connaught. It seemed to Hargrave these Irishmen 'must have felt they were transported to another planet'.[4]

Meanwhile Ivone Kirkpatrick had heard rumours that the division might indeed be sent to fight the Turks, and was witness to 'a great many jokes about harems, whilst one or two officers even thought about learning Turkish'.[5] Noel Drury, however, was busily engaged in the huge mock battle between the soldiers of the 10th and the 13th Divisions. During this exercise he was billeted for two nights in a spacious country house in the vicinity of the woods where the 'battle' was held. He was well looked after by the two elderly ladies who provided him with 'a good bath, and plenty of hot water and magnificent dinner with butler in attendance'. Drury also remembered several nights under the stars on nocturnal manoeuvres. One night, near Newbury, he was convinced he could hear a nightingale sing as he lay on the grass and gazed up at the bright moon in a cloudless sky.

At the 'Commons' camp Drury had had his car sent over from Ireland and before long was 'getting good value out of it, taking fellows for a breather in the evenings and sometimes going to London to see a show'. He noted some aggression and antipathy between the various battalions at the camp but divisional unity was never fatally harmed. Endless inter-regimental pranks and practical jokes at Basingstoke focussed on trying to pull down or damage the regimental flag hanging outside a rival battalion's HQ. Drury also found that there was quite a lot of friction between the men of the 6th Dublin Fusiliers and the members of their sister battalion. He found the men of the 6th Munsters made far better companions than the men of the 7th.

When two full-scale military reviews were held at Basingstoke, by Kitchener and by the King, Drury was impressed by the sheer size of the 10th Division. With a full array of military units on display – artillerymen, transport and medical corps, motorcyclists and armoured cars – he felt that any observer would be highly impressed by the spectacle.

During the royal review, King George looked like a highly experienced horseman and Drury did not doubt the rumour that General Mahon had had some top thoroughbreds sent over from Ireland for the occasion. However, the number of molehills at Hackwood Park made it difficult for men to march in line, and the armoured cars lurched about badly on the uneven surface.

Drury continued to focus on his highly enjoyable weekend leaves. One particular Sunday he drove as far as Salisbury, entered the cathedral for the morning service and motored back to Basingstoke via the south coast where he had tea in a hotel in Bournemouth.[6]

The song was for you and the ship was for me

Francis Ledwidge, although intrigued by the pretty Hampshire villages surrounding Basingstoke, still hungered for the familiar vistas of the Irish countryside. In his letters home he wrote: 'The birds sing here too but my thoughts are in Slane and on the road to the bog.' He regularly vanished at weekends. With a couple of bars of chocolate, he would disappear into one of the little copses of trees that dotted the Hampshire countryside to dream of his lover.

Ledwidge's melancholy intensified when he heard of the death of his earlier sweetheart, Ellie Vaughey. He wrote an elegy for her, which included the lines:

> A song in the wood
> A ship on the sea
> The song was for you
> And the ship was for me

He wandered the Hampshire lanes with his friend Robert Christie and they got to know the Carter family who lived near the Commons camp. The two Irishmen were soon invited to enjoy the luxury of hot baths in the Carters' house and to join the family for high tea in their garden.

Ledwidge was also glad to meet Lord Dunsany on several occasions. Dunsany and his wife had rented a house in Basingstoke for their stay in England. As Ledwidge's volume of verse, *Songs of the Fields*, had just been published, there was much to discuss between author and mentor. However, Dunsany was about to be sent back to Ireland to Inniskilling Barracks in Londonderry. This was prompted by Dunsany's failure to exercise the cold rigour of army discipline. One incident saw the Irish peer taking his men to a local pub for a battalion picnic of plates loaded with freshly baked bread and butter and pint glasses filled with ale, all to compensate for a particularly gruelling route march.

There was much banter between the nationalist Ledwidge and the unionist Christie over who was developing into a better British soldier. Christie struggled to hit the target as a rifleman, due, he claimed, to an inherited vision defect. Ledwidge claimed to be familiar with the entire training process already as the Irish National Volunteers had used the British infantry manual to train young nationalists! One day, the two men saw a 'cockney' soldier in the 5th Connaught Rangers fooling around with a pith helmet and impersonating a British gentleman abroad. The soldier turned around and said to Ledwidge: 'Wot, 'aven't you heard? We're goin' to the bleedin' East.'

As rumours about service in the eastern Mediterranean grew, Ledwidge visited the Carter household once again and promised Mrs Carter a fine Turkish carpet as a souvenir. He also wrote a poem for Molly, their little daughter. Later, when the Irish troops marched for the last time out of their camp towards the railway station, Mrs Carter and Molly waved a tearful farewell from the window as the 10th Division passed by their house. Mr Carter had gone to the station platform to present Ledwidge and his friend with some carefully prepared gifts for their onward travels.[7]

For William Knott it was a great pleasure to find two colleagues in the field ambulance brigade who were devout evangelical Christians like him. Their names were Bert Morris and Will Harrison and their friendship would soon be a source of sustained mutual comfort when the men were serving abroad. The mens' training for the delivery of emergency medical care on battlefields continued throughout May. On one occasion they all marched to Odiham and swiftly erected a field hospital there.

After the training was over, Knott and his two friends had the opportunity to seek out friendship with other believers. They attended local evangelical meetings and found them to be 'full of spiritual help'. Four elderly sisters invited the three lads to their home for meals and the trio cycled to the town of Tadley where they preached at some 'gospel meetings' – a memorable occasion because it was the first time that Knott had ever ridden a bike! Knott was quite horrified during his stay at Basingstoke to witness so many young Irish soldiers in the 10th, yielding to the temptations of alcohol, referring in his diary to these men as 'poor, blinded, sin-sunken wretches'.[8]

The young Dublin schoolteacher Reginald Ford, with the 7th Dublin Fusiliers, was less interested in the joys of faith and warmed more by memories of peacetime leisure and pleasure. On Whit Monday at Basingstoke, Ford thought back to the Baldoyle races and days spent as a fisherman, 'whipping the stream near Whitechurch'. He did enjoy the bayonet-practice at Basingstoke, if only because he found it amusing to rush seventy yards, then 'jump over a trench and bayonet a sand-bag lying on the ground'. Sometimes he saw how 'a man more use to a toasting-fork than a bayonet would stumble and fall into a trench. Another would miss the sack and in his hurry bayonet Mother Earth with great savagery.' For Ford it was also a source of much mirth to see men who were students or writers staggering under the weight of a heavy sack of potatoes or a box of ammunition.

It was sobering to contemplate their imminent departure for the war zone, however. Towards the end of June, news came that the 10th was leaving within a few days. The destination was the eastern Mediterranean where the infantry campaign to defeat Turkey had not had a smooth beginning. Casualty lists in Irish papers already featured Irishmen who had perished trying to land on a peninsula known as Gallipoli.[9]

What matter if for Erin dear we fall

Individual soldiers would later recall vividly what they did during the last few hours before their departure for the East. On Friday 9 July Noel Drury and his company of Dublin Fusiliers left the Commons Camp for the railway station, while the regimental band played and the men marched along the road singing the already famous songs of the trenches 'It's a Long Way to Tipperary' and 'Are We Down-hearted?' They sang with particular gusto the Dublin Fusilier anthem written several years before:

> Bravo the Dublin Fusiliers
> You're no craven mutineers
> You bravely stormed up the Glencoe height
> Put 5000 crafty Boers to flight …
> Bravo the Dublin Fusiliers

Soon the troop-train was on its way to Keyham dockyard in Plymouth. During another stop at the much larger town of Exeter, the Lady Mayoress laid on sandwiches, tea and cigarettes for all the soldiers. Later that night several hundred men of the 6th Dublin Fusiliers boarded a requisitioned Cunard liner, the SS *Alaunia*. Drury made his way to his cabin, which he was to share with two other officers.[10]

The 10th Division was dispersed to various ports. Some Dublin Fusiliers entrained for the naval town of Devonport while the Royal Irish Rifles, the Hampshire Regiment and many of the Connaught Rangers had departed two days earlier for Liverpool. William Knott and his friends, who left the

Basingstoke camp buoyed up by the prospect of a Mediterranean adventure, felt 'as happy as larks'. By July 13th they had boarded a liner, the SS *Canada*, in Devonport Harbour and had taken possession of their second-class cabin. On the following day after a breakfast of coffee and tripe they felt the boat glide smoothly out into the English Channel. Knott watched the shoreline recede and felt a little subdued, wondering if he would ever set foot in England again.

Bryan Cooper had been aware of the likelihood of a Mediterranean adventure for longer than men like Knott. However, on 5 July, as the final preparations began, he too was caught up in the unnerving experience. On the following day he paraded with his men through the dark, echoing streets of Basingstoke, lamenting the fact that there was little ceremony to send the men on their way. When a few voices from the ranks broke the silence the song they chose, despite their British army uniforms, was one of undisguised Irish patriotism:

> 'God save Ireland' say the heroes
> 'God save Ireland' say we all.
> Whether on the scaffold high
> Or the battlefield we die
> Oh, what matter if for Erin dear we fall

On arriving in Liverpool, Cooper boarded his vessel, the beautiful and gigantic *Mauretania*, famed for the fastest crossing of the Atlantic. He noticed, however, that it was seriously lacking in ventilation because it had been designed for a winter crossing. The sunlit Mediterranean being much warmer, it was likely that nights spent in cabins on the ship would be hot and oppressive, every aperture on the ship being tightly closed to prevent a submarine attack.

The moods of the men boarding their ships during the first few days of July were varied. Ivone Kirkpatrick boarded the SS *Novian* in Devonport with morbid feelings and anxieties. Godfrey Drage, on the other hand, was heartened by a last-minute encounter with his aged father, who had come all the way from Ipswich to bid him farewell. Looking out of his railway carriage Drage at first saw a bent but 'solid and chunky' figure on the platform, then realized it was his father, who had not been able to resist coming to 'see him off to the wars'. Drage proudly reflected that it was 'not bad for an eighty-seven year old.'

The 10th Division was now being randomly split up. It began with different departure dates and train journeys to various ports where the men boarded different ships. A unit as large as a division of Kitchener's Army could not be accommodated aboard one vessel and the logistics of ferrying thousands of soldiers to the eastern Mediterranean, while running what was by now a highly complicated war effort, were daunting. Divisional unity and efficiency were compromised in the process of sending the men to the East. The Royal Irish Regiment battalion, for instance, left Basingstoke in unison but were soon divided between Keyham dockyard and Liverpool.

On board a vessel called SS *Transylvania* were some men from the division's field artillery, while other artillerymen were sent to Devonport on 4 July, eventually setting sail for the Mediterranean four days later aboard the SS *Georgian*. Another group of artillerymen set sail from Devonport aboard the SS *Nitonian*, on which there was a disturbing lack of accommodation for the field artillery's horses. It finally left the harbour on 9 July escorted by two destroyers down the English Channel while a congratulatory address by King George was read out to the men and they were asked to give three loud cheers for 'His Majesty'.

By the middle of July various units, including groups as diverse as the Royal Engineers and members of the division's cyclist company, found themselves at sea. The men on board the *Mauretania* had a swift and uneventful voyage as their huge ship set sail for Gibraltar and then eastwards to the Greek island of Lemnos, the key infantry base for the Gallipoli campaign. They arrived on 16 July while the other men, on much slower vessels, were still journeying towards the East.

Among the luxuries left behind at Basingstoke were the officers' chargers, while very large quantities of ammunition were taken on board. The SS *Canada*, for instance, carried an alarming 180 tons of shells and bullets. The division's veterinary staff, meanwhile, had a busy time procuring the extensive foraging needed for more than 1000 horses and mules that were going to Turkey. As for the division's medical staff, most of them had been sent to Liverpool where they set sail on board the *Mauretania*, although a few provided basic medical support on board other ships.[11]

In contrast, at the regimental barracks across Ireland where men of the two other Irish New Army divisions, the 16th and the 36th, had also been recruited, trained and prepared for the Western Front, life was quiet and orderly.[12]

Home duties for officers left in charge of Irish barracks included training fresh volunteers who might be needed as the war intensified. Charles Brett, a young trainee officer from Belfast, was left in joint charge of the Munster Fusilier depot in Kinsale, County Cork. He spent some of the spring and early summer months practising night-time landings with his reserve troops on the beaches and headlands of the Cork coastline but also had time to indulge in card-games with his colleagues and to take leisurely drives around the county in motor cars belonging to the other reserve officers. He bought a two-stroke motorbike for £23 and rode it along the local roads. Occasionally he went salmon-fishing in the Bandon river. It was a more leisurely life than that of the fraught officers struggling on English quaysides to shepherd their men onto improvised troop-carriers travelling towards a secret destination.

The realities of war became clear to Brett when he met wounded soldiers who had returned from the battlefields of the Western Front and witnessed farm carts being piled with corpses washed ashore after a German U-boat torpedoed the *Lusitania* a few miles off the Irish coastline. In a few months' time, Brett would witness the horrors of warfare on an even greater scale when he was sent to France as a fully trained regular officer, serving in the trenches of France and Flanders as a boy of nineteen.[13]

Through the dark gateway of the straits

Aboard the *Alaunia*, Noel Drury was soon given the task of being the ship's censor and so was responsible for reading letters sent home from the men. He also got a chance to use his new-found skills as a signaller, exchanging semaphore messages with other ships making their way across the Bay of Biscay towards the straits of Gibraltar. The man in charge of the *Alaunia* was Captain Rostron, a figure of some repute, having been the skipper of the *Carpathia*, which had rescued the victims of the *Titanic* three years ago. Drury also attended the regular church services held on board, when the men sang 'Eternal Father Strong to Save', whose first verse concluded with a special prayer 'for those in peril on the sea'.

From the porthole in his cabin, Drury observed a school of porpoises accompanying the ship. On deck he helped to supervise his mens' drill but with the constant roll of the ship the precision of their movements often deteriorated into comic chaos. Despite the risk of seasickness, for the officers the day began with an excellent breakfast of porridge, omelette, bacon, fried eggs, toast and marmalade, washed down with cups of tea. Then there were duties to fulfil each morning . On 12 July, for example, Drury had to supervise the vaccination of his men against a range of tropical diseases. Meanwhile, at the rear of the vessel, a large tin box tied by a long line to the ship's stern was dropped overboard and some of the Irish officers practised their machine-gun skills on it.

On 13 July a number of men relaxed by playing bowls on the ship's deck and there were lectures on how to make life-saving rafts in the event of a successful torpedo attack from a German submarine. Then the *Alaunia* anchored at Gibraltar for half an hour before moving on. By 16 July, the men were sailing close to the North African coast, noticing the tall lighthouses on the Moroccan shoreline and the intensity of the sunshine. An official order stipulated that sun-helmets had to be worn on deck between 8 am and 6 pm.

By now, Drury was amusing himself chatting with the ship's wireless operator and familiarizing himself with the instruments at the officer's disposal. However, for a ship's censor the most entertaining aspect of the voyage was the task of reading the letters that the men composed for posting to their families when the boat reached Alexandria. One such letter-writer in C Company of the 6th Dublin Fusiliers was occupied with 'giving a most blood-curdling account of the battles he had been in and telling how he had had two of the enemy on his bayonet at one time and had to shove them off with his foot.' The letter ended with the improbable line 'the rule out here is "Die dog and eat the bayonet!"' When challenged by Drury, the writer told him that he had written it to 'cheer the old woman up a bit'. After a busy hour spent censoring the mail, Drury was glad to get some exercise in the small gymnasium on the ship. There were rowing machines, some weights and a 'patent bicycle'.[14]

The rhythm of life on board ship was different for the Dublin Pals, who were woken by the reveille bugle each morning at 6 am, with breakfast arriving an hour and a half later. Between nine and eleven o'clock were drills, followed by a bathing session in canvas tanks filled with sea water. Then the men would lie on deck reading and relaxing until dinner-time, after which there would be lifeboat drills and rifle inspections. When they reached the Mediterranean the men switched to a lighter uniform, putting on pith helmets to protect them from the sun. Looking out to sea, they could see sharks swimming through the clear blue water, opening and closing their cavernous jaws as they moved swiftly alongside the vessel.

The men were also entertained by a marathon race in which the soldiers ran around the perimeter of the ship's deck in their bare feet while other men took part in a popular battalion boxing competition. There was a battalion choir that was of great assistance to the chaplain during church services; two of its keenest members in the 7th Dublins were Private Elvery, who had been a church organist, and Private Coldwell, who had turned out to be not just a talented high-diver but a gifted singer!

Frank Laird found the queues aboard the *Alaunia* to be a source of perpetual tedium, noting: 'a queue stood outside the bathroom in the morning, a queue formed up at the water-tap to fill bottles, a queue was ranged outside the canteen to buy buns or cigarettes and the queue which waited for the beer issue knocked all others into a cocked hat'.[15] For William Knott, an uncomfortable feature of life aboard SS *Canada* was that the men were told to go barefoot when moving around the deck, as their hob-nailed boots damaged the wooden panels. The captain hoped that the ship would resume service as a passenger liner once the war was over, so the ship was not to be damaged. Because of this, on Sunday 18 July most of Knott's companions went to 'church parade' barefoot. They heard the chaplain's talk, which was based on a verse from the biblical letter by St Paul to the Philippians: 'Rejoice in the Lord always, and again I say rejoice.' In the afternoon there were less spiritual but nonetheless essential matters to focus on, as a pair of coal barges came alongside allowing the *Canada* to refuel.[16]

John McIlwaine was unhappy with the vessel he was sailing on. Unlike many of his Connaught Ranger colleagues, he was on board the SS *Bornu*, a dirty boat with its lower decks caked in palm oil from when it operated as a West African trader. They made slow progress across the Bay of Biscay as the ship managed a meagre ten knots. But by 14 July, having arrived at the gateway to the Mediterranean, the *Bornu* dropped anchor a mile from Gibraltar and the men could see the town's lights glowing brightly in the dusk. The voyage was resumed and the *Bornu* headed east for Malta, whose Grand Harbour was reputed to be an even more impressive sight. But it was between Gibraltar and Malta that the 10th Division experienced its first tragedy when Private Matthew Whyte died of pneumonia, the result of a virulent chest infection he had contracted within hours of his departure from Britain. He was buried at sea at six o'clock in the evening, a few hours before his ship reached Malta.[17]

Meanwhile, aboard the *Nitonian*, the officers of the 56th field artillery unit were having difficulty looking after their horses. There was poor ventilation on the horse-decks and no room for proper grooming, let alone adequate exercise. As their official war-diarist recorded on 11 July: 'The heat and foul air is terrible, one horse went mad from the heat during the night and had to be destroyed.' When the ship got to Malta it refuelled but there was no time for men or animals to disembark. The vessel was soon on its way to Alexandria in Egypt, followed by SS *Melville*, which was having similar problems. On one particularly hot night, four horses on the *Melville* expired before dawn and had to be thrown overboard. The heat was also extreme for many of the men of the 10th Division, including John Hargrave, who found that the boards of the deck blistered his naked feet and that each man soon had a 'sun-burnt V-shaped triangle on the chest' where he left his shirt open.[18]

On board the old coal-boat SS *Novian*, Francis Ledwidge and Robert Christie sheltered from the sun in the shadow of one of the ship's beams. They liked to sit in the same spot each day, playing cards, smoking cigarettes, writing letters and discussing poetry. Ivone Kirkpatrick, also on board the *Novian*, was content to stand on deck and watch the coastline pass by. With his keen eye for natural and historic beauty, as the ship passed Tangier he saw how 'the sun rose and streamed through the dark gateway of the straits like a searchlight'. The ship cruised eastwards, keeping a short distance from the North African coast and Kirkpatrick could see that the shores of Morocco and Algeria were dotted with scattered villages and ruined castles, beyond which he glimpsed the Atlas Mountains.[19]

My father was an Irishman

Malta was a source of fascination both for soldiers who were permitted to disembark and those who had to stay on board. They were amused at the appearance of a small craft that drew up alongside the Irish troopships with merchandise. On its awning were the words 'My father was an Irishman!' They were also astonished by the small Maltese boys who were swimming in the harbour, diving underneath the troopships and reappearing on the other side. Then a number of officers like Noel Drury were rowed ashore in a hired boat covered with a light green awning with curtains on each side to keep the flies at bay. Touring Valletta, Drury bought a scarf and a pair of dark glasses. He was struck by the vista of the long steep streets of the Maltese capital that led to the harbour where the Mediterranean sparkled in the afternoon sunlight. Also of great interest to Drury were the herds of goats driven through the streets by a goat-herd who would 'stop to give a pennyworth of milk to someone'.

Back at the harbour, small boys were diving for pennies thrown into the water by the soldiers. The men of the 10th had also let down baskets at the end of a length of string to do business with the hawkers gathered in a flotilla around the troopships. However, the stop-off at Malta was not just for leisure. Men of the Royal Naval Division and the Royal Marines who were being given a lift onwards to Egypt came on board the SS *Novian*, which was now seriously overcrowded. Also given a passage to Egypt was a mysterious interpreter who spoke excellent Turkish. Kitbags containing the mens' heavy khaki uniforms were handed in at Valletta and taken separately to the army depot in Egypt where they would be stored until required in the winter months.[20]

For many of the men of the 10th there was one more exotic port of call before their ships reached the Turkish theatre of war: Alexandria, a place of oriental mystique and a crucial command centre for Britain. When William Knott's boat sailed into this famous Egyptian harbour, his awe was amplified by a glowing African sunset.[21]

Noel Drury was also deeply impressed by the atmosphere. His shore leave was made even more enjoyable by the sight of 'some nice fine looking Greek ladies' who were bathing in Stanley Bay, but he and his fellow officers also sampled the delights of the Piccadilly Tea Rooms, where the men were presented with a gift by the manager, a copy of the words of 'It's a Long Way to Tipperary', which prompted Drury to wonder, 'When will we escape from this wretched ballad?'

The Dublin Fusilier officers also frequented an establishment known as the Moulin Rouge, named after the Parisian institution. Late one night, on returning to the harbour, Drury saw a small girl singing and dancing for money.[22]

The Dublin Pals' wider experiences of Alexandria were based on the route march through the city. The 7th Dublins marched for three hours and saw jugglers, sword-swallowers and countless other street-entertainers on the way. One Pal saw a man who made money by 'having nails driven into the nose and every part of the body'. To John Hargrave, Alexandria was 'like a scene from *The Arabian Nights*'.

The first striking feature of Alexandria for John McIlwaine were the 'Egyptian newsboys, scrambling aboard with papers hot from the press' but he too had to march through the city while a regimental band played 'Killaloe' and 'Brian Boru's March'. At night, having been granted passes, a number of his men spent a couple of hours in street cafes near the docks. It was here too that McIlwaine, like many of his 10th Division colleagues, received his first mail since leaving Basingstoke. Alexandria also offered opportunities for more elaborate religious services to be held than the ones that had so far been held on board. Men like Joe O'Leary in the Royal Irish Fusiliers made their way to Mass in a church not far from the quayside.[23]

A wide inlet called Suvla Bay

By mid-summer 1915 the attempt to invade the European shores of Turkey was a dismal and bloody failure, even though the full extent of the waste and

carnage was still hidden from the British public and the Irish soldiers travelling across the Mediterranean. Mass landings on precipitous coastlines and
into well-defended bays had done little to push the Turkish lines back inland.
Thousands of men in the Mediterranean Expeditionary Force were being
sacrificed in a war zone that increasingly resembled the Western Front, with its
static battlefield, its network of trenches and dugouts, and death by machine
gun fire as men were regularly told to break out from their positions.

Added to this was dysentery, caused by the terrible sanitary conditions in a
corpse-littered, fly-infested and waterless landscape. Among the dead were
hundreds of Irish soldiers who had perished when asked to wade ashore at
Cape Helles, on the Gallipoli peninsula's southern tip, and having been caught
in barbed wire laid under the surface of the water while the bullets rained
down on them. Farther north, at the stretch of coastline now known as the
Anzac Sector, Australian and New Zealand troops had mistakenly landed on a
narrow beach in a cove backed by steep hilltops where Turkish defenders held
all the odds. Called Anzac Sector because of the Australian and New Zealand
Army Corps who landed and disembarked from there, it was where the Anzac
fighters built a legendary reputation for themselves as fearless and resilient
soldiers, but at a terrible cost.

The British high command, who had been divided on the issue of the
Dardanelles enterprise, knew that the present stalemate could not be allowed
to continue and that fresh reinforcements were essential or they would be
defeated. It was crucial to find a new way to break through the Turkish lines of
defence and the idea was to launch a fresh invasion, using troops from the new
Kitchener armies on a loosely guarded part of the coastline to the north of the
Anzac Sector.

This part of the coast, surrounding a wide inlet called Suvla Bay, had broad
and accessible beaches and a relatively flat plain inland from the shore,
although it also contained a large salt lake. Beyond that rose the ridges of high
ground which it was essential to capture to withstand any sustained Turkish
counter-attack. A southward advance from this high ground could then be
attempted in order to link up with the Australasian troops, who would by then
have made a renewed break-out attempt, eastwards and northwards from their
own positions. Together these units were to join the British and French
soldiers at Cape Helles to the south and begin a march on Constantinople,
while the British navy would breach the Dardanelles Straits, sail across the Sea
of Marmara and start to shell the capital.

So that new landings would be more successful than earlier ones, the new 9th Corps of the Mediterranean Expeditionary Force, composed of five divisions from Kitchener's Army, would have at its disposal purpose-built armoured landing craft known as 'beetles'. They would also have access to improved aerial reconnaissance in the form of observation balloons and sea-planes. The lack of landing opportunities for large-scale divisional artillery units would be offset by the use of naval bombardment from British gunboats lying offshore.

These landings in Suvla Bay, scheduled for early August, would be accom-panied by substantial diversionary attacks that might tie up the Turks and add to the surprise further north. Wanting this surprise to be watertight, the leaders of the Mediterranean Expeditionary Force requested high levels of secrecy so that even high-ranking officers did not know their exact destination until the last moment.

Commanding this 9th Corps would be Lt General Sir Frederick Stopford. He was in his sixties, was physically unfit and had not, despite many years as a soldier and military strategist, commanded troops in action on a battlefront. Sir Ian Hamilton, the commander of the Mediterranean Expeditionary Force, had pleaded with the War Office for a general of the calibre of Sir Julian Byng or Sir Henry Rawlinson to command the 9th Corps. These men had recent experience on the Western Front but were still needed in France and Flanders, where the Germans were undefeated.

So most of the units of the 10th Division hoped to be reunited in early August, under the leadership of their commanding officer General Bryan Mahon. They expected to have to make hasty preparations for the new assault on the Turks. However, the precise location of the battlefield and their individ-ual military objectives when they landed were unknown in the division.[24]

Message unclear concerning a secret move

Noel Drury's voyage north from Egypt was enlivened by a new sight, which signalled that the men were drawing closer to the war zone. He spotted a Russian cruiser adorned with several long, cigarette-like funnels. The men around him immediately christened it 'the packet of Woodbines' after the brand of cigarette they smoked. John Hargrave, meanwhile, watched the sun go down on one of the most beautiful evenings of the voyage, and admired 'the wonder of a Mediterranean sunset … peacock blue, bottle green, emerald, pale gold, lemon yellow, deep chrome and orange, scarlet, mauve and purple'. The threat of sudden death, however, was always present as the ship once again cut wide zig-zag tracks through the ocean in response to recent U-boat attacks in the area.[25]

On 23 July several of the Pals stood on the port deck and saw Crete in the distance as their ship sailed onwards. Two days later, John McIlwaine saw the shores of the Greek island of Rhodes, passing it as they travelled farther north.[26]

The men of the 10th Division were not about to be reconstituted at a single camp as a complete division. A considerable number of artillerymen had been left behind in Egypt because their bulky guns, ammunition and horses were considered a potential liability in the early stages of a coastal military landing. Also, because Lemnos was already overcrowded and its harbour and dock facilities had never been improved to cater for the Mediterranean Expeditionary Force, plans had already been made for some of the troops of the 10th Division to sail south-eastwards to a base on the island of Mitylene, a hundred miles away.

When the 10th Divisional HQ staff arrived at Mudros Bay on Lemnos in mid-July, they supervised disembarkation from the *Mauretania* and found themselves surrounded by chaos. The soldiers coming ashore did not have cookers or water carts or even kettles with which to keep body and soul together. These items were being transported across the Mediterranean on another ship and on its arrival they would need to be located and retrieved. Meanwhile, equipment would need to be borrowed on the island. These difficulties prompted the division's official HQ war-diarist to comment drily in his notes: 'It is recommended units should be embarked complete with the necessary means for keeping them alive on disembarkation.'

Further problems arose when it was announced that General Mahon had to make his way to the 9th Corps headquarters on the island of Imbros, fifty miles to the north, to receive instructions from General Stopford. In an era when wireless communication was dominated by simple morse signalling, the only way that detailed instructions from Imbros could be accessed was by a painfully slow boat journey. Finding a boat to ferry Mahon to Imbros was in itself a long and frustrating task. There was further confusion in the 10th Division caused by the discovery that the ordnance depot at Lemnos was not on terra firma at Mudros but on a vessel anchored offshore, leading to great difficulties in giving and receiving instructions about the unloading, storage and utilization of weaponry.

Then there was the strange news from Imbros that two battalions from the division's 30th Brigade and 31st Brigade HQ staff had to move to somewhere called Port Iero on their arrival from Alexandria. It was the first of many perplexing instructions. Why send men of one brigade with the command staff from another? And where was Port Iero? A message was sent back to 9th Corps HQ asking for clarification. In due course the Irish commander was informed that the mysterious Port Iero was on Mitylene, that a basic telegraphic error had been made and that two battalions from 30th Brigade were to go to Port Iero with the appropriate HQ staff. However, a considerable number of other men would also have to move to Mitylene, including some companies of the Connaught Rangers, the Royal Inniskillings, the Royal Engineers and the cyclist's company. They would be billeted aboard the SS *Alaunia*, at anchor in a bay on the island's coastline.

Meanwhile, General Mahon returned from Imbros on 27 July to tell the men to prepare for departure for the battle-front. Although the destination had to remain secret, the division had to be made ready, and this included gathering weapons and storing rations. Divisional HQ at Mudros Bay continued to be a busy place to work in, as the new arrivals from Egypt were sent to their various locations.

HQ staff ordered men with specific tasks to practise their skills in light of their imminent departure to the front line. The signalling officers were told to practise with their flag semaphore equipment and heliographic mirrors, which would be most appropriate in the bright Turkish sunshine. However, the signallers in each battalion could only gain limited access to the division's small stock of heliographic equipment so practising thoroughly was impossible.

Other items were available to the division, including maps of the unchallenged region of Smyrna in Asiatic Turkey, many miles from Gallipoli. These maps were placed within sight of the troops as an elaborate bluff to thwart any attempts at espionage on the part of Turkish sympathizers on the two Greek islands. This move was to help ensure the absolute secrecy of the 9th Corps' real destination, on the deserted coastline of Suvla Bay. Respirators were also brought out of storage, although HQ staff noted that 'some are carelessly made, being deficient of the 3rd gauze streamer'.

For the men of the 5th Royal Irish Regiment, the division's pioneers, life on Lemnos was soon back-breakingly tough as they worked in the intense heat on a road for motor transport that would run from the dock at a place nicknamed Turk's Head to the divisional HQ at Pisparaghon. The majority of the Irish soldiers on Lemnos were based at a bivouac some two and a half miles from the point of disembarkation so the pioneers also had to carry vast amounts of equipment all this distance in the blazing heat of midsummer. At least the soldiers in the other battalions had a chance to operate in cooler conditions when they began to practise night operations at the shoreline.

By the end of July all the men had been inoculated against cholera, a necessary precaution given the sanitary hazards involved in having so many men on such a small island with so few facilities. Official war diarists with the division's field ambulance brigades noted looming problems with hygiene and health. The wells at Mudros Bay were particularly liable to pollution and the location of the latrines nearby meant that there was a serious risk of infection, particularly if rain fell and floodwater gathered. Initially, medical problems included sore throats and an occasional attack of scarlet fever but then, due to the huge swarms of flies attracted by the refuse that littered some parts of the camping ground, gastric and intestinal illnesses began to appear. Men reported stomach upsets and there were severe bouts of vomiting, cramps and what a medical officer called 'the passage of frequent putrid motions'. On 2 August the Medical HQ ordered the sterilization of the entire water supply in an attempt to deal with the problem.

Medical staff at Lemnos played a key role in preparing the men for battle. They faced dilemmas: although anti-cholera vaccination was crucial, there was a shortage of the vaccine, so who should be inoculated? Another problem was the use of the pith helmets, which were so crucial to avoid sunstroke. Some men did not stick to the rules and paid the price. There was also the danger of food poisoning from contaminated local produce and men were therefore forbidden to buy food from the local hawkers.

Added to the sporadic but increasing medical problems were continued difficulties with the location of vital equipment and with the process of command and communication. By early August a substantial part of 30th Field Ambulance Brigade's medical equipment was still on board a ship somewhere at Mitylene or Lemnos. The brief, encrypted telegram messages that the divisional HQ received from 9th Corps were also hard to decipher, as noted in their official war diary: '3 August ... 18.25: message unclear from 9th Corps timed 17.20 containing the date of a secret move of a field ambulance'. The garbled message which this referred to was important, as would be confirmed by a clearer telegram on the following day: the field ambulance men were among the first to be asked to prepare to move to the battle-zone.

Some members of the field ambulance services had already been on a brief reconnaissance visit to the front line at Anzac Cove, where they had seen some of the horrors of a battlefield at first hand. They recognized that the difficulty and distress encountered on the Greek islands were minor compared to what lay ahead for the 10th Division, once it entered into combat on difficult Turkish terrain with a highly aggressive Turkish enemy. Medical equipment was now laid out on the quayside at Mudros Bay and at Port Iero, including portable operating tables, operating tents, scores of stretchers and blankets, canvas buckets and what one observer referred to with bleak humour as 'a set of butcher's tools'.[27]

The sky lit up by the flames of burning Asia

Irrespective of the battle they faced, many of the men had been calmed and enchanted by life on the Greek island. They adored the deep, sparkling inlet of Mudros Bay and the tawny slopes that stood out in contrast to the blue water. Bryan Cooper always enjoyed his visits to the divisional HQ at Pisparaghon where General Mahon and his staff were at home, in the white-washed Greek village surrounded by shady trees. The island of Lemnos seemed to have an abundance of thistles, stones and blue flowers. However, when the wind blew, a blinding dust swirled across the landscape. Dust was one of Cooper's four 'Gallipoli plagues', along with flies, thirst and enteritis. Dust stung the eyes and coated food. Flies also lit on any morsel of food to hand, and the water, brought from Egypt by ship, was luke-warm and strictly rationed. At least there was a bathing drill after 6 pm on most evenings, when the men could be found diving off the end of the pier. Then, for Cooper and his fellow officers, there was an evening meal in the twilight.

Cooper watched his troops preparing for departure, packing into their bags razors and soap, sponges and towels and favourite books to read. Looking out on the Turkish mainland to the east, he could see what seemed like bonfires burning in the distance. They brought to mind the famous beacons lit on these slopes in ancient times to signal the fall of the city of Troy. It was in this part of the Mediterranean that the Trojan wars had unfolded. Would the men of Kitchener's volunteer army offer future poets similar material for a modern epic? Cooper, like so many of the officers at Lemnos and Mitylene, knew about how regular soldiers had been slaughtered in combat in previous months, including Irishmen from regiments such as the Dublin and Munster Fusiliers who, back in April, had struggled through the surf and the barbed wire to reach the Cape Helles shoreline that would turn out, for many, to be their grave.[28]

John Hargrave of the field ambulance service had spent his time on Lemnos attending to men who were suffering from stomach cramps and diarrhoea. He noticed that 'many men slept close to the latrines, too weak to crawl to and fro all night long'. However, by day the island was an intensely busy place. It was full of gangs of workmen, including Greeks, Armenians, Turks and Ethiopians. At dusk Hargrave would watch the Irish soldiers bathe in the harbour, swimming through the warm, clear water.

Ivone Kirkpatrick, with his Inniskilling battalion, arrived at Mitylene at sunset and saw for the first time the slopes covered in olive trees stretching steeply down to the shoreline. That night, from the deck of the boat where the men were billeted, Kirkpatrick thought that the bay looked 'like an inky pit in which the only light was the reflection of the moon on the water'. As departure drew near, some of the officers in the Inniskillings used their imperfect classical Greek to decipher local newspapers. Wags in the battalion, gazing at the sunlit bay and picturesque slopes, joked that they were all on a 'Kitchener continental tour' as a reward for prompt enlistment.[29]

Another Inniskilling officer kept a personal war diary under the pen-name of 'Juvenis', a word chosen because it could be translated from ancient Greek as 'youthful warrior'. Juvenis was, in fact, Lieutenant O.G.E. MacWilliam, who watched with amusement as his fellow officers passed the time in the final days on the island by playing shuffleboard, bridge and poker, and by drinking 'Gallipoli cocktails' consisting of gin, lemon, water and ice – but without the gin and the ice! Whilst sipping these cocktails on deck, one could look across the bay and sometimes see a 'cloud of dust creeping slowly round the zigzag harbour road where a battalion was keeping fit', while in the harbour rowing boats loaded with fruit swarmed around the troopships.

Fishing smacks were also moored in the bay, their bright blue sides decorated with paintings of red-headed snakes. Sometimes at night, before the moon was up, Juvenis could see 'the sky lit up a fiery red to eastward by the flames of burning Asia'. He and his friends felt sure that they were witnessing the burning by the Turks of villages that had belonged to members of Turkey's minority Greek population.

Sipping iced drinks and smoking cigars

The prolonged stay on a cramped ship in Mitylene harbour contributed to minor disciplinary problems among the ranks of the 10th Division stationed at this location, as fights about petty issues broke out on several occasions. Juvenis and his fellow officers, however, thought the landlocked harbour the most beautiful place they had ever seen. They fell in love with the white-washed villages, half-hidden by vines and fig trees, the short wooden piers belonging to the fishermen and the farmhouse lights twinkling on the silent hillsides at night. As the men marched along the roads, Greek women blew them kisses from nearby fields.

In leisure hours, when trying to decipher the only newspapers to hand, the officers engaged in a macabre game: taking bets about the date and cause of death of one of the deceased in the paper's death notices. The men in the ranks on the other hand were encouraged to expend their energy in regular swimming drills. They could often be seen floating nonchalantly in the bay, a cigarette perched between their lips.[30]

The Pals, whose first sight of the Greek islands had been the huge light-house at the entrance to Mudros Bay, were now a hundred miles away at Mitylene, where, with just days to go until departure, maps of Smyrna were passed around and examined by officers. Was Smyrna their real destination or was this an attempt to fool a Turkish spy network? Was this a case, as one officer later expressed it, of 'secrecy gone to seed'? No one seemed to know.

Another memorable feature of the Pals' stay at Mitylene was the arrival of fresh mail from Britain. They also enjoyed a concert on board the SS *Alaunia*, during which the Irish soldiers were joined by 300 troops from a French battle-ship. The evening's entertainment, provided by the men themselves, included a number of concertina tunes, several individual songs and a memorable pianoforte solo by Sergeant Clarke of the 7th Dublins. After the French and British national anthems had been sung, the Irishmen retired to their bunks and the French were ferried back to their vessels.[31]

Noel Drury was also at this concert and did not know whether to be moved or amused at the sound of three thousand men singing 'The Marseillaise' and 'God Save the Queen' loudly and with only a hazy notion both of the words and tunes of the two anthems. Since his arrival in the Greek islands, Drury had taken a particular interest in the clear night sky of this part of the world. On one occasion before his move from Mudros he had stayed out until after midnight looking at stars through the telescope. He could see that 'Saturn looked very well, the rings and four moons being clearly visible', then, as he gazed out to sea, he saw the moon begin to rise, leaving a silver path on the water.

Drury considered Mitylene an idyll, situated as it was so close to a war zone. He wandered the roads, trying to buy an illicit melon from the locals, using only the classical Greek he had learnt at school. Then one night, the officers who were billeted on the *Alaunia* again entertained officers from a French cruiser docked in the bay. They had an excellent evening, 'sipping iced drinks and smoking some of our famous Malta cigars'. The following day Drury hired a small boat from a local man and went for a short sail. On another occasion, he and a colleague walked high into the hills above the bay and looked down on a vista that reminded him of Ireland. That night he wrote in his diary: 'It reminded me very much of the road from the Sally Gap to Roundwood, high up over Lough Tay in County Wicklow.' On reaching a summit where an inn was located, the friends drank iced lemonade and saw, far off in the distance, the tell-tale smoke of burning Greek villages on the Turkish Asiatic mainland.

Drury and his friend met up with some Greek army officers for dinner in a cafe in Port Iero, smoking an ironically named 'Turkish pipe' and listening to a band play in the public gardens. It was here that Drury met the Harbinsons, an English-speaking family who were exiled on Mitylene, having left their business and home on the Black Sea coast, near the mouth of the Danube, at the outbreak of hostilities. They had many stories of what they termed 'the Turkish atrocities' carried out over many years against the Christian population of the Balkans.

Drury also regularly walked by the sea and picked up beautiful shells on the shore and a little seahorse that was dried out by the sun. The punishing sunshine was all-pervasive on Mitylene. Even on board the *Alaunia* it caused alarm when it made the rails of the ship so hot that they couldn't be touched. A sense of looming battle began to manifest itself when Sir Ian Hamilton, the Expeditionary Force commander, turned up suddenly one morning on board the *Alaunia* and the men swiftly lined up to be inspected by him.

Later that day, Drury investigated the interior of one of the flotilla of transport ships that would soon ferry the division to the war zone. He saw the shrapnel scars on the deck and hull and noticed the way the funnels were riddled with bullet holes, presumably inflicted during recent sorties. On 2 August the men of his battalion were given the opportunity to write their last letter home before departure for the front line. Once more, Drury was busy as the ship's censor but in a rather more sombre context now. On Wednesday 4

August he confided in his diary: 'This day last year the war started. 365 days and we have done nothing yet; it's disgusting and the delay is doing the men no good.'

Within hours the wait was over.[32]

Life springs from death

Stopford's plans for the deployment of 9th Corps were now becoming clearer in his own mind, if not quite so clear in the minds of his divisional commanders. From what Mahon could gather, in the late evening of 6 August, the soldiers of the 10th Division were to sail for the secret destination of Suvla and land in the bay where the 11th Division had come ashore a few hours earlier as the first spearhead of the 9th Corps attack. By the early morning of 7 August the 10th would also have arrived and they would storm the Turkish beaches.

Soon thereafter, the 11th and the 10th would both push inland while two other divisions of 9th Corps would be held in reserve until the initial divisions had made good progress. Stopford himself would watch the attacks from his offshore yacht and Sir Ian Hamilton would scrutinize and advise from his HQ at Imbros with regular investigatory trips ashore.

For the commander of 10th Division there was one frustrating and depressing detail in Stopford's plan. The 29th Brigade, under Brigadier Cooper, would not be attacking the Turks at Suvla, alongside their other 10th Division colleagues. They were to be separated and sent into battle a few hours before the departure time established for the rest of the division, landing at Anzac Cove, where they would assist Australian and New Zealand troops with an attack on the Turkish lines – a diversionary ploy to deflect attention away from the new landings to the north.

The process of splitting up the 10th Division as a cohesive military unit continued and Mahon was to attack the Turks with two-thirds of the troops he had expected to have at his disposal, while the other third would go into battle under the command of some unknown general, fighting alongside strangers from the other side of the world, rather than the colleagues with whom they had enlisted in Ireland or in other parts of the British Isles.[33]

These details of military strategy were hidden completely from the family and friends whom the men of the 10th Division had left behind in a country now becoming more aware of the calamitous nature of the war that engulfed

Europe. Hidden from the Irish troops on Lemnos and Mitylene were the details of political developments at home in Ireland.

One significant detail was the funeral in early August of the veteran Irish separatist, O'Donovan Rossa, an iconic leader of the nineteenth-century Irish revolutionary body known as the Fenian Brotherhood. An oration was delivered at his graveside by the nationalist visionary Patrick Pearse, in which he invoked a tradition of self-sacrificial Irish patriotism radically different from the one about to be expressed in tears and blood by the 10th (Irish) Division. Pearse claimed to be speaking 'on behalf of a new generation that has been re-baptized in the Fenian faith and that has accepted the responsibility of carrying out the Fenian programme'. This programme had always been focused on a challenge to British ownership of Ireland. Pearse went on to pledge, on behalf of the assembled crowds, ' to Ireland our love' and 'to English rule in Ireland our hate', and he then called for all true Irish patriots to 'stand together … in brotherly union for the achievement of the freedom of Ireland'.

For Pearse, the deaths that future generations of Irishmen would be inspired by would not be those of Irish soldiers fighting in British army uniforms on distant battlefields under the Union Jack, no matter how great their courage or sincere their motives. The graves that mattered were those of the Irish heroes who had fought and died to rid their country of the English invader. Standing at O'Donovan Rossa's graveside, Pearse spoke of how 'Life springs from death; and from the graves of patriot men and women spring living nations … while Ireland holds these graves, Ireland unfree shall never be at peace'.

Plans for a rebellion against the British empire in Ireland, aided where possible by German military assistance, were already being made by Pearse's ambitious cadre of Irish separatist leaders. Much of the national future would ultimately belong to them and to their political project. Meanwhile, a continent away, thousands of young soldiers, many of them talented, confident, and proud of their country, prepared to die for what future generations of Irishmen would consider to be 'the wrong cause'. [34]

The troopship *Mauretania*, robed in dazzle-paint.
Q65829 IWM

The Irish on a training march through Basingstoke on a hot summer's day in 1915.
HAMPSHIRE COUNTY COUNCIL MUSEUMS SERVICE

Lord Kitchener reviews 'the 10th'.

Lord Dunsany, Irish peer and literary patron, in Royal Inniskilling Fusilier uniform, 1914.

Francis Ledwidge – poet, nationalist, lover, soldier.
THE GETTY COLLECTION

Malta – first taste of the Mediterranean for many Irish soldiers.
Q57809 IWM

Stanley Bay, Alexandria – a favourite bathing place for some Dublin officers.
Q12816 IWM

Port Iero bay on Mitylene – to one Dublin man this Greek island was 'a veritable idyll'.
Q13751 IWM

Mudros Bay on the island of Lemnos – next stop Gallipoli.
Q 25766 IWM

IV
INVADERS

AUGUST 1915

The grey twilight shone faintly on many who were soon to die

THE EASTERN MEDITERRANEAN, 5–6 AUGUST

The 29th Brigade was the first to leave for Anzac Cove to assist the Australian and New Zealand troops with diversionary attacks on the Turkish positions to the south of Suvla. Three officers and 200 men from each battalion were told to remain at the divisional reserve depots on the Greek islands and the rest of the brigade began to pack for departure. John McIlwaine was told to leave his Connaught Rangers bivouac at 10 am on 5 August, carrying entrenching tools, cooking utensils, extra ammunition, bombs, and basic medical stores. He also carried his rations in a white cotton bag containing a handful of small biscuits, a small cube of oxo, half an ounce of tea and an ounce of sugar. He waited at the harbour with several of his fellow-soldiers until four in the afternoon when the men were placed on board the SS *Elector*, a cargo boat that transported the troops to within a few hundred yards of the Turkish coastline. Some soldiers from the Connaughts, unable to find space on the *Elector*, joined men from the Leinster Regiment on board another vessel that was drawn up alongside, the SS *Clacton*.[1]

The process of working out what General Stopford required of 29th Brigade from his brief and encrypted telegram messages was extremely difficult. Even the names of the ships to be used by the brigade in their landing manoeuvres tended to vary from message to message, despite calls for clarity in the matter. No instructions were given regarding the role of Irish brigade commander at Anzac Cove, so General Mahon went to Imbros to seek an urgent meeting with Stopford but this slowed down the whole schedule for departure. There was also the problem recorded by the Irish HQ war diarist of telephonic communication being 'interrupted by the cable getting fouled by ships in the port'.

Orders concerning which field ambulance brigade members, if any, should travel to Anzac Cove were particularly muddled. It was a situation compounded by serious shortages of equipment in the 29th Field Ambulance Brigade, which led them to borrow medical and transport equipment from their already under-resourced 30th Brigade colleagues. The omens for this new military campaign on the Gallipoli peninsula were not good.[2]

If such thoughts went through Bryan Cooper's mind, he did his best to conceal them. He had been busy with many tasks, not least of which was preventing Greek children from pestering his men with eggs, watermelons and lemons on the quayside. This was not made easier by the fact that he himself was beginning to suffer from dysentery. It also fell to Cooper to organize religious services for his soldiers in the last daylight hours of the final day at their base. He would later recall how 'the grey twilight shone faintly on the faces of many who were soon to die' as, just before departure, hundreds of young men stood solemnly at the water's edge with their heads bowed, many of them with up to 200 rounds of ammunition 'festooned around their necks'. Every man also carried either a pick, a shovel or a camp kettle.

Cooper also noted how carefully some of the battalions had attempted to improvise regimental badges of coloured cloth and to sew them onto the fabric of their sand-coloured khaki uniform or affix them to their large, mushroom-shaped helmets. The Hampshires had mounted a claret and yellow regimental patch while the Irish Rifles had improvised an emblematic display of their traditional green and black colours. The Leinsters had procured some ink and stencilled the letter 'L' onto their helmets but the Connaughts had ordered some professionally made shamrock badges from home and these had not yet arrived when the men went into battle.

At last the men of 29th Brigade boarded their vessels. In the end, they were travelling to war without their field ambulance unit and without their own field engineers, so it was assumed that the four infantry battalions of the 29th Brigade were going to be attached to another army corps and would be able to make full use of their medical and engineering services. On board, as the boats sailed northwards, the men kept close watch on their personal equipment and some soldiers tried to sleep. A few were allowed to come up onto the deck to see the island of Imbros pass by and then sink astern while the sun set beyond the Lemnos hills.

In the gathering gloom ahead, flashes of gunfire could be seen and the boom of explosions heard coming from a shadowy headland on whose summit an enemy searchlight pierced the surrounding darkness. As the Turkish coast drew nearer, Cooper saw a British destroyer focussing its search-light on a path leading down the face of a cliff. The circle of projected light looked like the beam of a 'magic lantern' in a village entertainment at home in Sligo. The 'cliffs' that Cooper could see were the infamous slopes behind Anzac Cove. The 10th Division had reached a battlefield at long last.[3]

We went to Gallipoli without any orders

THE EASTERN MEDITERRANEAN, 5–6 AUGUST

The two other infantry brigades of the 10th Division were now ready to contribute to the 9th Corps landings at Suvla. On the islands of Mitylene and Lemnos, thousands more Irish soldiers prepared for departure on boats that would take them to one of the three beaches in Suvla Bay that were at this moment being assaulted by the 11th Division in the first wave of new British attacks. The landing area for the Irish troops was to be A Beach close to the northern tip of the bay, ideally placed for an assault on a long rocky strip of high ground nearby known as the Kiretch Tepe ridge, the capture of which would be the division's first major objective. Only the highest-ranking officers in each brigade knew of these plans. The details of how to go about both the actual landings and the subsequent capture of the ridge were far from clear.

Few maps of Suvla were available and it is questionable whether even Brigadier-generals Hill and Nicholl had proper cartographic assistance to help them plan a careful battle strategy for the men who were under their command. It is not surprising that after the war many Irish officers claimed that they set sail for the battlefield, not knowing where in the world they were going or what to do with their men when they got there.[4]

When the Irish troops got ashore, having been conveyed from their flotilla of transport boats in new armour-plated lighters, what exactly would their relationship with the men of General Hammersley's 11th Division be? How would they liaise effectively while soldiering in completely unknown territory? How would the division maintain close contact with the 9th Corps' commander, General Stopford, while he was ensconced in his yacht, the *Jonquil*, anchored some distance offshore? How effectively could supplies of food and water be delivered to the men and how easy would it be for the much-reduced ranks of the division's field artillery to get ashore and then bombard the Turkish positions with accuracy? How efficient would the medical care be in a war conducted many miles from a proper hospital service? What did the 10th Division really know about the Turks whom they were to kill or capture on arrival? On Mahon's disembarkation, what would his role be as commander of a diminished fighting unit? Perhaps most crucially of all, how swiftly should the Irish soldiers press toward the inland stretches of the peninsula after the anticipated coastal breakthrough, and did individual battalion and brigade commanders have permission to improvise battle plans? If they could take advantage of Turkish defensive weaknesses where they came upon them, could they improvise or would that lead to accusations of individualistic recklessness?[5]

Answers to such questions were not be forthcoming from 9th Corps HQ, whose instructions thus far had been sparse and unclear. A telegram to Stopford from the 10th Divisional command on the morning of 6 August complained with increasing frustration and alarm: 'No orders sent ... you said you would send anything necessary ... there has been no means of communication'.[6]

The combination of inadequate telegraphy, a series of conflicting naval semaphore signals and a number of out-of-date letters from Stopford meant that Mahon and his staff now felt frighteningly unclear about their role in the impending battle. Things were not helped by news, later that morning, of more than 600 men who were suffering from gastric trouble which someone at HQ blithely suggested was the result of an excessive amount of potassium permanganate used to sterilize the water supply.[7] Mahon was assured that the problem of sickness was well under control but this was misguided optimism, given that many soldiers in the Munster Fusiliers were actually suffering from dysentery. Godfrey Drage would later explain that by 6 August he had been ill for ten days and was almost too weak to stand, due no doubt to the fact that almost everything he ate at Mudros Bay was covered in flies. Drage would recall how this growing swarm of insects 'sat on your very fork' and 'unless you shook them off you found yourself chewing and swallowing flies'. A number of the men from Lemnos went into battle using improvised remedies against such sickness. Drage procured opium pills and used them to settle his stomach and dull the pain.[8]

On the much healthier island of Mitylene, Juvenis joined his fellow Inniskillings as they received their official ration of tobacco along with shamrock-covered envelopes containing cigarettes from 'friends in Ireland'. The hardware for an officer going into battle included revolver, field glasses, compass, map case and mess-tin. Once this was assembled they went on board their transport ship and below deck on the cramped vessel the men huddled together in an atmosphere that seemed to Juvenis like 'an ill-savoured furnace'. By dusk the boat had left the harbour and was heading northwards.

As the vessel maintained its northward trajectory, the men knew for certain that they were not bound for Smyrna in Asiatic Turkey but for the Gallipoli peninsula, which lay on the European side of the Dardanelles. As darkness thickened, 'lights out' was ordered on board and shortly afterwards Juvenis mounted the steps to the deck and found that it was wet with salt spray and that a cool wind was blowing. At 3 am the men were allowed to drink some hot tea. Shortly afterwards, a hospital ship passed them on its way to Lemnos, with its red and green port and starboard lights burning in the dark.[9]

Irish battalions, packed onto crowded boats, followed in one another's wake as the flotilla moved ever closer to the battle zone. The boats themselves were endearingly named.[10] Some of the men of the Royal Irish Fusiliers travelled on board a vessel called *Honeysuckle*, while others were on board the *Snaefell*, named after the highest peak on the Isle of Man, a mountain visible on a clear day from parts of the eastern Irish coastline.

Soon the rumble of gunfire announced that they were approaching the peninsula and the boat now veered north-westwards, indicating that neither Cape Helles nor Anzac Cove but rather a new battlefield, several miles ahead, would be the 10th Division's peninsular destination. Ivone Kirkpatrick was excited to find his ship's captain heading towards this fresh and unknown territory past the thunder of explosions, the distant pyrotechnics of shellfire and the regular flares, which indicated the continuing battle on the heights beyond Anzac Cove.[11]

On first approaching Gallipoli from Mitylene, many Dublin Pals thought they noticed a resemblance between the dark silhouette of the peninsula and the coastal land around Dublin Bay. Then grim reality struck as the men watched the blaze of huge shells bursting on the Achi Baba hills above Cape Helles 'like a house going on fire with a sudden blaze and immediately going out again'. Before long the Pals were close enough to the coastline to be awe-struck by the noise of the rival artillery-pieces, which between them made a sound like one long and continuous roll of thunder.[12]

A range of skilled men, who would be as vital to the success of the Suvla mission as any infantry officer, were on their way to the peninsula. They included the field companies of the Royal Engineers who sat on board their vessel holding on tight to their hand-barrows piled high with tools and their empty sandbags. Their minds were focused on the tasks that lay ahead, including that most nerve-racking of tasks, the search for and destruction of land mines.[13]

Noel Drury had had a last lunch on board the *Alaunia* on 6 August when the officers of the 6th Dublins all drank success to their 'undertaking'. Then in the early evening they boarded the vessel that would take them to Gallipoli, a boat that in everyone's opinion stank to high heaven. A few hours after the voyage began, the men saw the pale, lemon-coloured flashes in the sky and an hour later heard the heavy boom of the guns. Unfortunately, the cushions on which Drury was sitting were alive with vermin, distracting him from the ghastly beauties of the night-time battlefield. Undeterred however, he managed to enjoy a breakfast of two bread rolls and a celebratory quarter bottle of champagne, something each of the officers in his battalion had managed to secrete in their baggage.

When Drury inquired, the naval officer in charge of the boat indicated that he knew very little about their destination. He had orders to dump the men onto some lighters that would appear at a given place indicated on his naval chart and then leave. The Irish officers were instructed not to use the boat's wireless equipment to try to contact Mudros Bay or Imbros for any further information to preserve the secrecy of the landings. Some of the officers now felt that this level of secrecy was reaching alarming proportions. As Drury himself later complained, 'We went to Gallipoli without any orders and without any maps.'[14]

Human blood soaking its way into sand

SUVLA BAY, 7 AUGUST

As the 10th Division neared Suvla Bay, orders did come through from 9th Corps HQ that were profoundly significant. The 11th Division, which had begun the attack on Suvla during the previous few hours, had encountered grave difficulties when landing at A, B and C beaches.

A Beach was particularly troublesome. It was very hard to locate in the darkness, and further problems occurred when the lighters carrying the men struck shoals in the bay, leaving the soldiers to struggle desperately towards the shore while under enemy fire, trying to hold their rifles above the surface so the salt water would not damage the guns. When the men came ashore, battalion command structure had been thrown into confusion. Despite this, the men of the 11th managed to move from A Beach onto the heights of the nearby Kiretch Tepe ridge to occupy some key positions.

Meanwhile, the men who had landed at B and C beaches to the south, had struggled badly in the face of remarkably accurate and heavy Turkish gunfire. They attacked their first military objective, the coastal prominence of Lala Baba on the southern tip of Suvla Bay. When dawn approached it was clear that the 11th Division would not have time to fight for their second objective, the pair of hills referred to as 'Chocolate Hill' and 'Green Hill', from which the Turks could fire across the intervening flatlands of Suvla plain in the direction of A Beach where the rest of the British troops had their landing place. Green Hill was fertile and lush, while Chocolate Hill had been ravaged and charred by recent bush fires, turning the hillside dark brown.

What was also clear to the few officers in 11th Division who possessed a map was that the great salt lake at the heart of the Suvla plain had disappeared, presumably due to summer drought, leaving a huge white marsh. Due to their inexperience, the unexpectedly stiff resistance they met and the difficulties of landing and fighting by night on unfamiliar terrain, the 11th Division did not make progress as anticipated.

This left the 10th with a much more dangerous and demanding task than expected. As news from Suvla Bay filtered through to corps HQ, Stopford decided to change the plan of action. At 5 am, the Irish soldiers approaching the Suvla shoreline were told to go to B and C beaches rather than A Beach, as these two seemed more accessible. B and C beaches were, however, just outside the southern tip of Suvla Bay and thus a considerable distance from the Irish Division's primary objective, the Kiretch Tepe ridge.

A couple of hours later, while the Irish landings at B and C beaches were underway, this order from General Stopford was amended because a new, approachable and relatively sheltered stretch of coastline had been located just north of the original landing spot. As a result of this double alteration of orders, some of the 10th Division were now landing at a position called A Beach West. The Irishmen were soon spread out across the full width of Suvla Bay, and the dispersal and fragmentation of the Irish division made Mahon's task increasingly difficult.

As part of this unforeseen dispersal, the two Dublin Fusilier battalions, the two Royal Irish Fusilier battalions and one battalion of the Inniskillings had all been diverted to the southern landing area while the two Munster battalions, the other battalion of Inniskillings and the men of the divisional pioneers had all been re-diverted to the northern landing area just after 7 am. When General Mahon arrived at Suvla a little later in the morning, he found himself at the modified A Beach landing place with only four battalions at his disposal to launch an assault on the Kiretch Tepe hillsides. He had anticipated having the thirteen battalions of an entire division when planning the Suvla battle at his HQ in Lemnos a few days before.[15]

The ship containing Noel Drury's Dublin Fusiliers anchored close to the southern headland of Suvla Bay. He sat on deck, perched on top of a pile of entrenching tools, feeling both conspicuous and vulnerable. At 6 am the first men left the relative safety of Drury's vessel and piled into the tiny, ugly, motorized 'beetles' for the brief journey to B Beach. Drury and his company awaited their turn at the stern of the ship and watched as hundreds of their fellow-soldiers were 'jam-packed' into the lighters until it looked like the vessels could take no more weight. These lighters set off slowly towards the low Turkish shoreline and then Drury saw through the murky early light the first Irish soldiers jump out of their beetles and run ashore.

He saw some of these men fall and assumed they were being picked off by Turkish snipers. Then he saw the bodies of two or three soldiers blown into the air by land mines concealed several inches beneath the sand. None of the men sitting around Drury in the relative safety of the ship showed any sign of emotion even though they had just seen and heard these explosions and knew that they too would be going ashore in a few minutes.

When his company's turn came, he urged his men down into their lighter, which was swaying violently in the water, then stepped down from the ship himself and very nearly ended his soldiering career. In his haste he slipped and one of his legs was left dangling between the hulls of the two vessels. His leg would have been mangled or crushed had he not been pulled to safety by an unseen pair of hands. Gathering his wits, he cast his eye in the direction of the ramp in the lighter's prow that was held in place by large chains. Presumably this ramp would be let down to allow rapid disembarkation when the beetle finally hit the sloping coastline.

A huge artillery shell suddenly whistled through the air and exploded in the water, half-way between Drury's lighter and the one ahead of it, leaving everybody soaked to the skin but unharmed. A few seconds later the lighter had landed and the men were running through the shallows onto a battlefield for the very first time in their lives. There was a random and terrifying carpet of debris on the beach from the 11th Division's engagement with the Turkish defenders: hand grenades, gas helmets and pistols lay everywhere while there was a tremendous cannonade overhead, caused by the British gunships that had now opened up on the Turkish defensive positions.

Drury traversed the beach, trying to locate a senior officer to give him orders but then found the colonel of his own battalion doing exactly the same thing. Amid the confusion and noise, he came across his first corpses: they belonged to Turks who were 'lying bayoneted, still in the attitude of firing from cover' and who had been left there untouched since the previous night's combat. They were already beginning to swell in the heat under a veil of hovering flies.[16]

Many of the Pals had seen a white sandy beach from their troop-carrier and beyond that the low, grey foreshore of Nibrunesi Point. Beyond that were some clay cliffs dotted with shingle and an area of scrubland through which several paths were visible, leading inland towards the heights of Lala Baba. The scene looked to some like the shoreline at Killiney Bay, just south of Dublin. The sand dunes, on the other hand, that stretched south towards Anzac Cove reminded one or two soldiers of the strand at Dollymount. Gazing at the farthest reaches of high, hilly ground where the Turks had their artillery positions, one man watched each British naval shell explode 'like a bright red flame edged with a black fringe of smoke, just like a tulip with the red leaves tipped with black'.

As the Pals' vessel anchored offshore, they could see human figures in the scrubland behind the beach who appeared to be working with spades, and the Irish troops took it as evidence that the 11th Division's soldiers were creating trenches and dug-outs for them on the peninsula. They could also make out what seemed to be stretcher-bearers, carrying wounded men down the slopes of Lala Baba.

After a brief trip on a lighter, the Pals prepared to disembark. As he stepped down the gangway, loaded down with what he called his 'impedimenta', Frank

Laird saw a young lad lying on a stretcher, blocking his way. He must have been one of the first 10th Division soldiers to come ashore a few moments earlier. He had been badly hit and left on the beach by stretcher-bearers for a lighter to pick him up and return him to the safety of a ship. Laird could see how the stretcher was filling up with blood and how it poured out as four of his colleagues heaved the injured man up and carried him on board before making their way once more to B Beach.

Before long, most of the Pals were ashore, feet crunching over the wet strand. The men immediately made for the shelter afforded by the clay cliffs they had seen from their troop-carrier. They could hear the sharp hiss of shrapnel whizzing through the air while the naval guns continued to thunder in the background. In the grass at the edge of the beach everyone could see mutilated bodies, both Turkish and British, the human debris from the previous night's fighting.[17]

Among the men of the field ambulance brigades arriving at B and C beaches was William Knott, who at this stage was only vaguely aware of where he had landed. He thought he was close to a hilly stretch of land surrounding a large plain but there was no sense of a coherent battle plan in his mind and as he watched the infantry ahead of him go ashore, some of them knee-deep in water, he wondered what lay ahead for all of them on this strange peninsula. On coming ashore he came across the blackened corpses of two men from the 11th Division's Manchester Regiment who had been blown up by a landmine. He resolved not to think about this and focus instead on what he could do to help the living, wherever he found them.[18]

John Hargrave was also a field ambulance man. As he approached Suvla, he kept focusing not on the shoreline but on 'the little yellow-skinned observation balloons which floated like a penny toy' above the ships that were anchored in the bay. Then, as he began to look more closely at B and C beaches, where shells were constantly exploding, his brain began to register scenes of immense horror and suffering as 'the dead lay there like little groups of dead beetles and the wounded were crawling away like ants into the dead yellow grass and the sage bushes to die'.

In the humid half-light of dawn he could see a widespread flicker of rifle-fire and hear the constant crackle of the guns. It looked to Hargrave as if the combatants were 'striking a thousand matches at once' out there on the peninsula. After just a few moments' acquaintance with the realities of twentieth century warfare, Hargrave felt that it was all incredibly wasteful and senseless.

He felt that he was watching 'mechanical Death, like some devilish ant-eater, eating up its insects, steel-studded and shrapnel-toothed'.

When he landed on Turkish soil, Hargrave immediately encountered two Irish corpses that lay sprawled on the sand. He noted with both fascination and revulsion how 'one had his stomach blown out and the other had his stomach blown in'. Then, as he searched for wounded soldiers to whom he could be of assistance, he first smelled the characteristic, ghastly Gallipoli odour of 'human blood soaking its way into the sand.' Before long, Hargrave had come upon a Turkish intelligence officer's deserted dug-out, with its store of tobacco, its 'field telephone, dried fish, earthen jar, fez, boots and fringed waistband'. A little later he also found the corpse of an enemy sniper who had been killed during the initial 11th Division landing. The Turk was by now 'a great heat-swollen figure, stinking in the sunshine. A swarm of green and black flies, which had been feeding on his face and up his nostrils, went up in a humming, buzzing cloud'. Clearly, death brought decay and degradation to one's enemy as it did to one's friend.[19]

Someone could be heard screaming out in panic

A BEACH WEST, SUVLA BAY, 7 AUGUST

As some soldiers fought to establish themselves on the beaches beyond Nibrunesi Point, other men had been diverted to land at A Beach West close to the Kiretch Tepe ridge. Among them was Ivone Kirkpatrick, waiting with the 5th Inniskillings on a ship moored in Suvla Bay. He, like William Knott, had little idea where he actually was. Ahead of him he could see troops who had already landed and were trying to make their way inland. These were men of the Munster Fusiliers and among them was the figure of Godfrey Drage, for whom the landing was an opium-induced blur. The only detail of the landing that he could later recall was the shocking mutilation of some of his fellow soldiers by a huge explosion that sent 'arms, legs and bodies flying up into the air'.[20]

Ivone Kirkpatrick had had a couple of hours waiting on board his carrier, which he spent watching an enemy plane circle over the bay although thankfully none of the bombs actually hit British shipping. Kirkpatrick could also see one of his own ships laying down a series of pudding-shaped mines in the outer waters of the bay, presumably to prevent enemy submarines from attacking the British vessels now gathered there.

The two companies of Inniskillings who were waiting ahead of Kirkpatrick then began to pile into their lighters and make for the shore. A few moments later it was his company's turn. His beetle was manned by a weary naval officer who told the men to cram into the confined but sheltered space below the armour-plated roof. Then the officer shouted at his passengers that they were all 'going to make a good trip' and Kirkpatrick's lighter surged towards the beaches, bumping against a terrible flotsam of soldiers' corpses en route. He stood up and gave his platoon orders to prepare immediately for landing. The Inniskillings dashed out into the knee-deep shallows across the drawbridge, then sprinted up the beach into the thick scrub that lay behind the sand. There, Kirkpatrick told his men to wait until orders came through to proceed inland. Nearby, they could all see the corpse of an enormous Turkish soldier who lay 'looking with open eyes at the sky'. Kirkpatrick saw how 'a fly walked along his teeth and his upper lip' and thought that 'it seemed incredible that he could not brush it away'.

The rush of adrenalin from his first few minutes in military action made Kirkpatrick feel exalted and powerful, despite the danger all around. An Irish soldier in another company was lying a few yards away, yelling fiercely after being hit in the shoulder. Minutes later someone else could be heard screaming out in panic that he had nearly pressed his hand down on an enemy landmine.[21]

A brilliant sunset behind Samothrace

A BEACH WEST, SUVLA BAY, 7 AUGUST

Meanwhile, Juvenis spent the morning and afternoon sitting on his transport ship. Around him the sea was becoming calmer except where the water was occasionally 'splashed up by rifle bullets and shrapnel and the waterspouts of shells'. Because of the danger from enemy fire, the men of Juvenis' company were ordered to lie on the deck while enemy fire targeted their particular vessel. For the first time since his rifle-training days in England, Juvenis heard the crack and hiss of bullets passing close by. He lay on his back on the hard wood of the deck, gazing into the sky. He was sure that he could see a bird of prey hovering high overhead, undisturbed by the din and the danger. Steeped in classical literature, he was at once reminded of how the warrior Agamemnon had seen an eagle in the sky as he set out for Troy. Then a more modern flying creature sailed into Juvenis' line of vision. It was a German plane, loaded with bombs and with two 'Iron Crosses' painted on its wings and fuselage.

Suddenly, there was a terrific explosion close by. An empty transport ship that was moored alongside had been hit by a Turkish artillery shell and began to take a heavy list to starboard. The inexplicable wait in the bay continued, so the men raised their eyes and watched the battle. They could see a flat area of marshy land and beyond that a broad plain girded by hills. This marsh was soon to be known by the Irish soldiers as the salt lake. In its dried-out summer condition, it was gleaming white in the sun. Through his field glasses Juvenis watched his 10th Division colleagues landing at the southern tip of the bay beneath the low cliffs near Lala Baba and scampering over the shore into the scrub, the sheen of their sunlit bayonets especially visible. When he stared at the Turkish defensive emplacements closer at hand on Suvla Bay's northern headland he observed 'huge mauve and yellow spurts of smoke and sand' bursting up as British warships pounded them with shells.

By now Juvenis and his men were growing impatient and tense and their feelings were intensified by watching the Turkish artillery achieve a direct hit upon a lighter nearing A Beach West. Thick yellow bursts of smoke suddenly surrounded the craft, followed by the crack and thud of an immense explosion. Juvenis watched as men were 'flung this way and that' and then saw some of them crawl up through the surf onto the beach and lie still, either dead or gravely wounded, while others disappeared from view beneath the reddening water. Explosions from other shells followed in quick succession and before long clouds of smoke and sand seemed to obscure the view. A few minutes later a brief but powerful thunderstorm erupted, after which the men watched a brilliant sunset behind the Greek island of Samothrace.

It was not until midnight that Juvenis got orders to bring his soldiers ashore. They made the 600-yard journey in an ugly lighter that Juvenis thought was an 'uncouth wave-washed monstrosity', piloted by an exhausted man munching 'a thick and oily sandwich'. The men landed under cover of darkness and then lay down and tried to sleep, either on the sand or in the scrub, until the next day.[22]

Crossing the vulnerable spaces

SUVLA PLAIN, 7 AUGUST

If it was nightfall on the first day at Suvla before Juvenis finally found himself on A Beach, what happened to the men who disembarked on B and C beaches beyond Nibrunesi Point during the earlier part of the day? They had been landed in a location far from their original disembarkation point, where they came under the general charge of General Hamersley of 11th Division. More specifically they were under the command of Brigadier-General Sitwell, whose English soldiers were the main force occupying Nibrunesi Point.

Brigadier-General Hill, the most senior Irish officer to come ashore in the southern part of Suvla, understandably felt that he was responsible for both the well-being and the military use of his men. Within a couple of hours, Hill and Sitwell had met up at a command post and clashed over what should happen to the 10th Division troops in the vicinity. Sitwell argued that the Irish soldiers should be part of an immediate dash to capture the untaken heights of Chocolate and Green hills. Hill wished to move his men north across the shoreline to join their divisional colleagues in an attack on the Kiretch Tepe ridge, as had originally been planned. Sitwell won his argument after several attempts to communicate with General Stopford aboard the *Jonquil*. So the Irish troops who had landed at B and C beaches, rather than being under General Mahon's command for an attack along the Kiretch Tepe ridge, were now to be committed to an assault on objectives originally assigned to the 11th under the directions of a brigadier from that English division.

The assault on Green and Chocolate hills was no easy task. The artillery support that was needed to effectively pound enemy trenches on these hills was limited and when going forward the Irish troops were probably best off moving along the periphery of the dried-up salt lake and attacking the hills from the north-west, as the preponderance of Turkish defensive fire-power was probably aimed in a southerly and westerly direction.[23]

There is evidence that aerial reconnaissance had already shown British commanders that there were several heavily fortified trenches on the northern slopes of Chocolate and Green hills. Photographs would also have shown that Hill 10, one of the interim objectives on the Irish division's circumlocutory route, also possessed a well-constructed Turkish redoubt. If Hill and Sitwell did receive this information on time, it did not affect their strategy: by early afternoon Irish and English soldiers in the southern part of Suvla had gone into action, moving along the edge of the salt lake bed towards Hill 10.[24]

Noel Drury, awaiting the orders that would propel him northwards, was shocked by the apparent inertia of his new colleagues of the 11th Division. These soldiers, whose natural rhythm was disturbed by a disorienting nocturnal battle for the Suvla beaches, seemed to be wasting the daylight hours by 'doing nothing but lying about and sleeping'. Galvanized by fresh orders to attack Chocolate Hill, however, a mixed group of 10th and 11th Division troops including Drury set out for a shoreline location known as the Cut. The Cut was a gap in the coastline where the lake overflowed into Suvla Bay during the wet winter season and therefore the perfect place to gain access to the dried-out salt lake. However, the margins of the salt lake that constituted the next stage of the journey turned out to be far from manageable terrain. The men soon sank to their knees in stinking, rotting vegetation and the Turkish gunners on the slopes targeted the troops as they advanced. Though no one in Drury's vicinity was directly hit, they were covered by the filth thrown up by the shells.[25]

Soon the Pals also joined the march towards Chocolate Hill. Many of them had already observed from their positions on the slopes of Lala Baba how the Munster Fusiliers had scrambled ashore on the far side of the bay, only to face death and mutilation on a beach strewn with landmines. Some of the Pals had worried desperately about the Munsters' welfare but then became entirely preoccupied with their own safety when bombarded by Turkish artillerymen who located the Dubliners' positions in the shallow Turkish trenches that had been captured during the first British landings during the night-hours.

When the order came for the Pals to advance to the Cut, bullets immediately began to whistle past while the occasional shell landed with a terrifying explosion close by. The Turkish gunners also had the Cut in their sights. The only thing to do was to take a deep breath, then hurl themselves across the dried-up channel between the salt marsh and the sea and hope for the best. Already, the Fusiliers' casualties were mounting at this spot and someone dubbed it, with dark Irish wit, Dunphy's Corner, after a well-known Dublin location that funeral cortèges travelled past on their way to Glasnevin cemetery. The Pals who had safely got past Dunphy's Corner then took the next step: crossing the plain towards what was known as Hill 10.

The journey to Hill 10 across yielding sand, salt and muck was as agonising for the Pals as it had been for the other soldiers. Some of them screamed for help because they became lodged up to their waists in mud. Some men wondered if their period without regular exertion since leaving Basingstoke had left them unfit for the rigours of battle. Crackling Turkish rifle fire indicated that this side of Chocolate Hill was not as undefended as Sitwell had presumed. Gradually, men were picked off by snipers as they crossed the exposed landscape of the Suvla plain.

During a brief rest in a sheltered place, the news began to circulate that Major Tippett of C Company had been gravely wounded by a bullet and shortly afterwards it was rumoured that Lieutenant Ernest Julien, the Law Professor from Trinity College, serving with C Company, had also been hit. They wondered about their chances of making it through the first day of combat every time they heard the distant cry of a fellow soldier being hit by a bullet. Lying down for cover during a particularly severe volley of rifle-fire, one man watched a bullet ricochet off the ground just a yard from his face.

And before long the most desperate of all their difficulties was the problem of thirst. Halfway through the trek across Suvla plain, a heavy shower refreshed the men, releasing the powerful fragrance of thyme and rosemary, but soon the punishing heat crippled everyone. Their faces were bathed in perspiration and they tried desperately to ration their water. Many of the Dublin Fusiliers had already used their supplies and when someone located what appeared to be a well, the men clustered to drink, making themselves an easy target for Turkish gunners.[26]

Bright wild flowers were growing

CHOCOLATE HILL, 7 AUGUST

The Pals arrived at Hill 10 to find it had been taken by another battalion. So the final advance on Chocolate Hill began with several hundred soldiers from other Irish regiments and a considerable number of troops from the 11th. They headed off across the salt lake bed in an easterly direction, then ran over a couple of empty water-courses and through a number of dry, ploughed fields, before crawling through hedgerows. The troops now entered a network of empty but well-constructed trenches at the base of Chocolate Hill, which some men assumed had been built under German supervision.

The enemy strategically withdrew to the very top of the hill. Now it was time for a wild and heart-stopping charge up to the summit, using both bayonet and bullet. Even those who were not in the vanguard of the assault could see that an officer was signalling the men for 'the off' with a green cloth tied to a stick. Then with a deafening roar and a concerted rush, the Dublins stormed Chocolate Hill. To many of the Pals it looked and sounded like a gigantic version of a forward rush on the rugby pitch at Dublin's Lansdowne Road.

By the time the Pals had reached the top, all the Turkish defenders had either been bayoneted or shot or had fled into the distance. Dead bodies lay in the brushwood on a hill-top that looked like a volcanic landscape in places, thick with smoke and pockmarked with craters of shells sent over earlier by British naval gunners. It was a bleak and lifeless scene, but the Dublin Pals had helped the Irish Division to take its first big objective and there was an intense satisfaction for many of the men in that fact.

As dusk fell, the troops who had occupied Chocolate Hill tried to rest and ignore their terrible thirst. Some men in the Pals heard rumours that scores of Royal Irish Fusiliers ahead of them had moved on and taken Green Hill, which lay 600 yards farther ahead. Lying on top of Chocolate Hill under the stars were many Irish troops who earlier in the day had left behind their packs, mess-tins and water flasks, believing that they would be an encumbrance. Now they were stranded inland, a long way from the supplies of fresh water which were supposedly being landed on the Suvla beaches. Many of the men on Chocolate Hill were so parched with thirst and weak with hunger that they could scarcely speak.

The grim task of making a casualty list for the first day's fighting had to be undertaken and in the 7th battalion of the Dublin Fusiliers the figures suggested that a hundred men had either been wounded, killed or simply could not be accounted for. In D Company, where the Pals were based, there were twenty-two casualties. It was also widely known that Lieutenant Julien and Major Tippett were casualties. His colleagues did not know the full details at the time, but Ernest Julien had been badly wounded by a gunshot wound to his back and had been taken from a casualty clearing station to a makeshift field hospital on the beach. He died the following day on a hospital ship in the bay and his weighted body was dropped into the sea after a short service.

As sniper fire crackled throughout the night, many Pals wondered what lay ahead and worried about the possibility that shells from their own artillery would start to land on top of them. Scenes from the day's fighting flashed before them, preventing them from sleeping. They recalled seeing the lighters being turned into floating ambulances to take back the wounded from 11th Division on their blood-stained stretchers on the beach.

Frank Laird recalled several scenes with horror, in particular the sight of a 'young Dublin chap' who had given a 'sudden choke, stiffened and lay dead, shot through the throat'. But he was comforted by thinking about how he had spent much of the day with his friend Charles Frederick Ball, with whom he had agreed on the troop-ship to stick together in the coming battle.

Some men were conscious that they were covered in sticky, half-dried blood, usually not their own but of a wounded colleague whom they had carried to safety. What stuck in one young soldier's mind most clearly was that while sand-bagging an improvised defence line on the top of Chocolate Hill, he and his men actually used the corpse of a dead Turk to fill a gap in the defence. [27]

Also trying to rest on top of Chocolate Hill was Noel Drury, whose company of the 6th Dublins had traversed the salt lake bed and assaulted their final objective without any significant losses. He felt proud to have survived his first day of battle but was both mentally and physically exhausted, not just because of the gruelling terrain but because he had had to lift and carry heavy loads of ammunition. Drury had been looking forward to a meal at the end of the day but when he opened his knapsack and tried his 'first dose of biscuit and bully beef' he realized that he 'couldn't face it at all'. It 'turned out of the tin in a horrible, slimy, multi-coloured mess.' He faced another day of battle on an empty stomach and seriously dehydrated. [28]

Fighting on the stony spine of the ridge

KIRETCH TEPE RIDGE, 7–8 AUGUST

Meanwhile, the assault on the division's original objective, the Kiretch Tepe ridge, was under way at the other end of Suvla Bay. This was a very difficult task, for as one senior officer reported 'the ridge is very steep and stony, with no communications except occasional goat tracks'. There were springs located half-way up the slope but otherwise it was barren and hostile territory. As the Munster Fusiliers fought their way up to the top of the ridge, Godfrey Drage's thirst was made worse by the fact that he felt obliged to give the last of his water to a badly wounded fellow soldier he encountered en route. As a result of this generosity, Drage's tongue was swollen and he could hardly swallow any food. [29]

The highest point on the ridge was soon known as the Pimple, a cairn of stones at about 650 feet. Soldiers from the 5th Inniskillings remained near the coastline and watched with awe as the two Munster battalions headed up the rocky slopes and out of view along the ridge towards the Pimple while gunfire rained down on them from the Turkish defenders. Also watching the spectacle were the men from the divisional pioneer battalion of the Royal Irish Regiment, who looked up from time to time as they unloaded ammunition and supplies on A Beach West and then went about the business of creating a divisional HQ for General Mahon and his staff, who had just arrived on the peninsula. Some of the pioneers were also instructed to create a small jetty where specialized lighters containing tanks full of Egyptian water could dock and begin to supply the men with fluids. Many of the pioneers also started digging the first lines in a network of defensive trenches.

The 30th Field Ambulance Brigade also busied themselves, erecting tents for a field hospital on the beach. Already the Irish stretcher-bearers were beginning to bring back blood-stained casualties who were lined up in rows on the sand awaiting medical attention.[30] In the vicinity of A Beach, one group of Royal Engineers searched carefully for land mines while another group tried to find a nearby spring or well to supply the medical services with water. By mid-afternoon only one well had been found. The water-lighters had also run into trouble, several of them grounding on a sandbank in the bay, one hundred yards from the shore, reducing the supply of water to a trickle.[31]

Throughout the long day, Ivone Kirkpatrick's company of Inniskillings lay near the beach and watched the heights for a sign of how the Munster Fusiliers were progressing. They knew that before long they too would be called on to climb those slopes and face the enemy. It came as no surprise then when Kirkpatrick's men were told by the commander of 31st Brigade to walk in single file up a marked route to a spot on the ridge where they would find some shallow trenches in which they were to try to sleep until dawn, when they would go into action.[32]

Juvenis, whose Inniskilling unit had landed much later than the other infantrymen of his brigade, was instructed that night to lie down where he had landed on the beach and try to get some sleep during the remaining hours of darkness. At 2 am he was woken by the sound of other men groaning loudly in their sleep.[33]

Meanwhile, during that first night at Gallipoli, the Munster Fusiliers were encamped somewhere on the heights above. The walking wounded and the graver casualties carried on stretchers made the slow and bumpy journey down to A Beach. News came down with the injured, of the day's heroic fighting on the stony spine of the ridge and in particular of fierce conflict at a place soon to be christened 'Jephson's Post', after the Munster officer who had led the assault. Men like Godfrey Drage, who had started the day drugged with morphine because of gastric problems, now fell into a sleep of exhaustion. He suffered from nightmares focussed on the devastating injury suffered a few hours ago by a fellow officer called Stokes, who had been hit by a bullet that had penetrated both thighs. Drage had been kneeling, trying to tend to his colleague's wounds, when there was a 'terrific crack' by his ear and a bullet 'furrowed his brow and knocked him out'. After this lucky escape for both men, Stokes was picked up by members of a field ambulance brigade and ferried to the rear of the battle. A couple of hours later he was taken down the hillside to the beach where he awaited transportation to a hospital ship for the medical care and attention which he urgently needed to survive.[34]

The commander ordered no further advances on Sunday

THE GALLIPOLI PENINSULA, 8 AUGUST

It became clear to General Mahon and his HQ staff, sitting in their newly prepared dugouts on A Beach on the morning of 8 August that the Turkish forces were stronger, more numerous and better equipped than had been assumed. The vague plan for an assault on Suvla by Stopford's 9th Corps had been made on the assumption that the forces garrisoning the area were of limited numbers and capability. With British soldiers still not completely in charge of the Kiretch Tepe heights and full control over the area around Chocolate and Green hills still hanging in the balance, the big concern was that Turkish reinforcements would soon be heading for Suvla. These troops would be fresh and keen and they would have had access to food and water.

To what degree Generals Mahon and Stopford or any of their fellow officers understood the danger posed by the Turkish defenders is hard to say. The young officers of the 10th Division who had joked about learning Turkish probably knew little of the proud culture, deep Islamic faith and strong national spirit of many of the Turks who faced them on the Gallipoli peninsula. Given that they were unclear about their destination until the last moment, it is unlikely that the Irish soldiers knew anything about the local 'gendarmerie', the defence force that met them there and countered the initial assault of 10th and 11th Divisions with surprising strength.

What is likely is that the officers of the 10th were influenced by the common British perception of the Ottoman empire as a crumbling, cruel and decadent institution. Like men in other, British divisions, the Irish troops might have believed that the Turks were a barbarous and sensual people, in thrall to a dogmatic, heathen religion. Former British Prime Minister W.E. Gladstone's view that a 'broad line of blood' marked the Turkish track through history still held true in many circles. Widepread attacks on the country's Christian Armenian population in the 1890s seemed to support this view.

The men of the Broussa Gendarmerie defending Suvla from the initial 9th Corps attack were part of a nation-wide territorial force consisting, for the most part, of young unmarried men trained at a special recruitment school and then scattered around the country in small military outposts called *karakols*. They wore a cornflower-blue jacket with scarlet collar patches and a black *kalpak* hat with a scarlet top and silver stripes, as well as a black leather belt. In later years it became clear that the behaviour of the gendarmerie in other parts of Turkey during the war was often unsavoury. Stirred by fears of an uprising and of being betrayed by their Armenian minority, many of these young men were involved in the horrific episodes of violence constituting the notorious pogroms of 1915.

Those Irish soldiers who had bothered to learn Turkish discovered that a gendarme called his bayonet *sungu*, a bullet *kurshun*, a gun *top* and a grenade *khumbasi* whilst the enemy was called *dushman*. They also discovered that the Broussa Gendarmerie was paid in *lira, piastre and paras*, while their units of measurement were a *parmak* and a *karish* rather than a foot or an inch. For these young Turks, the war did not begin in 1914 nor did the Suvla Bay landing occur in August because they used an Islamic calendar. Supervising their spiritual welfare were *imami* or Muslim holy men. The gendarmerie would of course have understood the meaning of the names of the invaders' military objectives. Tekke Tepe, for instance, means 'the hills with the holy shrine'.

Undoubtedly, the Irish troops knew very little about the men of the Turkish 7th and 12th Divisions who were, by the night of 7 August, closing in on Suvla to reinforce the gendarmerie. These regular troops, who were beginning to muster in and around the Anafarta villages, a few miles inland from Suvla Bay, had been raised in the vicinity of Egerdir near Smyrna. They possessed fine Mauser rifles, which could be fitted with a short bayonet, eighteen inches in length, and they sported a *bashlik*, a soft helmet with a long strip of khaki cloth wound around it. When they became prisoners of war, one compassionate Irish observer noted that they were fierce soldiers but also 'poor nondescript Anatolian peasants' whose uniforms were tattered and who had been used to surviving on a meagre diet of bread, crushed wheat and olives. These men were often illiterate, which made letter writing impossible. Sending an oral message from the Anatolian villages with a professional carrier who conveyed the news to the front line, was often the only way to get news of loved ones.

The men of 9th Corps were also unaware that a new and gifted commander was in place at Suvla. His name was Mustafa Kemal and he later became the venerated Kemal Atatürk who led the rebuilding process in the post-war years, when Turkey reinvented itself as a modern republic. In the shape of the Turkish 7th and 12th Divisions, he now had some 17,000 extra men at his disposal to start the process of dislodging the British army from their newly won and precarious positions. If there was going to be a military breakthrough, it would have to happen on the morning of 8 August, before the new Turkish defenders had a chance to rest and reorganize after their march to Suvla.[35]

No such attempt was made. General Stopford was troubled by the lack of artillery support for an operation like this, aware that his troops were under-supplied and dehydrated. Confused as to whether a swift but costly break-through attempt was the correct follow-up to the Suvla landings, he may have thought that perhaps a 'holding operation' could be maintained while the really vital military action took place, as before, at Anzac and Cape Helles. At any rate, the commander of 9th Corps ordered no further advances on Sunday 8 August.[36]

The shoreline looked like a disturbed ant-heap

SUVLA BAY AND TEKKE TEPE HILLS, 8 AUGUST

Sir Ian Hamilton, arriving at Suvla Bay in the course of the day, was amazed that there were no signs of military urgency. One of his entourage reported: 'a peaceful scene greeted us' with 'bathing parties around the shore' and 'no reali-sation of the overwhelming necessity for a rapid offensive'. He complained that the staff of 10th Division were settling themselves into dugouts and that their pioneers, who should have been 'making rough roads for the advance ... were engaged in a great retrenchment'. The officer blamed the siege warfare system prevalent on the Western Front for this. It seemed clear to him that the commanding officers of 9th Corps had transferred these unimaginative and defensive military attitudes to the operation at Suvla Bay.[37]

Perturbed by this stasis, Hamilton ordered a fresh advance as soon as possi-ble. He was troubled to hear that General Sitwell had recently ordered the advance troops of the Royal Irish Fusiliers back from the exposed trenches on Green Hill to the more secure positions on Chocolate Hill until better artillery support could be put in place. He would have been even more disturbed had he known of the views of the German officer Hans Kannengeiser, who was in charge of a body of Turks defending the Tekke Tepe heights on 7 and 8 August. Kannengeiser thought that the 10th and 11th Divisions, once ashore, had little intention of making advances and was not impressed by their calibre. He had seen on the Saturday morning how 'Suvla Bay lay full of ships' then how 'a confused mass of troops' arrived and disembarked, making the shoreline look 'like a disturbed ant-heap' before moving across 'the blinding white surface of the dried salt sea'.

Up on the Tekke Tepe heights where Kannengeiser was based 'all about was peace and quiet'. During the next forty-eight hours the German officer was not impressed with anything these British troops did. When they tried to assault the slopes that faced them it seemed to him that they 'approached slowly in single file, splendidly equipped with white bands on their left arms, apparently very tired'. When the Turkish soldiers opened fire at these easy targets, his impression was that the British troops lay down 'without answering our fire or apparently moving in any other way. They gave the impression they were glad to be spared from climbing.'[38]

On a sun-scorched, uncharted landscape

THE SUVLA SECTOR, 8 AUGUST

For most men in the 10th Division, 8 August was a day of military stasis and even of strategic retreat. Noel Drury became aware of the problem on the Sunday morning when he took some reinforcements up the slopes of Chocolate Hill, only to be told by a superior officer to take them back down again. As the minutes and the hours ticked away he became infuriated because of the delay in getting the men inland and he recognized that while there was no fighting all day, the Turks were probably rushing up reinforcements. The experienced soldiers in the battalion all seemed to be talking about 'the waste of valuable time' and 'grousing like blazes, saying we are throwing away our chance'. Drury was still particularly critical of some of the men in the 11th Division, whom he suspected of both cowardice and laziness, saying that 'the whole place here, near the Cut, and across to Hill 10, is thick with soldiers of the 11th Division, doing nothing'.

Drury was soon engaged, however, in assisting members of the field ambulance brigades, looking for missing colleagues from the previous day's action. Of particular urgency was the search for a young officer from D Company called Bridge, who had been wounded at 10 pm on the previous night. When he was found at last, after hours spent lying out on the slopes of Chocolate Hill, Bridge asked Drury for a cigarette. He was too weak to smoke it though, and had to lie back on his stretcher and wait to be taken to the beach and then the hospital ship lying offshore in Suvla Bay.

Drury also came across Turkish victims of the previous day's fighting, including an enemy soldier who was slowly dying from a wound to the stomach and refused to allow anyone to touch him. Compared to the rush and trauma of the previous day, Drury's first Sunday on the Gallipoli peninsula was relatively quiet. In the personal diary that he tried to keep throughout his stay at Suvla, he concluded on 8 August not with reflections on the terror and thrill of the previous day's activities but on the simple order given to his battalion not to make tea. This was considered wasteful because precious drinking water was lost in the form of steam. From then on, the men had to wash down their food with whatever cold water they had left.[39]

For Juvenis on the other side of Suvla Bay, Sunday 8 August began with the discovery of the cause of groaning from the previous night. By daylight he saw that his men had slept only yards from a casualty clearing station belonging to 11th Division, where scores of badly wounded troops awaited medical attention. Soon, the dangers posed by conducting a battle on such a sun-scorched, uncharted landscape became clear. Juvenis spent the entire morning trying to locate the 10th Division command posts where he was supposed to receive his military orders, but the task was as difficult as 'looking for plovers' eggs on a moor on a dark night' due to the absence of maps. He felt constantly vulnerable to snipers while moving across this terrain, especially when he was commandeered to spend several hours carrying ration boxes from the stores on the beach to the front line. The biggest problem was that the boxes were 'white and highly visible'.

Above all else, Juvenis was aware of the danger of fire, especially after someone dropped cigarette ash in the scrub and 'in half a second, yards of scrub were alight, tearing headlong up the hill among the stunted oak and vetch'. Luckily, Juvenis and his fellow-soldiers managed to put out the fire by emptying sandbags in its path.[40]

Sunday 8 August was a busy and solemn day for all those who had to gather the human debris of the Suvla landings. The 31st Field Ambulance Brigade brought back sixty-five casualties from the battlefield and were exhausted by the task of carrying injured men for up to three miles across rough and bullet-swept terrain.[41]

For the more exposed battalions in vanguard positions such as the 5th Royal Irish Fusiliers, who at one stage occupied positions on both Chocolate and Green hills, there was constant sniping from Turkish soldiers still lodged in the dip between the two hills. There was also concern about bushfires, just as there was at the other end of the Suvla plain. The danger of a conflagration was intensified by the severe artillery bombardment of the area by both British and Turkish gunners that sent showers of flame and sparks into the brushwood and undergrowth.[42]

The holy flower that bloomed beside the graves of enemy and friend

B BEACH, 8 AUGUST

The Dublin Pals, on the other hand, spent Sunday morning in much less danger than the previous day, although they watched helplessly as some thirst-crazed men from the battalion were killed by snipers while desperately trying to refill their water bottles from a couple of small wells that had been located in a very exposed part of the front line. Eventually, by 3 pm, fresh water supplies were ferried up from B Beach but they arrived too late for Irish troops whose corpses now lay swelling in the heat at the edge of the Chocolate Hill wells. An hour or two later, one man became aware of another Suvla hazard when heating up food over a small, carefully contained fire. A few cartridges that had been discarded on the ground beside the embers, exploded loudly. Later in the day the men grew more frightened of the brushwood-fires, which they could now see eating up an area of scrub several hundred yards away. Soon a number of Turkish corpses were incinerated by the wind-fanned blaze.[43]

John Hargrave slept lightly on the first night on the peninsula. All through the hours of darkness, as he lay a few yards inland from the shore, he heard the 'lap-lap of water on the beach of Suvla Bay' and on rising he ventured down a captured Turkish trench where a dead enemy pack-mule stood, still loaded with luggage. He noted the 'brass coins on the fringed bridle and coloured fly tassels over the eyes' as the animal stood, stone-dead and stiff, with only the deep sides of the trench holding it upright.

Hargrave was given the grim task of erecting memorials to many of those who did not survive the first few hours of battle in the vicinity of B Beach. That morning, he placed a cross made from pieces of a wooden bully beef crate over the grave of one young Dublin Fusilier. By the late afternoon he felt he had seen enough of 'stretchers loaded with men and pieces of men' to last him a lifetime. He developed a terrible sense of loneliness while venturing out into the Suvla battlefield in search of the dead and the wounded. When he encountered any of his own troops, sheltering in a trench or a dugout, he noted that the verve and ebullience which had characterized so many of the men just two or three days earlier, had completely gone – 'No-one whistled rag-time tunes, no-one tried to make jokes, each man you passed asked you the vital question – "any water?"'

At one stage during the day Hargrave came under attack from a Turkish sniper and when trying to crawl inconspicuously away from the line of fire he had had to move across the earth as slowly as 'the hands of a clock, about an inch at a time', propelling himself only by digging his toes into the earth.

Among the wounded men Hargrave attended to was one young Irish soldier who had in his possession a pair of nail scissors. With this awkward instrument Hargrave proceeded to 'operate'. After pouring iodine into a gaping wound in the man's right arm, he 'cut great chunks of his arm out' with the scissors because the flesh was gangrenous. Soon his fingers were soaked in a mixture of blood and iodine as he plugged the opening with gauze and put on an antiseptic band. The stretcher-bearers then had to carry the man a couple of miles to the ambulance tents on B Beach where the doctor discovered that the gangrene had spread and that the entire arm would have to come off.

It was on this first Sunday at Suvla that Hargrave became conscious of the white flower that grew everywhere among ' the scorched thorns' and which he would soon grow to think of as a 'holy flower' which bloomed beside the shallow graves of enemy and friend alike.[44]

The whiff of carrion and the whizz of a sniper's bullet

KIRETCH TEPE RIDGE, 8 AUGUST

For Ivone Kirkpatrick, fighting with the 5th Inniskillings on the northern side of the bay, 8 August was a day of intense thirst and complete ignorance about the next step. He supervised water-ration parties to and from A Beach where he could see 'a large iron tank in the shape of a trough,' floating offshore, with water being pumped into it. Plans had been made for a ship, the *Krini*, to draw up a few hundred yards from the shore, with water brought all the way from

Egypt. The crudely customized water lighters, one of which Kirkpatrick had seen, could then ply between the *Krini* and the small, improvised pier that had been constructed on A Beach West. Kirkpatrick and one of his fellow Inniskillings, on a trip to the pier, realized that the supplies were being delivered much too slowly and so they looked for whatever extra supplies they could find. At one stage they located a full water bottle on the corpse of a Turkish soldier whom they discovered lying in the scrub on their way to the beach and they shared the contents without any scruples.

The men of the Munsters and the Inniskillings were increasingly dependent for survival on the arrival of warm, insipid liquid that Kirkpatrick and his men were carrying up from the shoreline. Dehydration was now so bad that many Irish soldiers were unable to eat their rations. Kirkpatrick found that 'it was impossible to get a piece of food into one's mouth without swallowing a fly, which had probably only just left one of the putrefying corpses, with which the hillside was strewn'. Sitting on a ground full of sharp flints that night, he was glad, after the baking heat of the day, to feel a heavy dew wetting him.[45]

During his first full day on the peninsula Juvenis felt only confusion and uncertainty. He had tried to find a senior officer to give him precise orders but the only clear instruction he received was to take his men up the Kiretch Tepe hillside by a winding path towards the high ground that the Munster Fusiliers and some men from the Inniskillings had been holding for the last thirty-six hours. It was on this vague journey that Juvenis first learnt to crush a handful of wild thyme growing on the hills, holding it to his face so that its fragrance would cover the stench of the rotting bodies that littered the path to the summit.

On the Kiretch Tepe heights, some 500 yards above sea level, Juvenis was finally able to use his training in semaphore to send a message about the whereabouts of the Inniskillings to a ship anchored offshore. Even at this altitude he could still smell 'the whiff of carrion' and occasionally hear the whizz of a sniper's bullet. As darkness fell he watched two sweating men bear a familiar figure on a stretcher along a 'ragged little path' and recognized one of his own men who had just fallen victim to a sniper. Later, under cover of darkness, Juvenis was sent by his battalion commander back to brigade HQ to receive fresh orders. The journey was long in the enveloping darkness. When he reached the HQ he received his briefing about the next day's strategy, then lay down in a corner of the dugout, placed his head on a respirator bag and promptly fell asleep.[46]

Only a few of the officers in the 10th Division ever caught sight of their top brass on 8 August and those who did were not reassured that their commander had a worthwhile military strategy. Godfrey Drage, having come down from the ridge to enquire about the plans for the following day, encountered General Mahon standing in a newly dug trench, sheltering from the violent thunderstorm lashing the peninsula in the afternoon. Drage offered Mahon his mackintosh because he could see that his commander was 'coatless and drenched'. Mahon refused, saying, 'No, you keep it, thank you all the same.' On being asked about the battle plans for Drage's battalion, Mahon merely replied: 'try to get those lads on your left moving' and the encounter was over as the general moved on in a confused search for further information about his scattered and depleted division.

During the day Drage was also frustrated with the inadequacy of his equipment, like his set of wire-clippers that were so blunt that he threw them away. However, most distressing were the deaths of his second-in-command, Captain Cullinan, and 'young Bennett who foolishly went out to rescue him'. He then witnessed further mutilation, watching his 'excellent batman, Dewick, crawling away on his stomach and trailing a useless leg behind him' after being hit by a Turkish bullet.

There seemed to be snipers everywhere on the Kiretch Tepe ridge but for Drage the fear of these lone gunmen was no more agonizing than the revulsion he experienced when he had to recover service paybooks from the putrefying corpses of two Irish soldiers who had died early the previous day. The smell was so bad that Drage was physically sick before he could hand the stained documents over at battalion HQ. Given that Drage had problems with what the doctors had called nervous collapse in the pre-war years, it is not surprising that he was beginning to suffer terribly from battlefield stress and anxiety.[47]

We could have smashed the Turk defence

THE SUVLA SECTOR, 9 AUGUST

On Monday, 9 August, Suvla Bay witnessed another attempted forward assault on the part of the 10th Division. High on the Kiretch Tepe ridge the Munsters and Inniskillings, accompanied by an assortment of 11th Divisional troops, were ordered to attack along the high ground as far as the outcrop known as Kidney Hill. Sir Ian Hamilton had also pleaded for an attack in the southern part of Suvla but the assault, which should have taken place on the Sunday night, had been hopelessly delayed by difficulties between the Irish and English divisions in the hours of darkness.

It was decided that fresh attacks would be launched on several new objectives in the southern part of the battlefield at dawn. Their objectives included a prominence known as Scimitar Hill and the prized W hills that constituted a significant line of high ground and included the strategically valuable Ismail Oglu Tepe. Beyond all these objectives lay the road to the Anzac front. However, Mustafa Kemal had ordered a counter-attack on the British invaders by several thousand new Turkish troops on the morning of the 9 August, adding to the likely intensity of the fighting which lay ahead.[48]

For Noel Drury, this was a day of conflicting signals. At first he was informed that the 6th Dublin Fusiliers were to advance towards the W hills. Subsequent messages indicated that the 6th Dublins were to support the 6th Lincolns from 11th Division who were engaged in heavy fighting with Mustafa Kemal's new troops some distance to the north. The Dublin men acted on the second order and fought alongside their English colleagues, coming under heavy fire as Kemal's infantry tried to advance. Irish casualties began to mount and Captain Luke of C Company arrived at Drury's temporary command post with the fingers of his left hand cut off by a piece of shrapnel. However, like so many other young men, Luke was keen to prove himself and to continue to support his colleagues, so he appeared in the command post a short while later, having spent only a brief period at the nearest dressing station. His hand was partly bandaged and he was carrying a couple of water bottles under his arms so he could refill them at a recently located well situated nearby. Drury, however, could see the 'white bones of his hand sticking up out of the flesh' and ordered an officer in the command post to re-dress Luke's mutilated fingers. He then insisted that Luke leave the field of action to seek more effective medical attention.

During the day's battle with the Turkish reinforcements, Drury was very conscious of the enemy's added fire power. Wounded soldiers who were lying at dressing stations on the Suvla hillsides were now being hit for a second and third time by Turkish bullets. By late morning the battlefield atmosphere was one of total confusion and Drury became increasingly angry that no one in the Irish battalions was taking control of the situation or suggesting a strategy for a counter-attack.

Drury was intensely annoyed to find General Maxwell, commander of the 11th Division's 33rd Brigade, sitting in a sheltered position behind the front line, 'in a devil of a funk and incapable of giving proper orders'. Drury also deemed his own brigadier-general to be useless, recording that he 'doesn't know what is going on and doesn't try to find out'.

The intense anger and distress of men like Drury increased when they found that close friends were being killed on a regular basis by Turkish shell-fire. Long-term colleagues and friends like Major Jennings were killed on 8 and 9 August. These losses made Drury react furiously to any soldiers found hiding from the enemy behind rocks or bushes. He 'went barging about through the scrub, trying to find where people were' and soon 'found parties of Lincolns and Borderers lying in funk-holes.'

Drury was particularly critical of men from these two regiments when he witnessed 'a whole lot of them running away like mad, shouting out that they were cut to ribbons'. Unimpressed by the fact that the 11th Division soldiers had been at the front line longer than his own men, Drury took out his revolver and threatened to use it on them if they did not turn and regroup in a shallow ditch that lay ahead.

> I managed to persuade a party of Borderers to go back … but I could-n't persuade any of them to put their heads up and fire although I showed them good targets. The worst of them was a fat Sergeant Major who would only lie down in the ditch and announce ' we are all cut to bits'. Then a big hare got up behind us and raced out past us through a gap in the bank and on towards the Turk. The brave Company Sergeant Major and one or two others lifted their rifles and started blazing away after the hare although they were too much afraid to shoot at the Turks.

This deep sense of aggravation was not confined to Drury. His friend and fellow fusilier, Paddy Cox, hit some English 11th Division troops over the head with his telescope during a particularly heated exchange concerning their lack of action. There was not much to see by midday through Cox's telescope, as the scrub was burning fiercely and dust and smoke shrouded everything.[49]

Meanwhile, the Dublin Pal Frank Laird had run into serious trouble. He was crossing some open ground when he felt 'a sudden pang in the shoulder and a frightful thump in the back' and then did 'a high dive on the stony ground'. He lay there hearing a singing in his ears and feeling as if his whole body was strung up to its highest tension. After a while he fainted and awoke to hear a voice say 'don't leave the chap in the open', after which some fellow soldiers carried him into the shelter of a ditch where he fainted again. This time when he woke he found that his chest and shoulders were wrapped in bandages. He summoned the strength to ask someone to take his glasses and give them to his friend Charles Frederick Ball for safe-keeping. He was in grave pain from the bullet wound in one of his lungs but also from his ribs that had been fractured as he fell.

Laird ended up lying in this ditch for sixteen hours because all the stretcher-bearers in the area were too busy with more serious injuries to attend to him. He lay there overnight, closing and opening his hands every so often to check if he was becoming weaker. He eventually decided to struggle to his feet and in spite of 'the gurgling noises' in his back he staggered to where another wounded man lay, who told Laird that both of his legs were broken. A third figure nearby was silent and immobile. Just after dawn, stretcher-bearers finally came and took Laird to the hospital facilities on the beach where he lay all the following day waiting to be taken to a ship in the bay. A few hours later the boat set sail and deposited him at Lemnos where he stayed in an Australian hospital tent, sipping tinned milk from an invalid feeding cup.[50]

Tinder-dry scrubland, flames and smoke

SOUTHERN ZONE, SUVLA SECTOR, 9 AUGUST

By the early afternoon Drury realized that after the costly 'distraction' of supporting 11th Division against the Turkish counter-attack, the original objectives of Ismail Oglu Tepe and Scimitar Hill would not now be taken. He worried about the impoverished manpower situation in the southern part of Suvla and thought to himself 'if only we had our own 10th Division here complete, we would have smashed the Turk defence and got all our objectives'.

The waste of life continued all through the afternoon of 9 August and the Dublins had no progress to report by the end of it. Several 'runners' who were given the task of carrying messages between the Irish battalions and the brigade HQ died when they got confused about their whereabouts because of the way in which the brigade's command post had been shifted without warning. The statisticians at battalion HQ had to tally up the figures as best they could to ascertain their losses. They reckoned that since landing on the peninsula on the morning of 7 August eleven officers and 259 men from the ranks of B, C, and D companies had been injured, killed or gone missing. At this juncture no figures were available for A Company.[51]

Throughout 9 August, the wounded continued to come in. William Knott spent the day trying to avoid snipers as he scrambled around the southern edge of the battlefield, trying to fetch in the injured. He survived as best he could on a diet of biscuits, bully beef and a few mouthfuls of water. He used his last reserves of strength to piggyback one man with a severely damaged foot back from a ditch near the front line to the beach.[52]

The burning scrub was causing panic among all the men of the 10th Division, especially those who found themselves in the southern part of the battlefield. There were rumours that the Turks were deliberately setting fire to the scrubland in that area, having noted the way that the winds fanned the flames sending a deadly conflagration in the direction of the British. Apart from the danger to life and limb, the flames and smoke also hampered mobility, generated confusion and had the soldiers dreading the prospect of being burnt to death if they were wounded and reached by the fire before the stretcher-bearers got to them.[53]

The 5th Royal Irish Fusilier battalion had had a dreadful time during the early hours of 9 August. Just a few hours earlier they had advanced farther than any of their divisional colleagues, but were troubled by the inadequacy of their trenches on both Chocolate and Green hills. The trenches were too narrow to allow the movement of large groups of Irish soldiers and too shallow to provide shelter from the shells and rifle fire that Mustafa Kemal's reinforcements were now bringing to bear on the Irish battalions. Morale had not been helped when the men were ordered to vacate the exposed advance positions that they had obtained on Green Hill. They were eventually replaced by men from the 6th Dublins and took up defensive positions a few hundred yards to the rear. The Dublin soldiers found the 5th Irish Fusiliers to be tired, thirsty, hungry and very short of ammunition.

The 6th Irish Fusiliers, meanwhile, were given an opportunity to attack that Drury's battalion was denied throughout 9 August. They participated in a new assault on Scimitar Hill that it was hoped would wrest the military initiative from the newly energized enemy soldiers. This soon turned out to be yet another costly and ineffective operation, involving gun and bayonet assaults on well-defended Turkish trenches, conducted in smouldering scrubland where there was little protection from enemy fire except from the grey smoke that shrouded the landscape. By nightfall, five officers in the battalion had been killed and another twelve had been wounded or gone missing. In the ranks, twelve fatalities had been recorded and over 200 soldiers had either been injured or were unaccounted for.[54]

Trembling like aspen leaves

NORTHERN ZONE, SUVLA SECTOR, 9 AUGUST

On the northern side of the Suvla area on 9 August there was similar loss of life and failure to advance. Juvenis woke on the morning of 9 August and found himself immediately placed in a reserve position for a big assault on the Turkish position at Kidney Hill. Shortly after dawn the British naval gunners opened up with a barrage of shells launched on the remaining Turkish positions on the northern side of the Kiretch Tepe ridge.

Juvenis watched as the Munster men ahead of him set off on their early morning advance towards Kidney Hill, but a few moments after the assault got underway a dreadful rumour went around behind Irish lines: apparently hundreds of men had been ordered off on the attack while their water bottles were being filled at A Beach. If this was the case, many of the soldiers were doomed to run out of energy and fighting strength within a few hours of combat and at the very worst they risked dying of dehydration if trapped on the ridge for forty-eight hours with no hope of making their way back to their own lines.

Before long, there were other rumours that the battle was not going according to plan and that the numbers of Turkish soldiers manning the defences on the heights were much greater than before. Moreover, some enemy troops were launching forceful counter-attacks on British lines and it was a tough and desperate struggle for the 10th Division to prevent themselves from losing ground rather than gaining it.

Juvenis watched the morning's action from his position near the western end of the ridge, close to a regimental aid post. He witnessed soldiers returning from the front lines and saw how, every so often, 'the bush would rustle and a man dripping with blood crawl through, a great relief spreading on his grey face at the sight of the Red Cross brassards'. Juvenis watched closely as sometimes 'a man beside himself with thirst – lips all black and caked – would stumble past'. On several occasions, half-crazed soldiers tried to seize water bottles from Juvenis' men as they waited in their reserve positions. It was, however, forbidden to waste their own supplies on other men's needs and one of Juvenis' fellow officers actually had to place some thirst-maddened Munster

Fusiliers, who had escaped from the fighting, under close arrest to prevent them from seizing the Inniskillings' water bottles.

By midday it was clear to Juvenis that more and more men were retreating from the high ground and that the 'big advance' of 9 August was coming to a sorry end. A runner from 30th Brigade HQ conveyed the order that the Munster and Inniskilling Fusiliers were to make another attempt to advance. The order was impossible to carry out given the growing Irish casualty rate and the exhaustion of the survivors. By 3.30 am a retreat was under way. Despite the division's best efforts, Kidney Hill was still untaken and Juvenis had not had a chance to prove himself as a fighting man.[55]

The day's combat took its toll psychologically as well as physically. Godfrey Drage witnessed Colonel Gore of the Munster Fusiliers being sent away from the battlefield in the late morning, having been seen as 'a large, conspicuous figure … armed with a cane, smoking a cigarette … totally inert in a support line.' Drage not only observed how Gore was unable to move forward and do his duty as leader of several hundred men, he also witnessed the fear and distress of the Turks who lived in constant terror of the British naval shellfire being launched at their defensive positions. They sometimes ran out from behind rocks and 'took cover' in the open, right in front of the Irish infantry-men, rather than be blown to smithereens by shells.[56]

For John Hargrave, now serving with field ambulance colleagues on the northern side of Suvla Plain, the men who were psychologically traumatized were more difficult to deal with than the physically injured because there was nothing that could be done to help them. At one stage in the early afternoon, two Munster Fusiliers came down from the ridge, having made an unautho-rized and half-crazed exit from the battle. They were 'trembling like aspen leaves' and their eyes were 'roaming unmercifully' while 'prickles from thorn bushes still clung round their puttees'. He could see that 'their lips were cracked and swollen and they had lost their helmets and the sun had scorched and peeled the back of their necks' and 'their hair was matted and full of sand'. This was the first case of what Hargrave later termed 'sniper madness'.

When writing in his diary that evening, in the relative safety of a dugout near the beach, he recorded that he would prefer to deal with the dead and the dying than handle such mentally distressed human beings. Despite all efforts by the field ambulance crew to soothe them, these victims of 'sniper madness' could not keep their limbs still. Their ribs stuck out like a skeleton's and their stomachs were sunken in while they inhaled much too loudly and far too deeply, as if terrified that there was not enough air left to breathe. In the long term some of these symptoms became less acute but they nonetheless looked like broken men. At night they mumbled loudly to themselves and prevented other soldiers from sleeping.

Most men at Suvla encountered physical suffering and death constantly and it presented desperate dilemmas, like when Hargrave found a wounded man who had been transported down from the heights of the ridge with two gaping bullet wounds in his thighs. The man was bleeding to death despite the tourniquets that had been made out of handkerchiefs and bits of stick. There was little the medical staff could do to save the young soldier's life. Within minutes, Hargrave was focussing on another casualty lying nearby, whose less severe injuries meant that there was a real chance of a recovery. He eventually had to trudge past the body of the other man who had by now bled to death. He saw how 'the tourniquets were still gripping his lifeless limbs and the blood on the handkerchiefs had dyed red, rich brown'.

Hargrave realized that the price for the high ground around Suvla Bay was paid in shattered bodies and broken minds.[57]

There was nobody in control

THE SUVLA SECTOR, 9–10 AUGUST

Debate raged in years after about what might have been achieved had the men of 9th Corps made a breakthrough during the first three days of their August landing, especially if they had pressed home the attack before Turkish reinforcements were fully gathered. Although a few men from 11th Division did make the perilous journey from Chocolate and Green hills, establishing a foothold on the Tekke Tepe range, their stay was temporary. The overwhelming power of the Turkish resistance soon drove the English soldiers back to their previous positions. At no stage during the weeks ahead did any British troops again reach this key military objective again.

A breakthrough was arguably impossible. The British soldiers were too exhausted, too dispersed across the Suvla area, too lacking in supplies, too ignorant of both the terrain and the enemy and bereft of a coherent strategic plan. Even if Irish generals had tried to improvise a daring move across uncharted enemy terrain before Kemal's reinforcements arrived, what kind of progress could have been made when the 10th Division was hampered by its water-supply system? It was both haphazard and tortuous because most of the capacious water carts had been left behind in Egypt, so a considerable number of infantrymen and their officers had to be diverted from fighting duties to carry water to the front line.

Without shelter or clear objectives, the invading troops had had to make do with a few mouthfuls of tepid water and a couple of spoonfuls of liquidized bully beef. The enemy on the other hand had decent access to springs and wells dotted across the peninsula and a supply of bread and olives. [58]

Most of the Irish troops watching dusk fall on the night of 9 August knew that the assault had gone very wrong but in spite of this some men felt the strange exhilaration that comes from having survived. Francis Ledwidge had had moments of immense excitement throughout the day and was amazed by the bravery of some of the Inniskillings. He witnessed one soldier 'standing on the hill with his cap on top of his rifle, shouting at the Turks to come out' and he also saw 'stretcher-bearers taking in friend and enemy alike'. He would later tell a friend in a letter home that 'it was a horrible and great day' and that he 'would not have missed it for worlds'.

For Ledwidge's friend Robert Christie some of the most vivid aspects of the past three days were the sudden little details that connected Suvla Bay to his home. During their journey to the peninsula, for instance, Christie had recognized that the vessel the men were travelling on was the SS *Heroic*, which had once travelled from Belfast to Liverpool as a passenger ferry. Then while making a water supply rendezvous with a sailor in charge of a lighter at A Beach, Christie was asked in a familiar accent: 'What part of Belfast are you from?'

The two men had a brief chat about their Belfast backgrounds and the sailor expressed his wish to be back in Sandy Row where he could 'tell the oul' woman' how much he missed both her and the chip shop she owned. The two Belfast exiles parted with a cry of 'Up the Blues!' in support of Belfast's famous Linfield football club and a yell of disdain for their greatest rivals, Belfast Celtic. Christie also managed to ease some of the agony of thirst during the first few days because he took the advice offered by an officer who had served in the Indian army. He placed a few pebbles in his mouth and sucked on them as this kept up the regular flow of saliva.[59]

By the night of 9 August and the early morning of 10 August most of the surviving officers in the division were acutely aware of the plight of their expedition. One officer in the 5th Inniskillings who had been fighting on the Kiretch Tepe ridge was horrified by the stunted scrub his men had had to move over and appalled by the impossibility of digging adequate protective trenches in such rocky ground. He thought it militarily suicidal to have hundreds of troops supplied by mule along a path three feet wide beside a precipitous drop to the ocean while constantly under fire. On a journey to the water-lighters he discovered that the gangway that the vessels were moored at was so narrow that one-way traffic was the only option. And where were the scores of pack animals that should have helped the men carry the water to the front line? The answer was that many of them were still in Egypt.

This same man was equally unimpressed with the food supplies. He estimated that during the first few days of the battle, only 25 percent of the tinned beef was eaten because it had turned to a brown and sticky liquid that oozed out of the can and was soon devoured by the infamous Gallipoli flies.

Another officer with the 6th Inniskillings who landed near Nibrunesi Point on 7 August become aware very quickly that there was something gravely wrong with the system of command when the troops halted at Lala Baba within a few minutes of their arrival. In due course they got going again, only to be sent off towards 'that brown hill in the distance'. Clearly, 'there was nobody in control and junior officers who had been lucky enough to find out the general objective made for it by whatever route they liked.'

This Inniskilling officer was perturbed because he was not given orders at any stage and had to use his own judgment, pushing ahead until the enemy actually stopped him. Surely, aggressive orders were crucial if a rapid advance was to take place? The stalemate that occurred instead was difficult to understand. After the war he spoke of how his more experienced soldiers at Suvla reacted to the stasis of 8 August. Despite the immense hardship caused by thirst and water, there was 'not a man there who did not expect to continue the advance at dawn'. When no orders to resume the offensive were given, these veterans anticipated with dread the likely outcome: that the Turks would have 'a free hand on Sunday to bring up all the necessary reinforcements'. He observed, 'there was nothing to be gained by not evacuating the peninsula that night instead of five months later'. Sadly, his bleak assessment was correct.[60]

Connaught Rangers leaving Lemnos for Gallipoli, 5 August 1915

Q 532092 IWM

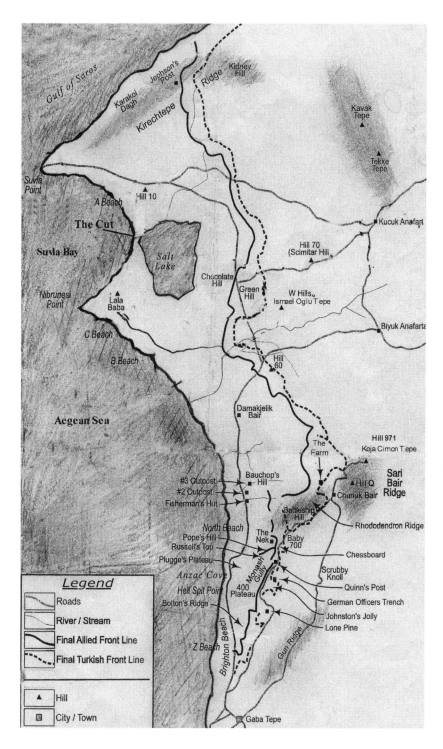

The Suvla and Anzac sectors, Gallipoli peninsula, summer 1915.
BOYD

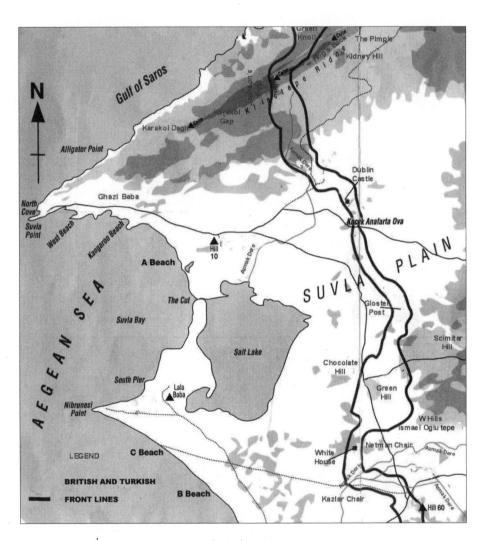

The Suvla sector.
BOYD

Looking north towards Suvla from Mustafa Kemal's command post on the Chunuk Bair.
BRIAN WILSON

Sand dunes on 'A' beach, summer 2004.
WILSON

'The Cut', summer 2004 – Turkish artillery pounded this spot remorselessly but for the Irish soldiers it had to be crossed.

WILSON

Professor Ernest Julian – mortally wounded, 7 August 1915.

O'H /H

Soldiers seeking shelter from the Suvla sun.

Q50209 IWM

Soldiers teasing Turkish snipers.
Q 13447 IWM

Shellfire near a Suvla mule track with the Kiretch Tepe ridge in
the distance.
Q13539 IWM

Francis Laird – he lay wounded in a
Suvla ditch for sixteen hours before
being rescued.
O'H/H

V

WARRIORS

Waste food and horse dung and a cloud of flies

THE SUVLA SECTOR, 10–11 AUGUST

On 10 August two new units from 9th Corps began to arrive at Suvla, sent by General Stopford to reinforce and relieve the men of 10th and 11th Divisions. One was the 53rd Division, which was officially Welsh but included men from several English counties. The other unit was the 54th Division, with troops drawn primarily from East Anglia and the eastern Midlands. Each of these Kitchener divisions had been recruited from the ranks of the Territorial Army, the part-time militia set up in recent years as a modernized force that could be called upon to guard peacetime Britain. These new soldiers stepped straight into the front-line, allowing the infantry who had already been fighting there to pull back into a temporary but welcome supporting role. General Mahon's exhausted troops had a chance to rest from the rigours of daily combat on or near the Suvla beaches.[1]

This was a far from relaxing time for many of the Irish soldiers. The beaches were not safe due to the continuing artillery fire sent over from the enemy lines and the two territorial divisions were soon struggling desperately to achieve their objectives, which meant that a continued 10th Divisional presence was still needed in some parts of the front. It was also a distressing prospect to watch the destruction of two inexperienced infantry units by Mustafa Kemal's forces, which involved the complete disappearance of one company from a Norfolk battalion in the 54th Division, apparently captured in its entirety while fighting on the Kiretch Tepe ridge.[2]

The work of the Royal Irish Regiment as a pioneer battalion continued unabated. Their activities confirmed the suspicions of Sir Ian Hamilton that his Suvla troops had picked up the worst habits of siege warfare. On 11 August the pioneers handed over some newly dug and very permanent-looking trenches to a brigade of the 54th Division and watched the new soldiers occupy them. The following day they completed a safe and strong dugout for General Mahon's Divisional HQ, near A Beach West. On 14 August they were still busy creating a piped supply from the few wells located at Suvla to the Divisional field hospital. By now, reinforcements to the pioneers' ranks had arrived from the base at Mudros Bay. The new men carried heavy tools with them, indicating that the division was indeed contemplating digging and staying longer at Suvla.[3]

The men in 30th Field Ambulance Brigade also found life very busy. The medical team was particularly troubled by their inability to find shelter from the sun for all the sick and injured. The equipment they had been allowed on the original landing craft had had to be kept below '58 hundred weight' so they had only one operating tent, which meant that many medical officers performed their operations under the punishing rays of the midday sun.

Someone in the brigade at last managed to get hold of tarpaulins and wood from the Royal Engineers and to construct a second makeshift shelter for surgical operations. By 11 August, finding themselves pressed beyond all endurance by the number of casualties, the Irish medical team wired Corps HQ, pleading for fresh supplies of hospital equipment so they could turn their base into a more effective centre for the care of the wounded and dying.

Not all of the patients seen by the medical staff were straightforward battlefield cases. On 10 August one young lieutenant with the Munster Fusiliers was found to be suffering from gonorrhea, contracted either on the Greek Islands or during shore leave on his voyage from Britain. On 12 August another young officer was found suffering from severe sunstroke because he had lost his helmet. Two days later, 30th Field Ambulance tended the needs of Lieutenant Everett in the 54th Division, one of the many young men now suffering from neurasthenia, a psychiatric disorder brought on by battlefield stress and often characterized by deep inertia and mental confusion.[4]

The Royal Engineer detachments of the 10th Division also continued to be busy. They were distracted from their usual preoccupation with landmines and wellshafts by the arrival of searchlights on the evening of 12 August. These lamps sent strong beams of light onto the high ground of the Tekke Tepe hills where, under cover of darkness, Turkish troops might be planning new offensive strategies.[5]

Meanwhile, the Quarter Master's Branch at Divisional HQ continued to puzzle over the supply of water. On 11 August their official war-diarist commented that 'the water question has assumed an acute shape.' He noted that some of the barges carrying water had broken down and that at least one barge had had its supplies contaminated by sea water, making it brackish and undrinkable. A limited amount of desalination of sea water had also been attempted near A Beach, using a condenser, but this had proved to be a slow and fairly worthless exercise. Adding to the problem was the fact that many barges dedicated to water supply had been commandeered for use in the mass landing of the troops of 53rd and 54th Divisions. However, the arrival on 11 August of more pack animals from the Greek Islands meant that no less than twenty-six loads of water could be sent up to the front line that evening, while one hundred more mules were sent from Mudros in the morning.[6]

Despite the arrival of the two new infantry divisions, 10 August was a day of continued Irish engagement with the enemy. The 5th Royal Irish Fusiliers still had men encamped on Green Hill where their plight was made worse by the absence of a medical officer and the continued scarcity of water at the front line. It was the early morning of 11 August before the Fusiliers would be relieved and sent to C Beach before being asked, later in the day, to move along the Suvla shoreline towards the base of the Kiretch Tepe ridge. It was becoming clear that in a few days' time, a fresh concerted Irish attack would take place on this ridge, the original divisional objective. Although the shoreline was a less terrifying place to be than Green Hill, the men still suffered from long range Turkish artillery fire, resulting in bursts of shrapnel at periodic intervals on or near the beach. The 6th Irish Fusiliers had also been relieved on 10 August, when men of the Essex Regiment stepped into their trenches and allowed them to return to the shadow of Lala Baba Hill. Then they too were ordered northwards along the shore to prepare for a new coordinated divisional assault on the ridge.[7]

During this lull many men continued to reflect on the ordeal they had endured and to question the possibility of success in this confused campaign. One officer with the 5th Inniskillings later claimed that by this stage he knew 'the whole show was a wash-out' because there had been 'no orders, no scheme, nothing told us as to what we were supposed to do'. In the troubled calm of a few hours spent behind the lines, he dreamt of what might have happened had General Felix Hill been allowed to act on his own initiative in the first few hours after the men stepped ashore on B and C beaches. Perhaps Hill could have 'taken the whole enemy position' in the southern part of Suvla, if he had been allowed to act independently and to marshal thousands of his own Irish troops to do his bidding. The feeling that the division had not been given a fair chance on the battlefield was beginning to grow.

There was also a lot of anger among the men of the Munster battalions. Some other Irish regiments were beginning to stigmatize them for what they considered the folly of setting out without water bottles in the 9 August attacks.[8]

The command staff of the 10th Division had plenty to worry about. Apart from promoting Irish morale and preparing for another attack on the ridge, they had to improve the poor sanitary arrangements at most of the divisional locations. The situation was particularly bad in the vicinity of the beaches where a mixture of waste food and horse dung was attracting thick swarms of flies. Divisional HQ also insisted that the two wells discovered at Suvla Point and Charak Chesme be properly policed, as raging thirst was still driving many men into making reckless forays in search of water.

At this stage, Irish medical officers were also recommending to Corps HQ that they place a hospital vessel painted with a visible Red Cross emblem offshore on the northern side of the Kiretch Tepe ridge because the long and arduous journey by stretcher to the medical facilities on A Beach was incredibly difficult. Any new attack on the ridge would result in a high number of casualties and place even more pressure on these stretcher-bearers.

For medical staff there was also the important task, given the shortage of food supplies, of preserving easily digested items like bread, beef tea and milk for patients whose survival depended on appropriate and sustained nutrition. By 11 August the medical services were also glad to report the availability of a mule litter, run by the recently arrived Indian Supply and Transport Corps, which brought the most badly wounded Irish soldiers down from the regimental aid posts that were an injured man's first point of contact with the medical retrieval process. At the medical aid posts on the battlefield, special areas were now set aside as convalescence depots, where men whose ailments were only minor could be treated quickly and returned to the front line where they were so badly needed, rather than being taken all the way to the field hospital for attention. The 30th Field Ambulance Brigade, meanwhile, had recently moved its chief station away from A Beach to the vicinity of the recently located Charak Chesme well in order to be able to make use of the forty gallons of water per hour provided by this source.[9]

If beauty could have stopped a war

THE SUVLA SECTOR, 10–13 AUGUST

The Pals started Tuesday, 10 August by taking on a supporting role behind 53rd Division, as the newcomers filtered into the front-line trenches. By the evening however, they were back in place, helping the beleaguered Welsh troops to garrison some of the more crucial front-line areas on Chocolate Hill. Many of the Pals now felt that the single most nauseating feature of their soldiering was the smell of the rotting bodies that no one had been able to retrieve from the Suvla hillsides.

Here at the front line, like at the Western Front, men lived with the constant threat of unseen sniper's bullets at a vulnerable trench junction or if they raised a weary head above parapet level. A notice had recently been erected near a spot where many of the Pals did sentry duty, warning of snipers, but the most dangerous place for a 10th Division infantryman was still a well or a spring and the Turks had ample opportunity to practise their marksmanship on Irish troops filling their water bottles. A pile of corpses close to a water supply was also a recipe for further contamination and disease and represented another threat to the troops.

By the end of 10 August many Pals were convinced that the Turkish artillery was able to avoid destruction by the British gunners. As far as the Irish troops could read the situation, the enemy's heavy guns were still able to move about on the far-off hillside, which probably meant that they were placed on wheeled platforms that could be pushed along a number of short, recently constructed railway lines. This enabled the Turkish artillery to elude anyone attempting to track their exact positions and to send over an accurate counter-bombardment.

On the night of 10 August watchfulness was an imperative on Chocolate Hill, due to fear of a big attack on British lines under cover of darkness. By day one man in eight was usually assigned to sentry duty but that night one soldier in four was watching out nervously for signs of Turkish movement. Eventually, dawn broke over the landscape and the dreaded renewed Turkish attack had not materialized. An order came for the Dublin Fusiliers to retire from the front line and make their way to B Beach. In the relative calm of their reserve positions near Nibrunesi Point, the men were given a quarter pint of neat rum and allowed to sleep.

During two days of rest spent at the shoreline, the Pals took some time to assess the enemy. In some men's assessment the Turks were 'a pretty brave lot' who 'fight pretty fair' but then others said that they had seen enemy artillery 'shell a Red Cross waggon and follow it with shell after shell for miles'. Everyone agreed that their greatest fear was not the Turkish artillery but the snipers who hid in the branches of small stunted trees that dotted the landscape. Some of the most feared marksmen were located in the disputed ground between Chocolate and Green hills.

In the early hours of Friday 13 August, 7th Dublin Fusiliers began to move north along the bay toward the base of the Kiretch Tepe ridge where they were ordered to climb to a sheltered part of the rocky incline on the north-facing side of the ridge, which faced the open sea. As daylight broke over the Mediterranean many of the Pals enjoyed scenic vistas they had not seen since arriving at Gallipoli. The sea lay before them, tranquil and blue and beyond this a number of Greek islands lay scattered on the western and northern horizons. In later years some of the surviving Pals echoed the heartfelt comment made by one officer with the Royal Irish Rifles: 'If beauty could have stopped a war that scenery would have done it.'

However, the Dublin men were also painfully aware of the dreadful appearance of the Munster soldiers they had met at Suvla Point who were week-old veterans of the battle in the northern part of Suvla. They had 'begrimed faces' and their hands were covered in dried clay. They were unshaven and their unwashed, close-cropped heads were stained with sand, soil and blood.[10]

John Hargrave was busily preparing for the casualties of the new advance with his ambulance brigade colleagues. He watch the newly disembarked Indian muleteers at work with interest, intrigued by their 'culturally distinctive activities … praying on prayer mats and cooking rice and chapattis'. He was upset at the chaotic state of the recently established field post office, noting some of the parcels that lay on the beach, open or un-addressed, strewn across the ground. It was heart-rending to see gifts from Ireland like a pair of socks or mouldy home-made cake in a cardboard box, lying uncollected on the sand.[11]

Juvenis still found that much of his time was taken up with the vexed and continuing issue of water. Organising a rationing system among his men was tortuous. Handing out water bottles led to intense discussion about who merited the greatest share. One ration-carrier who made it down to the beach for a fresh supply, returned so parched himself that he could not swallow any water because the inside of his mouth and throat were too swollen to admit a drop. These problems were not helped, in Juvenis' opinion, by the supplementary rations that the men now received. On one occasion he himself received a generous supply of 'salt beef'!

On one particular evening, just before the fresh assault – which was planned for midday on Sunday, 15 August – Juvenis sat on the stony ridge and gazed out towards Suvla plain, where he could see bush fires raging. The conflagration was too far away for him to hear the cries of the wounded English and Welsh soldiers who lay out there and whom the flames were swallowing alive. He felt as remote from the action and the pain of the combatants as 'Zeus reclining on Olympus watching the plains of Troy'. A few hours later some of the survivors from this distantly observed division made their way into rearguard positions at the base of the ridge as the Inniskillings prepared to move higher up to engage in the new assault.

Juvenis wondered to what extent his men were ready for the rigours and stresses of a fresh advance. Dysentery was widespread and he had just received a 'huge anti-dysentery pill' from the nearby field ambulance HQ. Water was still being carried from the beach in small, improvised containers like biscuit tins. During the last couple of days of rest behind the lines Juvenis also found moments for relaxation though. He had located a secluded cove near A Beach where he swam in the Mediterranean for the first time, ducking under the surface as often as possible for fear of snipers. There were of course other, natural dangers such as sea urchins. The sudden encounter with unfamiliar and dangerous-looking fauna on the Gallipoli peninsula certainly sent some soldiers into wild panic. While eating in a dugout, Juvenis was distracted from his half-opened tin of sardines when he discovered the horrible remains of a 'scaly vermilion monster'. The creature in question was a large centipede. Another officer then confessed to having hacked the thing to death, on discovering it crawling across the floor of his dug-out in the middle of the previous night.

Juvenis' main task as the attack drew nearer was to draw a useable map of the current British trenches in his sector of the battlefield. This involved him making regular journeys around the northern part of the Suvla sector, with all the dangers that such movement brought. But he never missed a chance to look out to sea and focus on the island of Samothrace in the distance which looked to him like the Scottish Isle of Skye in shape and colour. He could also see the British ships anchored here and there offshore. He dreamt of the comforts of life aboard ship where a bottle of beer could be obtained for a mere 6*d*. Juvenis also read newly arrived mail from Ireland, including three letters from his friends and family.

In the last few hours before the assault, a hamper from Fortnum and Mason in London arrived, to be shared with the entire battalion mess. Among the delicacies were a pot of herrings in tomato sauce and a large fruitcake, which the men cut into two slices each, one for the present and one for future consumption. After the devastation of 15 August many of the men did not reappear from the battlefield to claim their second slice.[12]

Those who were killed must have been burned

THE SUVLA SECTOR, 10–13 AUGUST

Noel Drury, soldiering with the 6th Dublins, did not have an easy time on Tuesday 10 August, because it was a day for registering losses. Among the officers his friend Major Jennings, second in command of the battalion, had died, Lieutenant Clery had been gravely wounded, two junior officers called Mortimer and O'Carroll had been killed and 2nd Lieutenant Carter had been badly injured and shortly afterwards died at sea on his way back to Ireland. The circumstances of death were often too awful for words and Drury was afraid that 'the bodies of most of those who were killed must have been burned' as their colleagues had had so little success in finding them.

On 10 August Drury was also incensed to find men from other divisions sheltering in terror behind the battle zone. He witnessed one tragicomic episode during which Colonel Shanahan and Father Murphy drove some of these men out of their hiding place with their bare fists. Drury was by now astute enough to see that the 53rd Division, to which these reluctant combatants belonged, had been involved in a demoralizing manoeuvre which had led to this behaviour. He had had a very clear view of a brigade of the 53rd Division 'deployed in the plain without a particle of cover, brasswork glinting in the sun.' These soldiers were 'simply plastered with shrapnel and long-range rifle and machine-gun fire' and in Drury's opinion, whoever ordered the manoeuvre 'should have been shot'.

On 10 August Drury also recorded a 'kill', shooting a Turkish sniper at eighty-five yards. He did not see the body of his victim at close range but he did, shortly afterwards, come across a 'sniper's nest' during a brief advance into Turkish territory. He found a brown blanket hanging in a tree and discovered bananas, raisins, an empty water bottle and a big leather strap for tying the sniper to the tree and preventing him from tumbling out if he fell asleep.

Later in the day everything became quiet in Drury's part of the line and he lay in a sheltered place and gazed out at the landscape. He noticed small details in the calm of the late afternoon. Around his feet crawled many beautifully coloured grasshoppers and from the corner of his eye he spotted the not unfamiliar sight of a small tortoise, making its way across the trench floor. Then at 6.30 pm the calm was disrupted when the 6th Dublins received their orders to relieve 5th Irish Fusiliers in a nearby part of the line.

If the night of 10 August was a relatively peaceful one, the next day provided more excitement. Drury 'bumped suddenly into a Turk' while walking up a seemingly empty trench. The man jabbed at him with his bayonet but missed and Drury 'did a world's record standing jump sideways'. He 'loosed a couple of rounds at him' from his Colt Automatic pistol but didn't hit the man. Eventually on 12 August came the news that some soldiers from the 11th Division would take over the positions being held by the Dublin Fusiliers and that Drury could therefore retire to the rest camp at C Beach.

The march back to the shore was a long and exhausting business for these men after almost incessant front-line duty since their arrival at Gallipoli. Even the lieutenant colonel of the battalion arrived back at the camp looking dirty and wretched and with 'one of his nice silk puttees missing'. The camp itself proved to be 'burningly hot with no shelter' and was infested with flies. Throughout the latter part of 12 August and much of 13 August the Dubliners also suffered from hunger as no arrangements had been made to provide meals for them on their arrival at the beach. Drury recorded that the men quite clearly had not been eating enough food. The bully was still 'simply awful'. He recorded in his diary how 'it pours out of the tin in a greasy mess and has no taste whatsoever' and he disgustedly wrote that 'a lot of the biscuits are weevily'.

At the end of the day the 6th Dublins crossed to the far side of the bay and prepared to play their part in the imminent mass assault on the Kiretch Tepe ridge. At the altitude of their new camp a light sea breeze fanned the men and brought welcome coolness. First evidence seemed to suggest that the food was rather better in this part of Suvla and that water was now being carried up in more satisfactory quantities from A Beach, transported by a mule train. Drury also had his most striking view to date of the Turkish coastline and of the Greek islands on the horizon, beyond which the sunset was 'most beautiful'. That night, he enjoyed the best sleep he had yet experienced at Suvla, although he started to feel quite chilly in the hour before dawn.

Numerous cases of trigger fingers shot off

THE SUVLA SECTOR, 14–15 AUGUST

The next day, Drury and his friends drank cocoa, ate sardines and enjoyed the luxury of a jar of marmalade. Letters arrived from home, the first that Drury had actually received since leaving Basingstoke. Feeling buoyed up and satisfied, he slept well once again on the night of 14 August. Waking the next morning in time to watch a Mediterranean sunrise, Drury thought to himself in a brief moment of euphoria: 'What a lot one misses at home.' A few minutes later he slipped down to the beach and had a bath. An hour later he was in position and ready for what promised to be the fiercest encounter yet between the Irish Division and its enemy.[13]

For Drury, as for the other men who now faced the ultimate test in battle, there was an awareness of the fact that they had been on the peninsula for a whole week and that it had been by far the most demanding week of their lives, a time of exhaustion, despair and occasional adrenalin-fuelled exhilaration.

Each man had constructed his own mental map of a few square miles that most of them had never even heard of prior to landing there. That mental map was full of improvised place names such as Jephson's Post, Dunphy's Corner and Scimitar Hill, the latter named after the curved sword whose outline it resembled. Suvla was a palimpsest on which a map of improvised militarism and black humour overlaid local cartography and indigenous place-names. Such names included 'the hill belonging to Ishmael's son' (Ismael Oglu Tepe) and 'the hill of the dragonflies' (now known as Scimitar Hill).[14]

For its Irish soldiers, Suvla was a place where everyone searched endlessly for shade from the sun and developed the famous 'Gallipoli stoop', caused by the incessant need to avoid snipers. It was a map out of which the green-painted face of that dreaded Turkish sniper might loom and where, it was rumoured, Turkish markswomen had been spotted, more ruthless and accurate than a man.

During their week at Suvla the men had also heard rumours about Turkish or German spies, clad in dapper British officers' uniforms who were suave, authoritative but strangely unfamiliar and who had been seen walking up and down behind the lines, gathering intelligence. As the Irish soldiers waited, on the morning of 15 August, they stared out at the now familiar skyline of the elongated chain of hills which constituted the high ground of the Gallipoli Peninsula. To one man it looked like 'the vertebrae of some antediluvian reptile'.[15] The Irish soldiers had also become familiar with the British naval searchlight that could be seen each night, raking the hillsides. They knew all about occasional downpours and the feel of rain-soaked clothes drying out against their skin or steaming in the heat. Many of them had known the impulse to run away from the battle or to feign injury.

William Knott saw his fair share of battlefield nerves, having witnessed soldiers turning to 'run like cowards' and having encountered in his field ambulance work, numerous cases of trigger fingers shot off in dubiously private circumstances to get immediate medical care and permanently exit the battlefield. Knott even encountered one man who 'bound up his own knee and allowed our stretcher-bearers to carry him right to the hospital where the doctor found nothing amiss'.[16]

At daybreak on 15 August, Ivone Kirkpatrick attended Mass with fellow Catholics from his battalion. He was in infinitely better form, having had a couple of days of rest from front-line fighting. He and a friend, during one of their bathing sessions, swam out into the bay as far as a British destroyer and climbed up a rope ladder extended over the hull to join the crew of the vessel and share a drink with them, standing stark naked on the deck while they teased the gunners about the accuracy of their firing. Now Kirkpatrick stood in a sheltered place on the ridge's steep seaward face as Father Stafford conducted the service and gave absolution. As the prayers continued, he kept gazing out towards the Aegean, where the sun rose over the 'shimmering bright blue sea' and 'the black rock of Samothrace' stood out in the distance.[17]

Meanwhile, at 10th Division HQ, senior officers busied themselves with the usual miscellany of pre-battle issues. Notice was taken of the recent directive from the Catholic chaplaincy that absolution should be given to all Catholic soldiers during Mass in the early hours before this next phase of the battle. Staff at the two Suvla brigade command posts were not so busy with battle plans that they could ignore issues like the tendency in recent days of men in the division to send letters by various means to ships that lay offshore, hoping that they would be inserted into the ships' mail bays. This unofficial communication with home was attempted because soldiers were spurred on by the prospect of a bloody renewal of the battle, but it was strictly forbidden.[18]

Other issues that HQ staff had to deal with just before the fight recommenced, were new arrangements for the confirmation of the identity of dead Irish soldiers. The memo from Corps HQ asked that the location of their demise be surrounded by wire and an improvised wooden cross erected. A few hours later, a huge attack began on the ridge, in which the men of two Irish infantry brigades fought side by side in full order, for the first time, strengthened by replacements that had been sent from Mudros Bay. So far these two brigades had lost over 100 officers and close to 3000 men in the ranks, due to injury, death or capture by the enemy. It was likely that they were about to lose many more.[19]

I prayed for renewed strength to endure to the end

NORTHERN SLOPES OF THE KIRETCH TEPE RIDGE, 15–16 AUGUST

The assault began at midday. It was General Mahon's best chance yet to achieve military success and lasting fame for his Irish Division. On the southern slopes of the ridge facing the Suvla plain were the 31st Brigade, made up of the Royal Inniskillings and the Royal Irish Fusiliers. On the north side, facing the open sea, were the Munster and Dublin Fusiliers of 30th Brigade. Their joint attack, aided by men from the other British divisions, was an attempt to force the Turks from the rocky Kiretch Tepe, then swing south-eastwards onto the Tekke Tepe hills en route to the Sari Bair ridge, which the Anzac soldiers were seeking to capture from the southern and western direction.

The midday advance began on the northern slopes with a great coordinated forward charge. Many yards to the rear, observers reported that 'our fellows could be heard cheering as they went forward and the bayonets were flashing and stabbing for several minutes before the Turks began to give way' and then went 'running before our men'.

According to another witness on the northern slopes of the ridge, as the Irish soldiers surged up the hill towards the stony skyline, the Turks 'leapt up from the crest and down over the ridge' onto the southern side and 'our men were standing up and firing down on them'. The Munster soldiers in particular seemed to charge at the Turks with great ferocity and verve, despite the numerous gullies that they had to cross and the by-now familiar scrub that grew on the Gallipoli hillside. The Munsters were led by inspirational individual officers like Majors Tynte and Jephson but as they pushed along the narrow ridge, within a few minutes of beginning the attack, Jephson was killed by enemy shellfire just a few yards from the stronghold to which he had given his name a week before.[20]

For Noel Drury, the midday advance made by his Dublin Fusiliers was adding up to a familiar tally of death and destruction. His personal friend, Lieutenant Richards, was hit in the face by a grenade hurled from the spine of the ridge and died instantly. Another friend, affectionately called Johnny Preston by Drury, was hit in the chest and died as he was carried to the dressing station. Other young Dublin officers received less grave injuries, like Bill Whyte who was hit by shrapnel in the neck. These walking wounded tried to continue with their duties, looking 'very game but very pale.' Another officer, 'Fritz' Cullen, was actually 'fielding Turk bombs and hurling them back before they could hit'.

Watching his fellow officers dice with death, Drury experienced the familiar frustration of being unable to communicate with his HQ via a field telephone. All afternoon he had terrible trouble with the company telephone lines getting cut. Semaphore communication was also curtailed when he lost several signallers. Drury felt particularly responsible for these casualties because he had not been able to get a proper shelter for them. By mid-afternoon, there was evidence that the advance was coming to a halt and clear signs that the attack on the southern side of the ridge had made even less ground. Not only were Turkish soldiers withstanding Dublin Fusilier assaults at the stronghold known as Kidney Hill but they seemed to be able to climb up the southern side of the ridge freely. They were now firing bullets and grenades at them from several vantage points well to the rear of the Dublin troops.[21]

Most of the Pals also began to feel the strain as the afternoon wore on. They felt demoralized and deeply unhappy with this disorganized and exhausting battle for control of what one soldier later called 'a rugged knife-edge above the sea'. They were aware of what a disadvantage they were at with their ineffectual missiles made from empty tins and charges of explosive, compared to the grenades the Turks were using.

Most distressingly of all, many men in D Company saw their popular commander Poole Hickman killed at midday, after which Major Harrison from A Company stepped into the breach. Leaping forward to take charge and striding bravely ahead while waving his cane, he shouted: 'I will lead you, men.' A few seconds later, he too was caught in the blast of an explosion from a grenade on the edge of an enemy trench. Captain Tobin, who was next to take charge of the company, was shot through the head a couple of minutes later. Thus the command structure of the Dublin Pals disappeared in a few minutes of savage fighting.

Later, while the Dublin Fusiliers were making a fresh assault on the Pimple, a popular young soldier called Cecil Murray also fell to the ground. Murray, the son of a County Wexford clergyman, had been a Bank of Ireland employee and was, like so many of his colleagues, a keen sportsman. A couple of Pals bent over their friend's prone body and asked him where he had been hit. Murray showed them his left hand, which had been shot to a pulp, but then while the men were talking to him, Murray was hit three times by a volley of enemy machine-gun fire which missed the other Pals by inches. As Murray died before their eyes he groaned in a heart-rending manner.

A few minutes later some of the Pals saw another young colleague being hit by enemy fire. One witness only knew this particular soldier as 'a young chap called Elliott who played footer'. The man in question was in fact T.C.M. Elliott from Strabane in County Tyrone. He had been a medical student at Trinity College and not only a talented sportsman but an excellent marksman in the university gun club. He jumped three feet into the air when hit, crumpled to the ground and then started crawling back to the Irish lines, when he was hit again. He died quickly, in full view of his colleagues who were unable to rescue him because of exceptionally heavy gunfire.

Later, while eating in an improvised dugout in captured territory on the ridge, other Pals were witness to further death and mutilation a few yards away when 'two shells came along and one fellow from A Company got his head blown off and Sergeant Kenny lost a leg'. Also lying close to death on the ridge was Lieutenant Fitzgibbon, son of a Westminster nationalist MP and a promising young trainee lawyer. Wherever one looked across the stony slopes and scrubland, bodies lay where they fell, often contorted in their last agonies.

As night began to creep over the Suvla headland, officers like Noel Drury sought advice from their senior commanders. Despite an immense effort and very serious losses, the big objective of Kidney Hill had not been taken and although they had advanced a mile or so, this had left the men stretched out and vulnerable to sporadic enemy fire. D Company of the 7th Dublins had been reduced to 106 by the night of 15 August, having landed on the peninsula so recently with a combat strength of 239.

The 6th Dublins were also losing men at a terrible rate and were now in a particularly exposed advance position on the ridge. Should Drury and his fellow officers order their men to retreat strategically to a safer location a few hundred yards to the rear? He sent a couple of messages to his superiors with a runner but received no reply, so under cover of darkness made the arduous journey back behind the lines, where he was ushered in to see his friend Colonel Paddy Cox, at 30th Brigade HQ. Cox, however, could provide no answers and asked him to travel a little farther to another command post where Brigadier-General Nicholl was holding a meeting with other senior officers.

Nicholl was in an awful temper at Drury's previous messages. Soon the brigadier was accusing him of 'having the wind up for no reason'. Then Drury also lost his temper and was, as he would later phrase it in his diary – 'a bit insubordinate', inviting Nicholl up to the front line to see for himself just how exposed the Dublin soldiers would be when dawn broke. Nicholl was somewhat taken aback by Drury's anger but did not journey up to the far reaches of the ridge. He agreed instead that the Dublin Fusiliers had best stage an immediate tactical retreat and that in order to facilitate this the gunners aboard HMS *Foxhound* should be ordered to open up and pound adjacent enemy positions with heavy explosives, keeping the Turks busy while Drury's men made their withdrawal.[22]

William Knott, meanwhile, still operating as a stretcher-bearer, found himself incredibly busy once night had descended on the peninsula. Earlier in the day he had felt optimistic about the chances of a breakthrough on the ridge when he had heard the wild cheer of the first Irish troops bayonet-charging the Turks. But now in the moonlit darkness he was scrambling around on the stony hillside, loading stretchers, dressing wounds and even helping to dig shallow graves. He called out to God as always and pleaded 'for renewed strength to endure to the end'.[23]

Reginald Ford, the Dublin schoolteacher turned volunteer soldier actually found the action of the afternoon and early evening of 15 August an exhilarating if terrifying experience as he watched the enemy being forced down from the crest of the hill at many points, then sensed the fighting petering out, as dusk gathered. That night, after he had helped build a narrow defensive rampart out of loose rocks and boulders, he was given some important nocturnal duties:

> I was one of a covering party who had to go over the top of the hill to watch for any movement of The Turks. It was a weird experience

crouching there in the darkness, ears and eyes alert. Sometimes there would be silence save for the creaking of the night-birds. The screams and shrieks of the wounded Turks were pretty ghastly but by degrees the sounds died down as the Turkish wounded were removed or put out of their pain ...

Unfortunately for Ford and his 30th Brigade colleagues, the brief quiet was interrupted when Mustafa Kemal ordered his soldiers to counter-attack along the ridge at dawn on the morning of 16 August. In the half-light, men awoke to hear the fearful cry of hundreds of Turks surging along the hill calling out 'Allah, Allah'. Soon the familiar terror of a grenade-attack engulfed the Irish soldiers and yet again some of the Dublin Fusiliers were seen catching the bombs that the Turks threw towards them, then trying to hurl them back again at the encroaching enemy. One young English soldier called Private Wilkin did this on five occasions, but his luck ran out on the sixth attempt and he was blown to pieces by the blast.

Reginald Ford was also aware that the Turks were charging towards the Irish lines in the early dawn. He saw that the enemy were not just firing rifles, machine-guns and grenades at the 10th Division but even big stones. Within a few minutes of the start of the Turkish counter-attack, Ford had received what he would later describe as his 'little dose', in the form of a severe shrapnel wound to the left elbow. A comrade bandaged the deep wound, mopped up the blood and sent him to the dressing-station – but not before he had helped Ford to fill and light his pipe to provide some consolation both for the physical pain and his distress at 'deserting' his comrades. At the dressing-station the medical team recognized that the damage to Ford's left elbow was severe and possibly irreparable. Within days he was on a hospital ship back to Egypt for further treatment and convalescence.[24]

Gradually, as the morning wore on, the British defence against the Turkish counter-attack on the northern slopes began to stabilize. When the enemy fire died down, Noel Drury began the less urgent but harrowing task of burying the bodies of dead colleagues and packing up the belongings of all the officers who had died or been injured in the last few hours. He collected Lieutenant Richards' personal possessions and sent them to a ship in the bay, whence they were conveyed to the young man's father at Merrion Square in Dublin. The items included three watches, obviously of sentimental value. One was made of gold, another of silver, and the third, much smaller wristlet watch was probably a woman's. There was also a gold signet ring, a clasp tie-pin, some religious medals and a purse. Later on Drury was choked with emotion as he helped dig graves in a 'brown patch' near the Dublin Fusilier rest-camp, for 'poor Billy Richards and Johnny Preston', then placed a cross made of pieces of board over their last resting places, with their names burned onto the wood.

Drury immediately had to focus again on the dangers of the current military situation. All through the day he had been requesting more improvised grenades to be sent to his men as they had completely run out of them. He received only one small box of extra bombs, despite his earnest pleas.

A smashed division, a fearful loss

NORTHERN SLOPES OF THE RIDGE AND A BEACH WEST, 16–17 AUGUST

Throughout the latter part of 16 August, once the Turk counter-attack had been repelled, brave attempts were made to bring back the bodies still scattered along the ridge. After nightfall, as the Irish soldiers withdrew still farther from their more exposed positions, one young Dublin Fusilier called Corporal Bryan, a stretcher-bearer and a drummer with the regimental band, stayed behind and spent hours searching in vain in the darkness for the corpse of a much-respected officer from C Company called Nesbitt.

By now Drury was confused and ludicrously over-burdened with responsibilities. He was placed in charge of communication between the companies of his battalion and so spent much of 16 August moving between different parts of the line in an attempt to get the surviving officers in each company to synchronize their watches for the now inevitable retreat to the rest-camp at the beach. Drury was sure that he would eventually be blown to bits by an exploding shell during these hazardous trips. He had taken over Billy Richards' role as adjutant while retaining his own role as signal officer, but he was also doing a range of other tasks once performed by men who had died. The experience made him feel like the street entertainer he had once witnessed in Dublin: 'the funny man we would see when we were children, who played all the band instruments at the same time'. Drury also saw some terrifying injuries, including the mutilation of Paddy Beard of the pioneers who had been 'wounded through both cheeks by shrapnel, messing up the bone and some teeth'.

By 17 August the Dublin and Munster Fusiliers had retired to sea level from the bloody heights where they had yet again failed in their attempt to achieve a breakthrough into enemy territory.

Despite the exhaustion, disappointment and grief at losing friends, there was a massive sense of relief. A canvas tent stood on the shoreline containing barrels of fresh water that were coming ashore in much greater quantities. There were relatively safe places to shelter and to bathe in the lee of the cliffs at the tip of Suvla Point. The men needed time and space to clean up: after two days spent fighting on the open ridge they were dirty, sunburned and un-shaven.

The men had not lost all of their sense of humour though. When Drury called at Nicholl's brigade HQ, he noticed a new cook called McManus trying to heat a tin of stew without punching a hole in the can, to let out pressure. This meant that McManus had unwittingly created a little bomb and Drury watched as the tin built up a good head of steam then blew to pieces and shot hot meat and vegetables over the brigade staff![25]

However, cheerfulness and sudden moments of humour could not lessen the impact of the casualty list. William Knott's non-combatant field ambulance brigade had suffered terribly and twenty-three out of thirty-three colleagues were killed, wounded or captured during the last three days. 31st Field Ambulance treated 117 casualties on the first day of the renewed offensive, 81 on the following day and 178 during the course of 17 August.[26]

After the attack on the northern side of the ridge, the surviving officers from the 30th Brigade discussed why an assault that had started with such a wild and successful bayonet-charge had eventually failed. There was deep frustration at the failure of 'the rotters' on the southern side of the ridge to make any advance and disappointment at the lack of satisfactory artillery support. As one officer later told the official historian of the Gallipoli campaign, 'The so-called intensive bombardment of twenty minutes meant throwing over some fifty shells at the Turks, this estimate has been agreed to by several of those present.'

The sense of frustration with the events of 15 and 16 August became even greater in the post-war years, when men of the 10th Division read accounts by German officers who had led enemy troops at Suvla. These indicated that the 15 August attacks constituted the greatest moment of danger for the Turkish defence of the Suvla sector. The Munster and Dublin soldiers apparently came very close to achieving a breakthrough on the afternoon of 15 August after their wild charge along the northern heights of the Kiretch Tepe.[27]

As this ridge became the site of yet another Gallipoli disaster, the command staff war diarist became aware of a pressing problem for the thousands of men in the congested few miles of Turkish territory they still held. This was the matter of men 'defecating where they will'. Human faeces was found everywhere, but in particular along the paths used by the soldiers. Latrines had been dug but were often hard to find and men feared that using them would make them sitting targets for the enemy. Bushy vegetation made it easy for men to relieve themselves wherever and whenever they felt the need, without being seen by their officers. The resulting filth was soon distributed around the battlefield as heavy summer rain sent polluted water cascading down the hills. Soon a more vigorous attempt was made to mark out latrines with wooden signs and flags and to enforce the exclusive use of them.[28]

For John Hargrave there were constant examples of stoicism and suffering to file away in his memory, such as an Indian service corps man who had been soldiering on the ridge and had his left leg blown off by shrapnel but was, incredibly, lying back against a rock and attempting to smoke a cigarette. Hargrave watched 'great tears rolling down his cheeks' but still the man 'said no word'.

Increasingly the field ambulance men felt that they were looking at 'a smashed division, a fearful loss'. But at least for the 30th Infantry Brigade there had been a measure of early success to record. No such successes attended the assault of the 31st Infantry Brigade on the southern slopes of the ridge.[29]

I no longer inhabited my own body

SOUTHERN SLOPES, KIRETCH TEPE RIDGE, 15–18 AUGUST

In the early afternoon of 15 August the vanguard units of the Royal Inniskilling and Royal Irish Fusiliers went forward and were annihilated. Officers and their men alike died in a hail of bullets, with the most sustained fire coming from the rocky outcrop of Kidney Hill. Ivone Kirkpatrick later put the failure of his troops down to the fact that the strength of the enemy had not been known. It was also impossible to locate and target the Turkish trenches on the southern slopes of the ridge as enemy positions were masked by the luxuriant growth of scrub.

In the last hour before the signal to attack on 15 August, Kirkpatrick had sampled tinned fruit, bottled asparagus, potted meat and a few dates from a Fortnum and Mason's hamper that all the Inniskilling officers had recently been sent. While they were eating, Kirkpatrick and his colleagues discussed what to do with each other's personal effects in case of death or serious injury. But, as he would later report, 'by evening no survivors would be left to carry out our complicated testamentary dispositions'.

At 1.15 pm, having received the signal to advance but without any idea where precisely the enemy was, Kirkpatrick gathered the men of his No. 6 platoon and headed in the general direction of the Turkish trenches, over a landscape dominated by new and unfamiliar vegetation. He was suddenly hit in the abdomen by a bullet, which felt like someone driving a golf-ball into his stomach from close range. From that time on, he felt as if he no longer inhabited his own body. It seemed as if, from a long way off, he was watching the aftermath of his own wounding. His soul seemed to hover at some height above his body and 'to observe its doings with a sort of detached interest'. He felt no fear, only a mild sense of curiosity.

He crawled into a sheltered hollow in the hillslope and tried to dress his wounds with iodine and bandages from his kitbag. A wounded man crawled past the hollow and Kirkpatrick asked him to get help as he felt unable to make his own way back to the rear of the battlefield. After waiting for half an hour he began the long, slow crawl back towards his own lines. He managed to cover 100 yards, with enemy bullets ricocheting off the boulders all around him. To lighten the load he was carrying, he got rid of his field glasses and revolver and then tried to crawl a little farther. At last he was spotted by a stretcher-party who took him to a dressing station. By now he was suffering from a violent cramp in his stomach and needed an injection of morphine to cope with the agonies of the bumpy journey back to the field hospital tent, situated on the beach. On the way, Kirkpatrick was violently sick over his chest and by the time he reached the beach he was not only covered in vomit but lying in a pool of greasy blood that now soaked his entire uniform from his helmet to his boots.

It was dark at the field hospital and a doctor examined his injuries by the light of an oil-lamp. A label was then attached to his uniform, indicating that he was a candidate for evacuation from Gallipoli, shortly after which he was placed on the open beach under the starlight, where all around him lay other men on stretchers, groaning, shouting and cursing. Then a Catholic chaplain came by and gave Kirkpatrick the last rites.

A couple of hours later he was taken to the nearby quay, then transported in a small craft to a hospital ship in the bay. The boats being used to take men to this ship clustered together in the swell and 'at every bump there was a chorus of groans and imprecations'. By now he was 'almost past suffering' and parched with a raging thirst. His mouth was also uncomfortably caked in dried blood. As dawn broke over the bay, his stretcher was hoisted up by a small crane and he landed on the deck with an excruciating thump. A few moments later he was lying in a bed and being asked to don a fresh, white nightshirt by a young nurse. Kirkpatrick's Suvla adventure was practically over. Once the bullet had been removed from his body, the days of gradual recovery that lay ahead offered a chance both for himself and the other wounded men on board ship to exchange what news they possessed of the fate of the 10th Division. Although his physical pain began to ease, the emotional pain intensified, as he heard of fellow officers and men from the ranks who had perished in the ill-fated attempt to capture the Kiretch Tepe heights.[30]

For Juvenis, the Gallipoli adventure was also nearly over. On 15 August he too advanced with his Inniskilling troops toward the objective that he could only identify as a large spur and which was, in all probability, Kidney Hill. It lay a mere 800 yards ahead but soon, 'an orchestra of bullets and ricochets' played as the men advanced, so no orders about how to close in on the spur could be heard over the excruciating din. Individual improvisation now had to prevail among the junior officers.

Juvenis charged with his men across an open patch of hillside, past a couple of dead soldiers whose bodies lay in the 'grilling sun' with 'their blackened faces in hideous contrast with the bright new khaki drill and helmet'. He kept on moving through the 'cloud of gaudy flies' which buzzed up from the corpses and he determined that he would not allow himself to fall wounded at such a frightening location. But suddenly, just a few yards farther up the hillside, he was hit by a bullet that pierced his right shoulder. Within seconds, blood was pouring down his sleeve. Another soldier stopped and tried to help him bandage the injury as he lay on the brushwood. Juvenis looked at his wristwatch. It was 1.45 pm.

The helpful comrade soon left and Juvenis realized he would have to lie there, waiting for help from passing stretcher-bearers. While stranded on this part of the hillside he watched as one man from his own battalion staggered about with a frantic expression in his eyes. The two canvas bandoliers full of ammunition that were slung around his body were ablaze. Wrestling to get them off, he disappeared from Juvenis' line of vision.

Suddenly he felt a wallop on the side of his head, his helmet rolled off and he could feel blood trickle from a shallow wound in his scalp. Although the wound did not seem to be serious, he was now panic-stricken and tried to get up and crawl towards safety only to feel himself being hit once again, this time in the left hip. He pulled from his trouser pocket the bundle of letters from home, which he always carried with him in battle. They were covered in blood and he could see that they had been pierced by the very bullet that had also hit his hip. He fainted with the pain and the shock but regained consciousness some minutes later.

Juvenis then tried to read the dial of his watch but it had been smashed, so he then tried to reach forward and gather a few stones to erect a makeshift barrier between himself and enemy snipers. After this, he wound his puttees around his head to shade himself from the heat of the sun, then placed a broken ampule of iodine in the wound in his shoulder, while flies gathered around the aching bullet wound. Whilst he was doing this, a Turkish shell landed close to where he lay and some of the sand that was thrown up in the air landed on his face, although the shell mercifully failed to explode.

Juvenis then heard the crackle of flames among the bushes and smelled smoke from the burning scrubland. He began to wonder if his fate would be incineration, as he lay helplessly on the Suvla hillside. At least there was little wind during the afternoon of 15 August and he tried to convince himself that the fire would not spread. By late afternoon he was hallucinating, seeing angels in the sky and imagining 'dainty nurses tripping through the scrub among the bullets, with neat red-crossed aprons and carrying bowls of nectar'. When he was lucid he held conversations with the occasional straggler who was making his way back from the front line, asking for directions.

After dusk, Juvenis heard distant screams and yells in an unfamiliar language, which indicated that a Turkish counter-attack was being launched somewhere on the heights. Then a water-carrier arrived, stopped briefly to give him a drink, placed a haversack under his head and assured him that a stretcher-party would arrive before too long. By this stage his shoulder-wound was filling with maggots and the mangled flesh was starting to stink. In the darkness the firing had begun to ease but this was replaced by the terrible chorus of the wounded, who called out feebly but persistently all across the southern slopes of the ridge.

Despairing of ever being rescued, Juvenis turned over and lay on his face in the sandy soil. Then he heard footsteps and familiar voices and he called out with all his remaining strength. Out of the shadows of the night emerged two men from his own company, who had been searching for him for several hours. They placed him in a blanket and carried him back to the nearest field ambulance station where he was given two morphia pills to dull his pain. As the dawn broke over Suvla, he lay on a piece of oilcloth in a row of 'stretcher-cases', next to another grievously wounded Irish officer.

Juvenis remained on his oilcloth for the entire day. His wounds were cleaned out and he was given ample water but there was such overload at the field hospital on the beach and aboard the hospital ships in the bay that many men had to wait their turn before being transported from the battlefield. As nightfall once again approached and the firing eased, Juvenis heard the renewed call of the wounded, still trapped on the smouldering scrubland, pleading for assistance. Eventually two men from 31st Field Ambulance Brigade came to where Juvenis lay and began the two-mile journey to the beach that was pure torture. He occasionally felt the stretcher-handles slipping from the tired, perspiring hands of the bearers. At the beach he received a fresh dose of morphine but it had little effect and he lay there shivering and aching, groggily watching the shipping in the bay, including an 'incessant stream of hospital ships'. Nearby he saw a gang of Turkish prisoners who worked all day long, unloading stores.

The beach was not an easy place to wait, for he was surrounded by mutilated and distraught fellow soldiers. A sergeant from his own company lay nearby with his right hand shot off and his face grey with exhaustion and bloodloss. There was little peace to be had because, not far away, some of the 10th Division artillery were busy launching high explosives and the ground vibrated and shook every time the guns were fired. Juvenis heard that one of the hospital tents had been hit by a Turkish shell that was sent over in response.

Many of the tents were by now so full that the wounded had to lie outside on the sand and there was a constant background noise of men groaning with pain from their injuries There was also the pervasive stench from wounds and clouds of flies. Every foot of space between the sea and the low cliffs was covered in stretchers and Juvenis watched an orderly walk up and down these rows, handing out Gold Flake cigarettes to those men still capable of smoking.

Then a doctor arrived and silently wrote out an identification label and a description of his injuries and attached it to Juvenis' buttonhole. Shortly after, he was placed on a small craft and towed into the centre of the bay. He looked up from his stretcher and saw the hull of a large ship looming overhead with the olive green band and a red cross emblazoned on the hull, which indicated that it was a hospital vessel. An electric crane lifted him high in the air and deposited him on the deck. Meanwhile, he saw a trail of walking wounded making their way up the gangway from the numerous small craft that gathered around the ship. He could pick out men 'stumbling, hopping, limping, bleeding, leaning on each other's arms and necks and one or two on all fours ...' as they boarded the vessel.

Juvenis was taken to a cabin for wounded officers and placed in a small cot, where he tried to sleep despite the remorseless ache from his wounds. The nurses had to cut off his uniform to free him from his stretcher because the mixture of dried blood, mud and shredded cloth had coagulated and no other way of releasing him could be found.[31]

It was Lady Day in Harvest

A BEACH WEST, SUVLA , 17–18 AUGUST

By 17 August the attack on the Kiretch Tepe objectives had wholly petered out. Mahon's pitch for a breakthrough using his eight available Irish battalions had turned into the most deadly and bloody few days of the Suvla campaign so far. The men from Munster, Dublin and the north of the island, and the many non-Irish soldiers who were in the division along with them, were now a broken military force. Even the pioneer battalion, the Royal Irish Regiment, designed primarily to service infantry attacks rather than to be in the front line, had suffered numerous casualties. Two officers were dead, one was missing and six were wounded. In the ranks, there were thirty-one men dead, ninety-eight wounded and eighteen missing.[32]

By the time the Kiretch Tepe debacle was over, the 5th Royal Irish Fusilier numbers were down to four officers and 537 men capable of fighting, indicating that half of the battalion had disappeared, and when the 6th Royal Irish Fusiliers returned to their support trenches they had lost ten officers and 210 men, merely from the last two days of battle.[33]

One of the most poignant anecdotes regarding the fighting of 15 August and its aftermath was offered by John Hargrave, who at one point thought that the 'parapet of crenellated rocks' along the ridge was strongly held by his own men because he could see so many British bayonets in the distance, glinting in the sun. He had not realized that these bayonets belonged to dead men who lay there on the rocky ridge with 'their rifles still pointing towards the Turkish lines …'.

It was also Hargrave who noted that 15 August was a time of special importance in Ireland. It is a day of rural celebration, known in the Irish Catholic calendar as Lady Day in Harvest but it had its origins in pre-Christian times when the Celtic peoples celebrated the Festival of Lughnasa to praise the bounty of the sun god, Lugh. Here at Suvla Bay, under the punishing rays of the August sun, the 10th Division reaped another kind of harvest.[34]

Dead Turks at Gallipoli, autumn 1915.
THE NEWPORT COLLECTION, ROYAL ULSTER RIFLES MUSEUM

Suvla Point – looking north-east along the Kiretch Tepe ridge.
WILSON

Wild flowers grew at Suvla
beside the graves of friend and
enemy alike.
WILSON

Cecil Murray, clergyman's son. He died
on 'the ridge', August 1915.
O'H/H

Poole Hickman, lawyer. He died on 'the
ridge', August 1915.
O'H/ H

Tom Elliott, medical student. He died on 'the ridge', August 1915.

O'H / H

Michael Fitzgibbon, son of a nationalist MP. He died on 'the ridge', August 1915.

O'H/ H

Reginald Ford, survivor of the attack on 'the ridge',
August 1915.
O'H/H

Rosemary – one of the herbs whose fragrance mitigated
the stench of the Suvla dead.
WILSON

VI
CASUALTIES

It had been the best division in the New Army

THE EASTERN MEDITERRANEAN, 15–19 AUGUST

Sir Ian Hamilton, who was deeply unhappy with the 9th Corps leadership, now contacted Lord Kitchener to indicate that Stopford needed to be replaced. The man brought in to replace him was Major General Beauvoir De Lisle, who had been in charge of 29th Division, which had made the costly assault on Cape Helles at the opening of the Gallipoli campaign a few months earlier. Sir Bryan Mahon was senior to De Lisle in army hierarchy and should have been the automatic choice to replace Stopford. The unceremonious way in which he was now leapfrogged in the promotion process was all the more hurtful because of personal animosity between the rival generals, apparently built up in the course of their military careers. Mahon was already distressed by the fragmentation of his own division as a fighting unit and by the terrible losses it had incurred in battle. This sense of being bypassed by a rival was the last straw. On 15 August, the 10th Division became leaderless. Mahon resigned.

Hamilton had already communicated to Lord Kitchener the concern he had felt on disembarking at Suvla Bay just after the start of the new offensive and finding 'most of the troops lolling about as if it was a holiday' rather than pushing inland. He had complained to the War Secretary that the senior officers at Suvla seemed 'to have no drive or control over the men' and Mahon was clearly one of the senior officers who were being criticized. Mahon's pioneer battalion was, according to Hamilton, 'making a devil of a trench as if he was going to defend himself to the gasp'. Clearly, in Hamilton's eyes, a more visionary and forceful leader was required. In the long term Sir Julian Byng might have been right for the job, but he was in France. Meanwhile, De Lisle was the best option as an immediate replacement for Stopford.

On hearing of De Lisle's appointment, Mahon sent an immediate message to Hamilton that said that 'for private reasons' he did not wish to serve under De Lisle and requested to be relieved of his command. Shocked but keen to avoid further top-level chaos at the front-line, Hamilton ordered him to go down to the pier at A Beach and board a vessel for Lemnos. Mahon penned a letter for circulation among the troops in which he wrote, in hurt tones, 'it is the saddest day of my life leaving you all … you are better off without me … I feel certain you will serve my successor with equal loyalty and devotion.'

He remained on the Greek island for a few days, in splendid isolation from his fellow officers and his Irish troops until, in a rush of regret, he expressed the desire to return to Suvla, whether serving under De Lisle or not. Hamilton had been horrified by Mahon's behaviour but nonetheless allowed him to return. Subsequent letters to Kitchener reveal that he was now very nervous of his temperamental Irish general who had 'refused to play up and sink his personal jealousies during a difficult period'. Hamilton expressed his fear that if he was 'bowled over' when he visited the lines, Mahon would be next senior British officer at Gallipoli and therefore would assume supreme command. That, in light of Mahon's recent behaviour, was a truly terrifying thought.

A later letter from Mahon to Kitchener reveals his deep distress at what had happened to the 10th Division, which he believed to have been the best in the New Army. It had been broken up before the men had actually commenced operations, when one brigade had been sent to Anzac Cove. Mahon had then 'heard nothing about it in five weeks.' As for the divisional artillery, Mahon claimed that he did not know where the majority of the artillerymen and their guns actually were. They certainly had not been sent with the division to Suvla Bay. It seemed to him that 'the division's value as a fighting unit was decreased 50 per cent by being broken up' and that 'their treatment will have a bad effect on recruitment in Ireland, especially in the south and west where the best soldiers come from'.

Mahon stayed on with the division which he had so swiftly left and equally swiftly rejoined, acting as their commander until December when they were soldiering in a new and less onerous campaign in the Balkans. Surprisingly perhaps, he was now temporarily elevated to the status of Commander in Chief of the British army in Macedonia.[1]

On Anzac Beach's narrow strip of sand

ANZAC SECTOR, 5–11 AUGUST

What became of the 29th Brigade that was sent into action at Anzac Cove? They had been picked to contribute to an assault whose main function was to be a sideshow. But instead of merely helping to deflect attention away from the Suvla engagement, the brigade soon found itself caught up in something bigger – a substantial attempt to break through the Turkish lines on this particularly precipitous part of the coastline and to capture the high ground of the Sari Bair ridge to link up with the troops advancing southwards from Suvla Bay.[2]

On the night of 5 August the brigade landed on a narrow strip of land, facing Turkish-dominated hilltops. The men transferred from their transport ships to the ubiquitous Gallipoli lighters that took them ashore. No one spoke in more than a whisper as they changed vessels in the pitch-black night. The big hope was that the whole landing procedure for 29th Brigade would go unnoticed and up to that point secrecy seemed to have been preserved. Then on Anzac Beach's narrow strip of sand, the Irish soldiers stood in the darkness and saw in the first light of dawn the busy figures of the Australian and New Zealand troops handling piles of forage and rations and reinforcing the sand-bagged dugouts. What they could not yet see were the infamously steep and scrub-lined gullies like the Aghyll Dere and Asmak Dere that led inland and upwards to the summits where the front-line troops had been trying so hard to establish a permanent presence since the month of April.

During the landing 29th Brigade was placed under the command of General Sir Alex Godley, GOC of the 1st Australian and New Zealand Division, who would later write an autobiography entitled *Memoirs of an Irish Soldier* due to his Anglo-Irish family background and his early soldiering with Dublin Fusiliers in the South African wars. Under Godley's command, 29th Brigade's task was to advance for a short distance up a dried-out riverbed which had been ominously renamed by the Anzacs as Shrapnel Gully. They stayed put in a series of dugouts there until a suitable moment for the Irish Brigade's first big assault could be found.

Bryan Cooper and his men were led to these emplacements by a group of New Zealand veterans and it was their first encounter with the legendary Anzacs. Overhead, in the pale light early morning, they saw the silhouettes of the towering hills that made this part of the peninsula such a daunting military objective. There were sturdy sand-bags all around the trenches and saps in Shrapnel Gully to protect the new troops from the bullets and shellfire that rained down regularly on the British positions, even here behind the front lines.[3]

Individual Irish soldiers like John McIlwaine of the Connaught Rangers were aware only that they had landed on a narrow beach at about 4 am. They were quite ignorant of the topography of their first Gallipoli battleground, but McIlwaine did notice that the light was growing swiftly as the men marched towards Shrapnel Gully and he worried about the added visibility for enemy gunners that full daylight would present. The Connaughts took up a position just behind some Australian soldiers and waited nervously for 'the off'. There was some light shelling to contend with, and it was the first time that most of the men had ever been under fire in a 'real' war. Soon the first Connaught casualty occurred when a man in C Company was hit by a burst of Turkish shrapnel. All through the daylight hours of 6 August the brigade continued to wait, looking up at the barren Gallipoli cliffs, hearing the sound of battle at the front line and then, towards evening, watching the British fleet heavily bombard the Turkish positions on the hills.

Mental exhaustion grew when three of the battalions of the Irish Brigade were ordered to remain in reserve throughout 6 and 7 August. Particularly upsetting for these soldiers was one false start when the men were marched farther up the gully only to be ordered back down again, an hour later. However by Saturday 7 August the fourth Irish battalion, the 5th Leinster Regiment, had been ordered to leave 29th Brigade's command and allotted to 1st Australian Division as their reserve battalion.

On the morning of Monday 9 August these Leinster men were ordered by their new commander to go up to the front line and relieve a number of New Zealand soldiers who were holding an exposed ridge known as Rhodendron Spur. At three in the afternoon they reached the foot of this ridge after a dreadful journey across open territory raked by Turkish gunfire. The hillsides were carpeted with the Irish dead just as had happened at Suvla. However, by nightfall on 9 August, two columns of the Leinsters had nonetheless advanced to their objectives and were standing high on the Spur, while the New Zealand troops whom they replaced were being given the chance to retreat.

Then, at daybreak on Tuesday, the Turks began a massive attack on the Rhododendron Spur sector where the Leinster Regiment were recently encamped. The day that lay ahead would prove to be costly for them, as officers and men in the ranks fell side by side.

By Wednesday, Turkish attacks had died down but the Leinsters had not only suffered a large number of casualties but those who had survived were exhausted. Many had reached the end of their tether and knew they had probably missed death by a hair's breadth on more than one occasion. On being relieved from the front line, they looked for food and water and a chance to lie down and sleep. One small consolation for survivors was the fact that the system of water supply among the Leinsters was relatively good. The battalion quartermaster ensured that a reserve store of petrol tins filled with water was available in key dumps along the battalion's route into and out of battle.

A process of annihilation began

ANZAC SECTOR, 8–11 AUGUST

Meanwhile, the men in the Royal Irish Rifles and the Hampshire Regiment had long since left their reserve positions and faced the full heat of battle, while John McIlwaine, Bryan Cooper and their Connaught Ranger colleagues had to wait much longer for their battalion's first major contact with the Turks.

On 8 August the Rifles and the Hampshires were sent on a painstaking march to the front line. Nervously, the men had made their way towards the enemy, past the disconcertingly long line of wounded Australians who were being ferried back down the gully to the beach. Accompanying the Irish battalions on their ascent were local ration parties and water carriers climbing the thin rocky paths that threaded the dried-up riverbed. Within minutes the men were stumbling into the front-line trenches in the darkness while enemy shellfire exploded around them. Their job was to extend the British positions on the slopes of Chunuk Bair, where Mustafa Kemal's command post was based.

Throughout 8 and 9 August the two battalions tried to advance across this key objective accompanied by a range of troops from the English regions and the British colonies, including Maoris, Sikhs and Gurkhas. As one observer noted, 'the scrub was so prickly it was impossible to crawl underneath it', but no one wanted to lie exposed to the Mediterranean sun shining over-head.

As at Suvla, food supplies were problematic and salt beef, when it was eaten, made the men thirstier. There was also the fact that the positions that the men now occupied were miles away from the hospital facilities on Anzac Beach. Another problem emerged when commanding officers asked the Irish soldiers to entrench themselves – this was easier said than done, as the men were too exhausted to do heavy labour.

Each of the men in the 29th Brigade had by now been given the customary white identification patches to place on their backs or on their arms. This was to prevent men being shelled by their own artillery, but there were disquieting warnings from the Anzac veterans that the patches only made it easier for Turkish marksmen to pick them off. By now the Irish troops were aware of some of the idiosyncrasies of life at Anzac that endured for the future generations who learned about Gallipoli through history books. These included the sight of Australasian soldiers stripped to the waist as they made their way along the shallow trenches, apparently fearless and devoid of respect for British military etiquette. McIlwaine was impressed by what he called their 'magnificent physique and condition' but he was unimpressed by the conditions under which these men had had to work since April, including the 'cold bully-beef and lukewarm water' that constituted the men's unhealthy and demoralizing daily rations.

Then at dawn on 10 August came the very same Turkish attack that did so much damage to the Leinster men at another location. A slaughter began that would surpass in intensity everything experienced by the Irish soldiers a few miles to the north at Green Hill and on Kiretch Tepe ridge. Within a couple of hours the central command staff of 29th Brigade were shot to pieces. The brigadier, General Cooper, was wounded severely in the lungs and spent the next few days fighting for his life. Then his assistant, Captain Nugent, died of his wounds and by midday the brigade's entire command structure had been wiped out. By early afternoon the Royal Irish Rifles battalion, which back in the late summer of 1914 had had the most successful recruitment programme, had suffered a devastating number of casualties. The commander, Colonel Eastwood, had been killed and only three of the officers had not fallen as casualties and it seemed that several hundred men in the ranks had been mown down.

The Hampshire Regiment suffered even more. Only one officer had been left unscathed and by nightfall a mere 200 men in the ranks survived uninjured. They had set out a few hours before for the Chunuk Bair with twenty officers and over 700 men. Several stragglers and those who had lost their way returned to base in the hours that lay ahead but by the evening of 10 August, the Hampshires and the Rifles had both been broken in what amounted to a cruel massacre.

At last by early morning the Connaught Rangers had also been ordered to move to the front line. As they marched forward they could see the terrible condition that the men in their three sister battalions were in. John McIlwaine looked at these men who were returning down the trenches and gullies and saw their 'drawn, set faces, half-masked by dry and clotted blood'. Many Connaught Rangers stared into the eyes of the wounded and wondered what might lie ahead for them.

After marching several miles northwards in the severe August heat they caught sight of their objective, a small building known as the Farm, which was surrounded by distinctive green fields on the otherwise dry Chunuk Bair foothills. This building had been British-held but the troops had been expelled. No enemy soldiers dared to occupy the position due to its exposed nature and two companies of Connaughts stormed the Farm and found inside stinking corpses, abandoned equipment and a few wounded survivors from the recent British occupation who cried out for water. The Turks opened fire from the hills on the Irish soldiers in the Farm and the chances of surviving there, never mind advancing, were clearly nil.

The best the troops could do was to collect those men from the East Lancs and Wiltshire regiments who had, in Bryan Cooper's words 'lain out from dawn to dusk under the burning rays of the Mediterranean sun without food, water, or attention, suffering agonies'. They also tried to attend to the needs of the recently injured from their own regiment. As Cooper later recorded: 'The sun was setting and the pilgrimage of pain began. Each wounded man had to be carried by his shoulders and legs. The mountains were pathless and in the growing darkness the bearers made many a false step. Some shrieked with pain.'

By the night of 10 August the Farm was deserted again and any hope of a breakthrough on the Sari Bair ridge was given up. Bryan Cooper reached the point of exhaustion due to continuing dysentery and towards the end of the Connaughts' spell under the shadow of Chunuk Bair, a friend and fellow officer found him in the shade of a small shrub, his face a congested red. Colonel Jourdain had summoned Cooper to HQ to receive some vital information but he felt too ill to move. His friend gave him a drink from his flask of brandy and once Cooper had regained his resolve the two men discussed how to dash to safety across open ground. That friend later remembered their conversation:

> 'Did you ever see a snipe, Bryan?' 'I did of course', he answered. 'Then for God's sake run like one now.' Over the wire, over the bushes, over the corpses, with bullets hitting the sand, flicking up stones, ripping and splintering, Bryan sped zig-zagging like the best cock-snipe in Sligo.

Exhausted and feverish but otherwise uninjured, Cooper made it to safety and was ferried to Mudros Bay for a period of recuperation, where he read voraciously whilst waiting to be recalled to the Anzac Sector.[4]

The men tore forward like driven birds

ANZAC SECTOR, 12 AUGUST– 6 SEPTEMBER

The Connaught Rangers, not having suffered as severely as the other three battalions in 29th Brigade, were asked to make yet another attack on Turkish objectives. On 21 August, as part of the strenuous attempt to create a stronger link between the Suvla and Anzac positions, they were ordered to assault the Kabak Kuye wells at the foot of Hill 60, north of Anzac Cove. Men who had survived thus far waited in their trenches for the signal to charge. Bryan Cooper noticed that 'here and there a man murmured a prayer or put up a hand to grasp his rosary'. Then at 3.40 in the afternoon the British bombardment stopped and he witnessed how 'the leading platoon dashed forward with a yell like hounds breaking cover'.

Advancing rapidly across open ground for 300 yards, the Connaughts took the wells, watched from the far side of Hill 60 by men of the Dublin Fusiliers who had advanced far enough south to witness this charge. This brief sighting was the closest that the men of the 10th Division's three separated brigades ever came to participating in the same field of action.

The Connaughts lost over 200 men at the wells and later in a further attempt to take Hill 60. A few days later the battalion also participated in another more limited assault on Turkish positions, resulting in 150 casualties. After this they returned to reserve positions where they stayed until the division's period at Gallipoli came to an end. The Rangers were a regiment who prided themselves on their illustrious military past, particularly during the Duke of Wellington's Peninsular campaign against Napoleon. They lost more men at the Kabak Kuye wells than at any of those far-off and famous engagements in nineteenth-century Iberia.

John McIlwaine was one of those who had to pick up the human detritus of these ill-fated battles. The Turkish command, aware of the fact that the heights at Anzac were the key to success at Gallipoli, threw thousands of young Turkish soldiers into the battle. Soon the bodies of enemy casualties covered the battlefield and so, along with other men from No.14 platoon, he was given a new job that consisted of what one officer termed 'interment of the unbeliever'. In consultation with the authorities, McIlwaine usually placed the bodies in any disused trench that he could find and quickly covered them with soil. But in their seemingly endless counter-attacks throughout the month of August the Turks left behind so many dead bodies that piles of swelling corpses obscured the view of the trenches from the parapets and stank dreadfully in the stifling heat. McIlwaine and his comrades went out at night to tie the decomposing corpses together with ropes and drag them away for burial.

They soon discovered, however, that to dislodge enemy corpses from some parts of the line would lead to the collapse of British trenches whose parapets and walls were sometimes structured around the rotting limbs of the dead. At times, McIlwaine had to use a pick to dig trampled bodies from the floors of the trenches. After this grisly and arduous work he had no appetite for food and was unable to sleep.

McIlwaine was also painfully aware of his own side's appalling casualty rate. Hurrying down communication trenches, carrying messages from one command post to the next, he sometimes spotted familiar faces staring up from stretchers. On 10 August he was particularly saddened to see the dead body of Captain Nugent being carried past, an officer whom he had known and loved.

McIlwaine was glad when the practice of placing identification patches on the Connaughts' backs came to an end. Earlier evaluations of the usefulness of these patches offered by the experienced Anzac soldiers had been proven right: the patches attracted accurate enemy rifle fire. Even more dangerous was the experiment of placing tin discs on the men's backs. The sunlight glinted off the metal and drew the attention of every Turk gunner within a two-mile radius. On occasion, Turkish soldiers wore similar metal discs, passing themselves off as British infantrymen to avoid British fire.

Throughout his weeks at Anzac Cove, McIlwaine got to know the notorious local danger zones like Dead Man's Gully. He filled countless sandbags and experienced the privations of thirst, noticing how many of the 'young fellows' suffered desperately, partly because they were unable to conserve their meagre personal water supplies and because they did not have 'mental stamina'. He experienced the usual Gallipoli problems of gastro-intestinal sickness and volleys of shots fired by unseen snipers, but there were unexpected compensations, such as the quart of rum handed out to the five members of his grave-digging party one night after a particularly exhausting and dangerous session in which the men brought in twelve British bodies from no-man's-land and buried them. Another compensation was that a wide range of Turkish souvenirs could be retrieved from enemy corpses. At one stage McIlwaine rescued a beautiful blue Turkish greatcoat only to be told to get rid of it by an officer.

McIlwaine's most vivid memories of military action in Anzac territory were those connected to the attempt to take the Farm at the head of the Aghyll Dere valley on 10 August when he joined his battalion colleagues rushing over a tomato field toward the distant farmhouse. After dark, this small party of Connaughts had to retire, carrying their wounded until they reached their old trenches, now occupied by a company of Gurkhas. The following day, McIlwaine reported on what had happened at the Farm to his battalion's commanding officer, Colonel Jourdain. The commander was, in McIlwaine's opinion, almost hysterical with the emotions of the past two days' fighting: deeply distressed that so much blood had been shed, he was also nervous in anticipation of further enemy attacks.

By early September, despite damper, cooler weather and fewer flies, dysentery kept affecting him and several of his friends. Fatalities also continued with terrible and relentless regularity, even though his own company were by now mostly employed on support duties rather than in front-line fighting. There had been no fewer than 155 casualties in D Company since they had landed on the peninsula.

On 2 September, McIlwaine witnessed another distressing scene when a shell burst nearby, injuring ten men and killing their officer, Major Money. That evening he reflected in his diary on the physical horrors of what he had just seen and on the way his own morale and health were sinking because he had not had a wash for a month and was frequently feeling nauseous and generally unwell. By 6 September the sickness had developed into fever and disease continued to afflict him for the remainder of his stay at Gallipoli, making him a much thinner and weaker figure than when he had first stepped ashore.

McIlwaine was also disgusted by the behaviour of Colonel 'Savvy' Jourdain and 'his unspeakable adjutant' Ross Martin, particularly Jourdain's habit of lecturing. He had a tendency to tell the men off at length for the slightest misdemeanour and in some of his writings after the war he did little to dispel McIlwaine's depiction of him as a hectoring, highly strung, self-righteous man.[5] In the 1920s, he told an officer compiling the official history of the Gallipoli campaign that 'one thing ruined the operations more than anything … the habit of the New Armies to drink water at every turn and all dirty water when found'. He boasted that he had made his own men refuse to give way to the desire to drink and that they were therefore 'far more capable of enduring thirst than the other regiments'. He was proud that he himself 'hardly touched a drop of water all day long' and was 'never ill in Gallipoli'.

Jourdain also condemned the 'mass of malingerers of 13th Division' who fought alongside the Irish troops and then went on to criticize the 'poor' soldiers in the 6th Royal Irish Rifles. As far as he could see, the majority of the men in this battalion ran away in disorder when faced with the enemy. Jourdain claimed that he spent days hunting these 'cowards' out of the places 'where they had dug holes to hide themselves in the Aghyll Dere'. In correspondence with the same author, Jourdain also made a rather dubious assertion: 'I found if one only would advance with determination, The Turk would give way.'[6]

A new sense of identity in the midst of conflict?

THE ANZAC SECTOR, SEPTEMBER 1915

Other officers of 29th Brigade who spent time at Anzac spoke with less confidence about their experiences when corresponding with the same author. F.E. Eastwood of the Royal Irish Rifles, who had been a company commander in Gallipoli, told his correspondent that most of their time was spent 'following about like sheep' as they had no idea why or where they were to perform any of their military tasks. Often the troops in the trenches rushed together in a desperate and undignified 'rugby scrimmage' to find cover during enemy artillery bombardment. When ordered to attack, the men were no more organized and 'tore forward like driven birds'. In the post-war years, Eastwood still had scars on his body that showed the cost of these chaotic and perilous frontline experiences. He had one wound in his neck, another in his wrist and a third in the flesh at the top of one of his ears.

Bryan Cooper, who spent some of August in a hospital tent on Lemnos, felt deep guilt at being absent while his friends continued to fight and die at Anzac. Cooper's distress about 'not being there' intensified when he was informed that the battalions of the 29th Brigade had now been reduced from nearly 1000 to two or three officers and two or three hundred men in the ranks, although reinforcements began to replace many of the missing soldiers. In the post-war years, Cooper's memories of physical details of the battlefield did not fade. He still recalled the dark silhouette of the Rhododendron Spur against a night sky in which the stars always seemed to sparkle. He remembered the faint line of the paths along the gullies that glimmered before him when there was moonlight. Sometimes he recalled the exact outline of the constellation known as the Great Bear, 'hanging low over the hill-tops'. However, the memory of being reunited with his devastated battalion when he returned from hospital also endured. He later confessed that 'to look in vain among the thinned ranks for any familiar faces' is the hardest ordeal that any soldier has to face, harder even than extreme physical suffering.[7]

What became clear to some Irish observers in the Anzac sector, where the Australians forged a new sense of cultural identity in the midst of terrible conflict, was that many of the Irish soldiers in 29th Brigade were also able to console themselves with a sense of national identity. It gave one observer with the Connaught Rangers pause for thought when he watched Irish wounds being dressed by an Irish doctor, named O'Sullivan, and saw the Irish Catholic chaplain, Father O'Connor, administering last rites to nearby Irish casualties. Then, listening to the distant sounds coming from the front-line, he was certain he could hear 'amidst the din of battle our lads shouting "A Nation Once Again!" and "God save Ireland!" although the air was filled with the moans of the wounded.

That some of the 10th Division's troops remembered Thomas Davis' poem about the enduring dream of Irish national renewal is perhaps an indication that many Irishmen fighting and dying with the British army at Gallipoli saw themselves as part of the patriotic project of Thomas Davis's famous ballad:

> When boyhood fire was in my blood,
> I read of ancient freemen,
> For Greece and Rome who bravely stood,
> Three hundred men and three men.

And then I prayed I yet might see
Our fetters rent in twain
And Ireland, long a province, be
A Nation once again

The spirit with which the regimental band of the Connaught Rangers had once taunted Brian Cooper had not been entirely extinguished by the ordeals suffered in the Dardanelles.[8]

Turks stood everywhere victorious, masters of the heights

THE SUVLA SECTOR, 18–31 AUGUST

The attacks on Anzac objectives by the Connaught Rangers throughout August were just one part of a masterplan for coordinated action both at Suvla and at Anzac. To create extra strength at the former location, the famous 29th Division was brought from Cape Helles. Depleted by several months at Gallipoli, it was nonetheless a force to be reckoned with and included in its ranks regular battalions of the Inniskilling, Munster and Dublin Fusiliers. The 29th were assisted by the 2nd Mounted Division, who served as a unit of infantrymen and arrived for the purpose from Egypt. Units of the 11th, 13th, 53rd and 54th Divisions supported the attack and 10th Division, which was acknowledged to be close to exhaustion, was to be held in reserve.[9]

Noel Drury and his comrades in 6th Dublins gradually recuperated from their recent combat experiences. By 18 August more divisional reinforcements from Mitylene arrived to fill the massive gaps in the Irish ranks, but the pressures of the last week and a half of soldiering took their toll. One young officer in Drury's battalion was hospitalized 'quite off his head' with hysteria. He had to be restrained by the field ambulance brigade members charged with his removal. This young officer was, according to Drury, 'the last I would have thought would have broken down under the strain'.

Drury was quite delighted, on arriving at A Beach after the horrors and privations of battle, to find that his quartermaster, 'Stuffer' Byrne, had prepared a comfortable billet for him. The surviving Dublin Fusilier officers found a 'grand meal and hot tea ready for the troops' and a comfortable place to sleep. Byrne had even 'raised a piece of cold roast beef for the officers' and 'had all our valises already laid out for us to turn in and have a pyjama sleep'.

Then on 19 August, after more than eight hours of uninterrupted slumber, Drury and his colleague Arnold bathed in a little cove near Suvla Point, well out of the range of Turkish gunners. He felt much better for the bath and 'a good rub of a rough towel and a change of underclothes'. The two men then ran up and down the little cove to dry themselves but their exercise was cut short when they examined a notice erected nearby that displayed a warning from the Royal Engineers that the beach was mined!

At this point preparations for a renewed offensive on 21 August were well advanced and the beaches at Suvla Bay were busier than ever. Piles of rations were stacked on the sand, including bags of oats and flour for baking bread to improve the Gallipoli diet. Several new items of equipment landed at A Beach West, including a number of bicycles and motorcycles. However, for the men of the 10th this was still a time of welcome calm. Drury was able to camp at a safe spot at Karakol Dagh that was the site of an old Turkish gendarmerie post and offered 'a grand view' of Imbros across the blue waters of the Aegean. There was good shelter from the sun under some large rocks and a refreshing sea breeze. The men also entertained themselves by watching the Turks trying to shell the British destroyer *Foxhound* that was moored offshore. They admired how the navigator almost seemed to know where the shells were going to fall and turned the ship just in time, as a result of which the explosives would 'drop in the swirl where the stern had been'.

Drury's battalion now had the luxury of four pints of water per man every twenty-four hours, although spills, leaks and evaporation were all still a problem and supplies were reduced when the mules and water bags were hit by flying shrapnel. On 20 August Drury attended a Church of England communion service on the sheltered northern side of the Kiretch Tepe hillside. Chaplain Canon McClean officiated and as Drury and his colleagues Arnold and Cox all knelt to receive the bread and the wine, they felt at peace for a while despite the shells that screamed over during the service. This service was one of those occasions of stillness and reflection when men could consider the gravity of what had happened to them during what they had once matter-of-factly termed their Gallipoli undertaking. Drury recorded the bald statistics that night in his diary: 'When we left the *Alaunia* we were 30 officers and 952 men. We are now 4 officers and 487 men.' His joys and sorrows from now on were those of a privileged survivor.

On 21 August the 6th Dublins marched over the salt lake bed by a now well-established route to Lala Baba to occupy positions some distance behind the new British assault which was focussed primarily on Turkish positions at Scimitar Hill. Although front-line troops were fighting to the death only a couple of miles away, the soldiers of the 10th and other reserve formations waited their turn.

In their positions by the shoreline, having learnt to cast off anxiety and sobriety whenever possible, they spent a few hours of relative safety in maximum comfort. That morning thousands of men swam in Suvla Bay. Shells dropping in the water here and there only provoked laughter at the expense of those who were nearly choked by the spray they threw up. Drury watched with fascination as one soldier caught fish by 'throwing into the sea bombs made of old milk cans' and then swimming out and catching those that were stunned by the underwater explosions!

By mid-afternoon Drury's battalion had left these carefree pursuits behind and been asked to occupy the reserve trenches directly behind 11th Division. Many men were now openly worried about the ordeals that lay ahead on the front line. Some of them had met a handful of fellow Dubliners who were serving with 29th Division. They learnt that 1st Battalion of the Dublin Fusiliers now had only one of their original officers left and that since arriving in the Dardanelles in April, they had 'got through over three thousand men', including a couple of thousand reserve soldiers from all across the British Isles drafted into their formerly Irish ranks.[10]

One Catholic padre with the 10th Division, Father Charles Henry Devas, remembered how on 21 August he 'crept about hearing a good many confessions' and recorded that 'men of every denomination' showed pleasure at seeing him and one or two even clung to him 'as if they were little children'. The rising fear and panic was increased when every so often 'strange lost men from other regiments' ran back from the battlefield and burst into an Irish-occupied trench, their faces white with terror.[11]

At one point in the afternoon, in an attempt to boost the British assault, a new naval bombardment opened up with an 'ear-splitting noise'. Drury watched how 'some of the guns made magnificent smoke rings which circled up in the air for hundreds of feet', but despite the intimidating sights and sounds from the gunships, it was hard to determine whether the British troops at Scimitar Hill were making any advances. There was a lot of fog and mist floating across the peninsula and this made it very hard to observe the progress of the fresh attempt to advance. Eventually, smoke and flames from burning vegetation also thickened the fog. By late evening whole swathes of hillside were ablaze and brought to some men's minds the fiery hell of medieval paintings.[12]

Initially, William Knott had no part to play in the 21 August offensive. He was released from duty on 19 August and used this time to catch up on his diary entries. It was here that he first expressed his doubts that the Turkish positions at Suvla would ever be taken. On the morning of Friday 20 August, despite a few shells that were falling around them, Knott and his colleagues decided to use their spell out of the line attending carefully and slowly to their early-morning ablutions. Knott washed his face and teeth methodically in half a pint of water but sadly a friend who was doing the same thing just a few yards away was hit by a piece of stray shrapnel that pierced his jaw and shattered his teeth. Knott was still learning that at no stage in the Gallipoli campaign could one entirely relax or feel out of the way of danger.

By 22 August, in response to increased military activity around Scimitar Hill, Knott's field ambulance brigade was at last summoned back across the salt lake bed. They marched on soft sand towards a camp on B Beach, not far from a location referred to by many men as Two Tree Hill. On the following day the wounded arrived yet again at the regimental aid posts across the Suvla sector in frighteningly large numbers, some of them presenting 'heavily mut-ilated bodies'. On the same day, Knott received minor shrapnel wounds of his own. He was hit in the shoulder and had to spend a few hours getting treat-ment behind the lines.[13]

The division made several other active contributions to the campaign on 21 August, including helping the 2nd Mounted Division. In another part of the line, a field company of the 10th Division's engineers were busy building barbed-wire entanglements, deepening wells and constructing safer stores for ammunition.

A small number of other Irish troops also supported the assault, and men from various regiments soon found themselves on drearily familiar territory as they set off towards Chocolate and Green hills and beyond. Despite the fresh attempts to make substantial advances on 21 and 22 August, however, the Turkish defence was high quality and the familiar stasis reasserted itself. Further attacks were guaranteed to cause massive casualties. Six days later some Irishmen were still on Chocolate and Green hills, yearning to be relieved from front-line duties.[14]

By this stage Mustafa Kemal had at his disposal five regular divisions. He also had a number of well-supplied artillery batteries to offer support to his infantry. A number of German officers were also in key positions at Suvla, adding their military experience and expertise to the defence of the peninsula. One such officer had watched the British troop movements from his command post during 21 August and felt completely confident that the British would make no substantial advances. Despite the fog and the dense smoke from the fiercely burning bushes, by late afternoon the officer could see that the attacking infantry were too thin on the ground and too daunted by Turkish gunfire to advance far beyond Green Hill. Writing about his experiences after the war he described how 'as the sun sank blood-red behind the Gulf of Saros on the Thracian horizon, the Turks stood everywhere victorious, masters of the heights', though he admitted that it had come at a high cost for the Turkish army and that many thousands of wounded soldiers had to make their way to hospitals in Constantinople.[15]

All hope of victory at Gallipoli was gone by the end of August for the 10th Division and their other 9th Corps colleagues. The next few weeks saw the Irish troops perform a holding operation at Suvla Bay. Then came evacuation.

The seed from which may spring mutual understanding

THE SUVLA SECTOR, SEPTEMBER 1915

If the final few weeks were a less daunting experience for the men, they were nonetheless marked by several macabre and poignant experiences. Noel Drury, sent out into no-man's-land, found the corpse of a young English officer from the Manchester Regiment that had lain there since early August. Drury noted how he had been shot through the forehead and how his body had shrivelled up and his skin was like hard parchment with no visible decay. The young man had been equipped with every imaginable gadget, including a full pack and haversack, spare socks and handkerchiefs, a little medicine case with a lot of small bottles, a pair of Zeiss glasses, a periscope, a compass, a sandwich case, a revolver in a holster, an ammunition pouch, a map case with celluloid sides, a platoon roll book and some notebooks. Drury wondered how the man had ever managed to heave himself out of the trench and make his way forward. For a moment the dead Manchester officer almost amused Drury, who pictured him staggering along 'loaded like a Xmas Tree'. But then as he examined the man's personal possessions more carefully, the full force of the human tragedy struck home and he 'recovered some letters for dispatch to his people'.

By now Drury was alert to all the features of trench life at Suvla, like the wooden trench signposts bearing Irish place names, including the one erected by a company of Munster Fusiliers, which welcomed the soldiers to Patrick Street, a busy thoroughfare in the city of Cork. And there were the constant 'Suvla Bay rumours' about 'black Turks', who could crawl, naked and invisible, across no-man's-land. There was the familiar nightly sound of Turkish ration parties who were heard supplying the enemy trenches at half past nine every evening. There was also the daily worry of being fired at by the Turks when the 10th Division's own ration trucks arrived, creaking noisily as they approached along a path from the beach.[16]

Throughout August and September, the chaplaincy service continued to minister to the needs of the troops. Anglican, Roman Catholic and Nonconformist chaplains all operated out of the same church tent on the main Suvla beaches. Each day an intercessory prayer session was held in the tent. On Monday the chaplains prayed for their own welfare and for the welfare of the HQ staff of the division. On Tuesday they prayed for the men in the trenches, on Wednesday for those who were resting behind the lines, on Thursday for the medical services, on Friday for the sick and wounded, and on Saturday the Catholic chaplain prayed for the souls of the departed.

Padres like Reverend Davis Jones, who was stationed at Suvla throughout August and September with another division, nonetheless helped care for the needs of many men from the 10th. He found that he had more time to gaze out to sea now that autumn approached and so spent time gazing at the 'towering pinnacles' of Samothrace and Imbros. As a keen birdwatcher he believed that he could spot buzzards, vultures, kites, larks, snipe, pigeons, plovers, robins, curlews, jays, wheatears and sparrows in the vicinity, none of whom had been banished from the peninsula by the last few weeks of war. On one occasion he came across a snake winding its way through the bush and reckoned that it must have been three or four feet in length. In late September he also noticed how the evenings were darkening much earlier and dawn was coming later, indicating the approach of the Turkish winter.

Jones later reflected closely on his Suvla experience and dwelt on the way that war was a great leveller. He saw how 'place, position, intellect and religion all count for little on the field of action' and how 'men of diverse opinion at home pull together, Nationalist and Ulsterman, labourer and capitalist, liberal and unionist, nonconformist and churchman'. He noted that 'if discussion arises it ends in jokes and jibes'. Jones then went on to ask himself what significance this levelling might have. 'May there not be from here the seed from which may spring a flower that one might call "mutual understanding"?'[17]

Time seemed to slow down like a clock with its hands stuck

THE SUVLA SECTOR, SEPTEMBER 1915

September was also a less exhausting time for John Hargrave at Suvla. In previous weeks he had begun to develop 'stretcher-stoop' from having to carry so many wounded and dying men while keeping his head down to avoid being hit by a bullet. But September provided him with a host of quieter memories and he recalled tiny natural details such as the Gallipoli thistles that he could see from the sheltered vantage point of his dugout, 'all bleached and dead and rustling in the breeze like paper flowers'. With revulsion he thought back to the 'great black centipedes' that crawled under his blanket one night. Much more pleasant were the baby tortoises and the tiny lizards.

During his quieter and more pensive moments throughout September, Hargrave dwelt on the bizarre ethics of the organized slaughter that he had witnessed and thought to himself, 'Queer thing this civilized Christianity'. He had time to reflect on how he 'had seen men, healthy, strong, hard-faced Irishmen, blown to shreds' then how shortly afterwards, he had had to help 'clear up the mess'. He contemplated that by now 'thousands of armless and legless cripples' had been sent back to the hospital ships from Gallipoli and so far it had all been 'for nothing'. Time seemed to slow down 'like a clock with its hands stuck'.

Hargrave conversed with the Indians who ran the pack mule service with its two-wheeled cart that brought supplies to the trenches throughout September. He learnt expressions like *Jhill-O!* which, he was given to understand, was the Indian expression for 'Giddy-up!' He became aware of the religious customs of one particular group of men that included the daily use of prayer mats and abstinence from tobacco and alcohol. He tentatively admired the large, sharp knife that they carried everywhere with them and early each night he saw them make their way across the salt lake bed from the supply depot on the beach toward the firing line somewhere beyond Chocolate Hill.

With his friend Hawk, Hargrave managed to create a 'little underground home' in a sandy hillock on the shoreline near the mouth of the salt lake. Hawk was a fifty-year-old veteran who had served time in India and been Lord Kitchener's dispatch rider in the South African wars, more than a decade and a half ago. He was from a northern English mining background and was, when the opportunity arose, a heavy drinker.

By day the two men took care of the medical needs of the sick soldiers who were now less likely to present terrible wounds and more likely to suffer from less pressing afflictions like sandfly fever, scabies, dysentery, cracked lips and foot-sores. By night, their work done, the two friends would scan the sky that was invariably lit up by stars, or stare across to the island of Imbros that looked like a 'long jagged strip of mauve' on the horizon. Later in September, Hargrave's field hospital was shifted to C Beach, just as the wet season commenced and storm clouds obscured the sky, 'coming up over the hills in great masses of rolling banks, black and forbidding'.[18]

Meanwhile, William Knott returned to work as a member of the field ambulance team following his minor injury and after re-consecrating his life to God. Knott, as an evangelical Christian, was firmly convinced that any unbeliever who died in a state of sin was destined for eternal punishment by a righteous and angry God. He was therefore increasingly concerned about the eternal destiny of many of the men he watched die. In his diary entry for 1 September he recorded his fervent prayers for a man to whom he spoke about God, just before the man was badly wounded by shellfire. The man cried 'Jesus Save Me!' in his dying agony and Knott hoped that this desperate call for divine mercy had been accepted by God.

Knott's brief rest from battlefield duties was enjoyable. Back at work he found himself in a makeshift dugout with his eyes full of grit and sand as the swirling autumn winds blew the dry earth into his face. Then on 9 September he became an invalid once again with a temperature of 104°F and was diagnosed with malaria. The illness occasionally debilitated him throughout the rest of his army career but he was still able to perform light duties during the last few days at Suvla at the new field hospital on C Beach, even though the autumn winds chilled him to the bone in his thin khaki drill uniform, so appropriate in the intense heat of early August, but not warm enough now.[19]

There is considerable slackness in the matter of saluting officers

THE SUVLA SECTOR, SEPTEMBER 1915

With General Mahon restored to command, divisional HQ remained busy throughout September. There was particular emphasis on good intelligence on the whereabouts and movements of the Turks. It seemed important to assess the likelihood of another big assault from Kemal's troops, who might aim to push 9th Corps back into the sea. Using aircraft and airship reconnaissance, the commanding officers in the division tried to find out if clouds of dust on the road from the W hills to Anafarta villages meant that substantial reinforcements were marching towards Suvla for a fresh attack.

Staff officers stressed the importance of lightning trench raids to obtain prisoners who could be interrogated for information about the morale and battle plans of the Turks. It was also crucial to apprehend Turkish soldiers suspected of engaging in espionage, as noted by the Division's HQ war diarist, who on one occasion wrote that:

> A Turk was caught hiding behind our lines in the brush wood between Green and Chocolate Hills. At first he feigned incapacity to stand, speak or open his eyes. Our medical officer examined him and he recovered, took food and proceeded to Corps HQ.

The divisional quartermaster's concerns were more mundane than previously. He needed to procure luxuries like arrowroot, brandy, cocoa, cornflour and sago to treat gastric upsets. There was also the issue of replenishing supplies of rifle oil and flannels, to maintain clean and efficient rifles, as well as the urgent matter of establishing a pound next to the divisional post office on A Beach, to store the increased number of unlabelled goods that had arrived at Gallipoli from friends and family at home. The pound was also needed to hold that melancholy pile of goods that, although properly addressed, had remained unclaimed due to the death or hospitalization of the recipient. The pound soon filled with packages containing personal belongings brought back from the farthest reaches of the battlefield on empty ration carts.

There was also the matter of military discipline. Men in the division faced court martial for insubordination or falling asleep on sentry duty. On 14 September one private in the Dublin Fusiliers was convicted of the latter and sentenced to death, although the sentence was immediately commuted to penal servitude, in line with the majority practice at Gallipoli of not imposing the death penalty in military courts. General Nicholl was particularly concerned that indiscipline was setting in, in all kinds of small ways and noted that there was now 'a considerable slackness in the matter of saluting officers'.

There were other military indiscretions. The men tended to use their rifles to prop up a piece of brushwood that served as an improvised shelter. They also continued to urinate in the trenches rather than using latrines and carelessly exposed shiny objects like biscuit tins to sunlight, attracting Turkish fire.

Discipline had to be maintained, especially as men might be asked at any time to steel themselves and go out into no-man's-land on a 'listening patrol' which meant staying there until the dawn. Bayonets had to always remain fixed for sentry duty in case of unexpected Turkish raids. Neglect of personal appearance and hygiene was also frowned upon as the first sign of deteriorating discipline, so men had to be instructed not to neglect to shave. They also had to report the first sign of lice and travel to the field ambulance stations for immediate attention. Dubbin supplies constantly had to be restocked to maintain the durability and good appearance of the men's boots. And although there certainly were no shops at Suvla Bay to spend one's wages in, army pay was handed out for the first time since arrival when a field cashier arrived from Lemnos and set up his stall at Lala Baba on 17 September. Clearly the 10th was settling down to a grim spell of trench warfare, so familiar to fellow soldiers on the Western Front.[20]

Meanwhile, the cyclist's company of the 10th Division that had initially been retained in Alexandria had arrived from Egypt in the latter half of August. With their bicycles carefully stored at A Beach, the men set about a variety of tasks, including stretcher-bearing and trench-digging. During the attacks of 21 August some of the cyclists acted as provosts behind those elements of 30th Brigade that were still in the front line; this meant that they had the duty of rounding up any Irish stragglers and of picking up any Turks who were captured before leading them into custody. They were also sent out to perform the hazardous, unpleasant duty of obtaining rifles from the dead and wounded men lying on the battlefield, to prevent these guns eventually falling into enemy hands. In the weeks that lay ahead the cyclists replaced damaged field telephone wires, reinforced trenches with corrugated iron and sandbags, disinfected the filthiest parts of the line with creosote and performed a variety of other mundane and sedentary tasks that they might not have anticipated when they first enlisted.[21]

Working through the arithmetic of death and injury

THE SUVLA SECTOR, SEPTEMBER 1915

The men of the field ambulance continued to know some of the most grim aspects of the war. Towards the end of August, despite the Red Cross flag fluttering over the 30th Field Ambulance hospital, a Turkish shell landed in the camp, causing death and injury among the most vulnerable of all the 10th Division's soldiers. The Irish troops tried to make sense of this breach of the normal 'rules of war', taking into account the suggestion that the mosque at one of the Anafarta villages had recently been damaged by a British shell and that this may have prompted a vicious act of revenge. On recovering from this, the men of the field ambulance found themselves coping with the difficulties of cooler September weather. Nights were chilly for the patients and a supply of warmer blankets had to be ordered from Lemnos.

By now the Royal Engineers had a more sophisticated water supply system: they placed pumps on the best wells to assist the flow and sank experimental well shafts in many fresh locations. Large water tanks were built to store fresh supplies being brought from Egypt. Midway through September plans were afoot for a covered approach road to Chocolate Hill and possible refuges on other pathways where soldiers could shelter from sudden artillery attack.

In September the staff officers were also able to make enquiries about several missing elements in the division, including the artillery units stranded at various locations from Egypt to Cape Helles. General Mahon was also upset that when new officers arrived to 'plug the gaps' they were not Irish reserve officers but men from English and Scottish regiments, diluting even further the sense of Irish divisional identity.

Then there was the depressing task for divisional HQ, in the final days before departure, of working through the arithmetic of death and injury. Final statistics showed that the two Irish Brigades at Suvla had been cut down to 132 officers and 4981 other ranks. The Irish Division at Suvla Bay had been more than halved since the warm summer night when they set sail from Lemnos and Mitylene.

The casualty rate throughout September, however, was certainly diminished. Between 29 August and 16 September only sixteen men died. On average some forty men reported sick each day with a variety of afflictions such as dysentery or malaria. The food was getting better though, and luxuries like lime juice, jam, rice, bacon and tobacco began to make an appearance.

For the division's veterinary corps an unusual task needed to be performed. The carcasses of scores of horses and mules needed to be disposed of and the only solution in a place like Suvla, where deep mass graves were hard to dig, was to take them out into the bay, disembowel them so that no internal gases were left causing unwanted buoyancy, and, weighting them down, to bury them at sea. By 28 September the veterinary war diarist reckoned that he had dealt with sixty-three mules in this way. Some assistance in preventative veterinary care was available once a protective dugout for mules and horses had been constructed.

Medical services continued to be concerned throughout the last few weeks of the division's stay at Gallipoli with general hygiene in the Suvla area. The

Medical Corps HQ war diarist complained that 'troops at present enter an area, dig latrines where they will and perhaps leave in a few hours', leaving the landscape covered with an array of human waste. By the end of August a permanent sanitary fatigue party drawn from men of the pioneer battalion, the 5th Royal Irish Regiment, was cleansing whole areas of the bay area of its 'tips, refuse and faeces'.

It was difficult to maintain standards of personal cleanliness in a battle zone where men rarely had a change of clothes, where there was little soap and where men resorted to using the tail of their shirt as makeshift toilet paper. The official Medical Corps war diarist, investigating the poor health of the Irish troops, recorded that the men's motions were 'mostly watery' and that 'a few cases complain of passing blood and mucus'. Few men had not suffered from the painful bowel and rectal spasms known as tenesmus that accompanied incessant loose bowel movements. Adding to the problem of hygiene were the loose toilet rags, soiled with excrement, that blew around the battlefield and wire netting was placed around many of the latrines in a bid to solve this problem. At the end of September the medical services requested new baths and a boiler with a hut to place them in to assist the men with their ablutions. New and deeply dug latrines were also under construction, in which it was hoped that 'anaerobic organisms will liquefy the faeces, which will soak away'.[22]

Every now and then the ship stopped and buried her dead

THE EASTERN MEDITERRANEAN, AUGUST–SEPTEMBER 1915

By now hundreds of soldiers from the 10th Division had left Suvla Bay far behind. Frank Laird spent the time in his bed at Mudros Bay writing short letters to his fiancée and sister. He shared a tent with several wounded Australians and a Welsh footballer whose right hand was 'gone from the wrist'. He spent three weeks in the tent, sleeping with a muslin cloth over his face 'for the myriad flies to walk on', eating increasingly substantial meals and conversing with his neighbours. When he regained his strength he played card games even though two of the players had 'only one hand each available' and so had to 'draw out the cards with their teeth'.

One day a man in the next bed died and the nurse proceeded to wash down the body while Laird ate his dinner. Hardened to such matters by then, he was nonetheless perturbed to hear the nurse burst into a fit of exhausted and hysterical laughter because the instructions he had been asked to follow included the usual custom of tying the corpse's feet together. Turning to the other patients he cried out, 'Look here boys, here I am, trying to tie this chap's feet together and he has only got one!' Eventually Laird was glad to leave the macabre world of his Lemnos hospital tent behind and return to England and eventually the Temple Hill convalescent home in Blackrock, County Dublin.[23]

Reginald Ford, who injured an arm in battle on Kiretch Tepe ridge, also arrived back at the hospital base on Lemnos where in the safety of his tent he received treatment for his injury and began to think about his uncertain future. A few days later he travelled by ship to a hospital in Egypt where he was attended by a doctor and a sister who were both 'genial Irish people' and by an Egyptian orderly, dressed in blouse and loose trousers, who 'went home in a fez and robes with a daily wage plus a bread allowance'. Ford was soon well enough for a short visit to the famous pyramids at Giza and a boat trip on the Nile. However, it was clear from his doctor's diagnosis that Ford would never be mobile enough to participate in battle again, so he was put on a boat for England, returning from his Mediterranean adventure to a rest home in Buckinghamshire where he spent a few weeks 'leading the life of a stricken warrior' while receiving physiotherapy to regain the use of his arm.[24]

The hospital ships on which so many Irish soldiers returned from Gallipoli were supposed to be places where medical care could be given in a calm, methodical manner unknown on the peninsula. The interior of a hospital ship was meant to be a sophisticated, well-organized place, containing specialized spaces like a ward for infectious diseases, a purpose-built laundry and a mortuary, all of which were placed strategically at the rear of the vessel. The main decks were to be used as large wards for the 'rank and file' and the saloons and cabins of peacetime were to be adapted for use by wounded officers.

By the later stages of the war, floors on a hospital ship were covered in easily cleaned linoleum and a number of comfortable cots filled each ward, made of metal and screwed to the floor in case of a heavy storm. Attached to the head of each bed was a linen satchel in which a patient could keep his brush and comb, letters and other personal belongings. Above each bed was a lifebelt made of cork. Surgical operations were performed in the operating theatre with porcelain tiles and a frosted skylight. There was a cot carrier aboard each vessel with a winch to assist with the embarkation and disembarkation of bed-bound patients. On an admission board nailed to the wall in a central place on the vessel were a series of brass tokens engraved with a number for each patient carried on board.[25]

On the first two legs of his voyage from Suvla, Ivone Kirkpatrick had no such facilities. Having been wounded on 15 August, he was brought on board a boat that was dank and ill-equipped for the task in hand. He lay on a mattress on a dirty floor where large red earwigs crawled about. The vessel entered Mudros harbour and stayed there for several hours while ammunition was unloaded from the hold. When it finally began its journey to Alexandria, Kirkpatrick discovered that there were just two doctors and twenty nurses on board to care for 500 patients and that only two thermometers were available. As for spiritual care, Kirkpatrick found his Roman Catholic chaplain to be a melancholy and off-putting man, quite unsuited to the emotionally demanding role he had been given. It was not comforting to learn that the vessel was still carrying a range of ammunition and would not be carrying a Red Cross flag.

As he regained some of his strength he tried to make one round trip of the deck each day. The daily food supplies were much improved once he joined a new and better appointed vessel for the voyage from Egypt to England. It was the *Aquitania*, a sister ship of the *Lusitania* and *Mauretania*. As a wounded officer, Kirkpatrick found himself placed in a luxurious oak-panelled room, sharing the huge boat with over 4000 sick and wounded men from a variety of regiments. When the ship stopped at Malta, fruit, cigarettes and books were purchased, making the final stretch of the journey a lot more bearable. A stop at Naples provided an opportunity for some fine Italian ladies to bring lilies and carnations on board. Several days later the ship left the Mediterranean, crossed the Bay of Biscay and reached Plymouth. Kirkpatrick was taken by train to Sussex Lodge Hospital in London for further convalescence.[26]

Juvenis, who was wounded on the same day as Kirkpatrick, had a long, slow recovery. During the first few days aboard his ship he was unable to eat solid food and instead sipped red lemonade and nibbled at chocolate. Meanwhile, the medical team had removed the last of the maggots from his wound, cleaned it thoroughly and gave him more morphine for the pain. He vaguely noted through his blurred senses how 'every now and again the hospital ship slowed down, stopped, and buried her dead.' On some occasions he could actually see the corpses, covered in Union Jacks, being carried along the deck to the rear of the ship before a short funeral service was held and the bodies committed to the deep.

In Egypt, Juvenis was taken ashore for more specialized medical care and then placed aboard the *Aquitania*, for the final voyage home. He watched, on first coming on board the vessel, how the broad deck was covered with mattresses with row after row of wounded men lying on them. Revelling in the luxury of the wounded officers' quarters he was struck by the huge chandeliers, the linen of 'dazzling whiteness' and the beautiful pyjamas he was given. The *Aquitania* even had Neapolitan lager beer and special Cunard souvenirs. With his convalescing fellow officers he talked about the disappointments and miseries of the Suvla campaign, exchanging information about who had died and who had survived. They all speculated about the fading chances of an allied victory at Gallipoli and leafed through piles of old newspapers that had been brought on board to learn how the war as a whole was progressing. Most of all, they read and re-read the mail that had been waiting for them at Alexandria.

By night, as the ship sailed westward, Juvenis watched the moonlight on the water, trying to benefit from the tranquillity of the view that was so at odds with the sounds of suffering in the wards. He later recalled how 'the most characteristic sound was the shout of a wounded man awakening from a nightmare', and how, in order to calm Juvenis in such difficult conditions, an Australian orderly called Ralph recited poetry as he sat by his bedside. Ralph knew Tennyson's elegy 'In Memoriam' by heart. It expressed the poet's grief for the untimely loss of a close friend, and his hunger to find meaning amid the suffering:

> Oh yet we trust that somehow good
> Will be the final goal of ill
> To pangs of nature, sins of will,
> Defects of doubt and taints of blood.
>
> That nothing walks with aimless feet,
> That not one life shall be destroyed
> Or cast as rubbish to the void
> When God shall make the pile complete.
>
> That not a worm is cloven in vain,
> That not a moth with vain desire
> Is shrivelled in a fruitless fire
> Or but subserves another's gain.
>
> Behold we know not anything.
> I can but trust that good shall fall
> At last – far-off – at last to all,
> And every winter change to spring.

So runs my dream: but what am I?
An infant crying in the night,
An infant crying for the light
And with no language but a cry.

As the voyage progressed and many of the patients began to make a recovery, it became clear that one or two had a macabre sense of humour. One man sat the skull of a dead Turkish soldier, complete with a fez cap, on his bedside table. By the time the ship reached British waters there were even occasional outbursts of laughter as some of the amusing if grisly anecdotes about Suvla were exchanged. However, a number of men in the ward continued to inhabit a world of private mental suffering, and 'made a great noise, shouting and swearing, carrying on their battles in delirium'.

Sometimes, with the aid of a crutch, Juvenis hobbled toward the ship's stern to stare at the creamy wake of the ship, stretching for miles behind the liner. Increasingly, he thought of the evenings he had once spent in the subalterns' rooms in the Inniskillings' Dublin barracks, when the men with whom he enlisted had 'contemplated the wildest schemes' for 'smuggling themselves out to France' so that they would not miss the war. He could still hear the tinkling of the pianola with which they had entertained themselves in the mess, and he remembered with amazement how they had only had to press a button for cigarettes, evening papers and drinks to be brought by a servant! At the end of every melancholy reverie came the same heart-rending image of 'empty armchairs by the fire' in an empty room in that far-off barracks.

Before long, Juvenis was in a convalescence ward in an English hospital, having been transported through a disorientingly noisy London railway station. As winter approached, he contemplated his first return visit to Ireland and increasingly felt that he had returned 'from travel in a land of dreams' and that the months spent at Gallipoli were now 'timeless and unreal, the folly of some other man's imagination'. He did not know how to connect this strange and terrible experience to the mundane world that he was about to re-enter. Although the physical wounds were almost healed, emotionally he was still unwell and he was distressed for many months to come.[27]

Many soldiers who set out on a hospital ship from Suvla did not make it home. One young clergyman witnessed the aftermath of the Suvla Bay landings when over 500 young soldiers were brought on board the ship where he was a chaplain. Among the patients he watched die were many men from the 10th Division. As the ship pulled out of Mudros harbour the chaplain 'carried round a bucket of hot milk, giving each one a mugful' but many of these soldiers were so weak that he 'had to give it to them as a little child, holding the mug to their lips'. The chaplain recorded how some were advanced dysentery cases who had shrunk to 'a living skeleton' and how among the scores of limbless men, there were some 'with limbs missing altogether'.

Then one evening, very early in the voyage, while searching for inspiration for the ten-minute homily he was supposed to deliver each day in the ship's wards, he looked out of a porthole window and saw the island of Patmos on the port side, where St John was reputed to have been exiled while he composed the 'Revelations' that make up the final book of the Bible. This was, after all, the part of the earth where Paul's missionary journeys were undertaken and the Christian message was first spread from Palestine to the wider world. The padre knew at once that he should simply speak on the short statement by St John that summed up the essence of his apostolic faith: 'God is Love'.

A couple of hours before dawn, one young soldier finally gave up the battle to stay alive and the padre was summoned to his bedside. The young minister stayed by the dying soldier's side during his final minutes, listening as the lad whispered 'I'm so tired' and then 'faded away like a shadow'. The soldier was 'conscious almost to the last minute but prostrate with exhaustion' so the padre read him a few verses from St John's gospel, then leant over to hear him whisper his last words – 'I'm very ill', – after which the padre recited Psalm 23 quietly to him while he held his cold, frail hand and intoned: 'Yea though I walk through the valley of the shadow of death, I will fear no evil …'.

A few moments later the boy died and was buried at sea after a simple service while the rest of the men were still at breakfast. Even after the ship passed Malta and was approaching Gibraltar, the suffering of many of the men continued unabated. One man tried to jump overboard when being exercised by the nurses and had to be physically restrained for the rest of the voyage.[28]

A company of latter-day Argonauts?

ANZAC COVE, 19–30 SEPTEMBER 1915

By the late summer of 1915 the overall dynamic of the war in the eastern Mediterranean had changed with the decision of Bulgaria to enter the war on the side of Germany, Austro-Hungary and the Turks. It was now crucial to prevent the Bulgarian army from marching through Macedonia and capturing the seaport of Salonika, which would give the Central Powers a key Mediterranean outlet.

Given that a Gallipoli breakthrough was looking less and less likely as the weeks went by and that there were those inside the British High Command who doubted the validity of the whole Dardanelles enterprise, a 'winding down' of the campaign began to look like a possibility. It therefore made sense to Lord Kitchener to send some of the troops from Gallipoli to Macedonia to defend the Greek city of Salonika. Weary and with a huge casualty list, and with a commander at odds with Sir Ian Hamilton, the 10th Division was the perfect candidate for service in what might prove to be a less bloody campaign against the relatively untried Bulgarian army. The withdrawal of Irish troops took place at the end of September, less than two months after their arrival on the shoreline of European Turkey.[29]

On 29 September the survivors of 29th Brigade – the first to arrive on the peninsula – were the first to leave, gathering for disembarkation in the evening light at the piers in Anzac Cove. For Bryan Cooper it was a poignant moment. Despite his absence from the peninsula in August because of severe dysentery, he had many memories of Gallipoli etched into his mind. There were recollections of swimming at night at Anzac Beach, his body outlined by phosphorescence. For Cooper it was a moment when 'the bather could free himself of the burden of responsibility which weighed him down onshore'. There were pleasant memories also of the arrival of a Red Cross supply of whisks and veils that came in late summer and helped ease the affliction of flies and mosquitoes. There were the wonderful parcels from home containing tinned fruit, lemonade tablets and curry powder, and the sudden arrival of swallows that swooped and hovered around the gullies at Anzac in spite of the noise of the guns, bringing back Irish memories of 'warm spring evenings and long twilight'.

There was, above all else, the memory of the people with whom it had been such a tragic privilege to spend the last few harrowing months in the British army. Cooper thought with respect of the way in which the handful of 'tinkers' who had been recruited from Ireland's itinerant peoples into the 29th Brigade had coped so well with the privations of Gallipoli life, as it 'was no new thing for them to eat sparingly and sleep under the stars'. He thought about the Catholic padres whom he had got to know well since they had begun their journey, 'the robust cheerfulness of Father Murphy, the recondite knowledge of Father Stafford, Father O'Farrell's boyish keenness and the straightforward charm that made Father O'Connor such a good sportsman and a good friend'.

Of course there were remarkable individuals like Lieutenant Johnson, a Connaught Ranger and former Irish soccer international who in a mad fury bayoneted six Turks and shot two others at the Kabak Kuyu wells. There was the redoubtable Sergeant Nealon from Ballina, County Mayo, who had been a soldier in the pre-war years and had joined up again in 1914, fighting with the vigour of a youth at the base of Hill 60 with the Connaughts. Sadly, there were also those Irish veterans who did not return from the peninsula. As he stood for the last time on Anzac Beach, Cooper thought of Private Glavey from Athlone, a company cook in his battalion who was so proud of his three sons fighting with the army in France. Glavey died in a volley of machine gun and rifle fire at the foot of Hill 60, a few weeks before the end of his battalion's Gallipoli campaign.

The personal tragedies of the badly injured were another unforgettable feature of Gallipoli. Cooper thought of Captain J.C. Parke, the brilliant tennis player and Irish rugby captain whose arm was severely wounded, so he would never be a sportsman again. He kept smiling to maintain his composure as he was ferried towards hospitalization.

Cooper's memories spoke only of the infinite sadness of war. As he stood at the pier awaiting departure he thought of the piles of letters from home that he could not deliver to the intended recipients because the men were either dead, missing or hospitalized. He thought of letters he had read from bereaved relatives in Ireland and England who were begging for details of how their loved ones had died. Then there were the 'useless parcels' that arrived 'filled with broken cigarettes, crumbs of crushed cake and a mass of cardboard, brown paper and string'.

Cooper also reflected on the various ways he had tried to make sense of this disastrous Gallipoli campaign during the past two months, persuading himself that the 10th Division were the last of the Crusaders or else a company of latter-day Argonauts. None of this alleviated the distress he felt when he stood on the boat and gazed at the Turkish coastline that he had just left, packed with 'friends lying in narrow graves on the scrub-covered hillside'

Early on the morning of 30 September, those men of 29th Brigade who managed to sleep on the voyage back from Anzac Cove to the Greek islands were woken by the firing of the morning gun in Mudros and shortly after by the peaceful sound of the British national anthem being played by the bands aboard the numerous battleships that lay anchored in the busy harbour.[30]

Someone had blundered

SUVLA BAY, 29 SEPTEMBER–1 OCTOBER

Then on Friday 1 October at four in the afternoon the rank and file of 30th Brigade who were at Suvla Bay also received their order to assemble at the recently built south pier by half past seven that evening. Everything was to be done as quietly and inconspicuously as possible to avoid Turkish fire. Thus the men of the 6th Dublins boarded their motor launches silently in the darkness, though as usual Noel Drury noticed the inimitable Stuffer Byrne playing the fool to lighten the sombre mood by melodramatically miming being scared when he found out that he was sitting on a box of shells.

Then the motor launch found its way across the bay to a steamship called *Osmanieh* and everyone climbed aboard with their baggage. From here, the men could see the Suvla camp looking like a small town, with its lights blazing and shining out from the dugouts and shelters and the openings of tents that faced seawards. Drury also noted with detachment and surprise how everyone around him expressed sadness at departing, born perhaps of disappointed hopes and a strange bittersweet attachment to the site of so much comradeship and bereavement. Drury, however, felt nothing like this.[31]

William Knott received his order to pack on 29 September and as he prepared to leave, three words from Tennyson's 'Charge of the Light Brigade' ran through his head: 'someone had blundered'. Tennyson's famous poetic evocation of military bungling and doomed, obedient courage seemed to express Knott's own growing conviction that the generals who devised and ran the Suvla campaign were to blame for the pointless bloodshed. On 1 October he boarded his vessel, fell asleep for a while on the bare deck and then awoke as the boat left the bay to watch 'the shores of a land of tragedy gradually disappear from view'.

Knott's thoughts turned yet again to the God whom he felt had preserved him ever since he stepped ashore at Gallipoli. In his journal he remembered that his heart 'overflowed with gratitude' to his 'Great Preserver and Paraclete' because while others 'found early graves in such a desolate, uninhabited land', he was spared. Before long the boat carrying Knott was sailing towards Lemnos where the harbour was as busy with hospital ships, destroyers and troop-carriers as on the day he had left it for the peninsula back in early August.[32]

All across Suvla, men from the division packed their bags for departure. The Royal Engineers piled their equipment into their tool-carts and handed over the job to the 88th Field Company who replaced them. A few stayed on at Gallipoli until 15 December, when they embarked on SS *Perdita* for Cape Helles, where they did vital work destroying the munitions that the allies did not want to leave behind once orders for a final evacuation had been given.[33]

Most of the men of the 10th Division's infantry brigades were also relieved from their positions in the final hours of August. The 6th Royal Irish Fusiliers marched to the beach, boarded the SS *Abbiseyah* and before long found themselves sailing back to Mudros Bay where they trekked to a camp situated a couple of miles east of the town. There they were stationed in twenty-two capacious tents and in the understated words of the official battalion war diarist, 'the battalion was given a complete rest, the men appearing to be exhausted'.[34]

A glorious memory for the example of future generations

THE EASTERN MEDITERRANEAN, OCTOBER 1915

Resting on the island of Lemnos, Bryan Cooper reflected on the disastrous yet heroic events of the last two months and recalled the lines of the poet and patriot Thomas Davis who commemorated the achievements of an earlier generation of Irish soldier-adventurers:

> For in far foreign fields, from Dunkirk to Belgrade,
> Lie the soldiers and chiefs of the Irish Brigade

In his darker moments Cooper reflected that 'all the effort and all the suffering seemed to be futile. The 10th Division had been shattered.' Yet in his brighter moments he believed that the bravery of the men whom he had led would stand 'as a glorious memory for the example of future generations'. He fervently tried to believe that if the young soldiers who died at Gallipoli had 'added a single leaf to Ireland's Crown of Cypress and Laurel, their death was not in vain.' During his time with the division he became convinced that 'a unit trained to arms' had 'a spiritual as well as a material being' and that the 10th Division going to Gallipoli was a community held together, despite the political and social differences of its members, by a love of Ireland as well as pride of regiment. As proof of this he noted how every company in every battalion had cherished somewhere in its possession an 'entirely unofficial green flag'. However, he also lamented the tragic side of this strong community network. When a casualty occurred, 'It was not merely number so-and-so

Private Kelly who was killed, it was Kelly, the only son of a widowed mother who lived on the Churchtown Road, three miles from home.'[35]

For many other survivors there was a similar sense of despair at so much pointless bloodshed but also amazement at the working bond forged during the months of the war between Irishmen of very different convictions like Canon McClean of the Church of Ireland and Father Murphy of the Roman Catholic chaplaincy, who worked so well together. One of their admirers called them 'two splendid soldiers of Christ'.

Most of all, the survivors carried away with them the terrible sounds and sights of the campaign. One Dublin Pal remembered, weeks later, the boom of the Gallipoli naval guns 'like someone slamming a gigantic door 700 yards in front', the slow leisurely tearing of the air as Turkish shrapnel fell to earth and the harsh scream as one of the enemy's high explosive shells arrived, followed by a miniature earthquake nearby during which one could see 'rocks, rifles, equipment, limbs, all going up in the air'.

There was also the memory of Gallipoli's incessant rifle fire 'with its sharp crackle, like innumerable whips being cracked without ceasing' and the irregular sounds of nearby machine guns, rattling and coughing 'like an asthmatic motorbike'. And no Suvla veteran could forget the sound of bullets passing close by with hisses 'much worse than a thousand snakes'.

Some Gallipoli scenes that came to mind involved comradeship in injury, like when a man who lost his sight was guided by a friend who needed support for his shattered shoulder-blade. Other scenes underlined the indignity of injury, like when a wounded man being stretchered along was 'dropped like a hot potato every few hundred yards while the stretcher bearers ran under cover from shellfire'.

Other men remembered most vividly the blinding glare of the salt lake, in its white and half-dry summer condition, the minarets of the untaken Anafarta villages in the far distance or the mundane reality of the Gallipoli ration biscuit in their hands – 'large, square, possessing the appearance of a dog biscuit and the consistency of rock'.[36]

The silence of the waste places reigns supreme

THE EASTERN MEDITERRANEAN, WINTER 1915

For John Hargrave, the warmest memories of his stay at Suvla were of his pal Hawk with whom he had survived several weeks of the campaign in a little dugout carved from solid sandstone near A Beach West, where they delighted in the menagerie of beetles and lizards that were their daily companions. Hargrave relished being on the strand once darkness had fallen. At the same time each night he saw the black shadows of ambulance wagons making their way to and from the field hospital. Throughout his stay at A Beach Hargrave constantly quoted lines from *The Tempest*, deliberately adapting Ariel's invitation to the golden beaches of Prospero's magical island: 'Come unto these *silver* sands …'

Hawk busily gathered souvenirs for 'the kiddies at home' including a little Turkish teapot, retrieved from a bombed enemy dugout. He and Hargrave christened their dugout Buccaneer Bivouac because of their piratical hoarding of stolen battlefield bric-a-brac. It was there that they often talked long into the night about 'politics and women's rights, marriage and immorality, drink and religion, customs and habits'. Hawk read whatever English newspapers he could get hold of and soon resented that the papers portrayed the Australians as the 'the big heroes' of the campaign. Foreshadowing later Irish feelings about this treatment of the Suvla story, Hawk exclaimed, 'the 10th and 11th Divisions are simply a myth according to the papers!' while reading yet another article about Gallipoli that made no mention of the Irish troops.

The Catholic padre, Father Stafford, joined them regularly at the bivouac, adding to its growing store of books and magazines and joining various discussions. Using a stick, he drew a map in the sand of their particular part of the eastern Mediterranean and traced the route Agamemnon took on his way to the battle of Troy. Occasionally he looked up at the night sky and wondered if these were 'the same old stars as looked down on Darius and his Persians'.

During his last weeks at Suvla, Hargrave was particularly alert to the natural beauty of his surroundings. For him 'the bay was always full of surprises, with its ever-changing colour and the imprints of the ripples in the gleaming silver sand'. He never forgot how throughout his stay at Gallipoli he came face to face with mortality. On all too many occasions he was forced to make the gravestones of the dead out of bully beef packing cases and then to inscribe the name, number and regiment of the slain in purple copying pencil. At Suvla he was 'tombstone maker, and engraver and sometimes even sexton' all in one.

Nor could he forget individual encounters with the young, dying men he had helped to collect from the battlefield, many of whom he helped through the final moments of their short lives. On one occasion he found 'a little

Welshman lying on a ridge of rock, with a great gaping shrapnel wound in his abdomen, imploring the medical officer in the Gaelic tongue to "put him out". Hargrave stayed with him during his last few minutes and gave him a morphine tablet. Before he passed away, assisted by the impact of the opiate, the young soldier sang a ragtime song at the top of his high-pitched voice:

> When the midnight choo choo leaves for Alabam!
> I'll be right there,
> I've got my fare,
> All aboard! all aboard!
> All aboard for Alabam!
> Midnight choo choo ...
> Midnight ... choo choo

For Hargrave, Suvla consisted of this and a thousand other indelible memories. He remembered 'the blankets soaked each morning by the heavy dew, the snort and stampede of a couple of mules bolting down the beach with their trappings swinging and rattling under their panting bellies, the smell of iodine and ideoform around the hospital tents and the long, wobbling moan of the Turkish long-distance shells'. There was also the unsettling feeling of having been one of the lucky ones who came through the campaign unscathed. As the motor launch finally left the bay, carrying Hargrave to safety, an old sea-shanty went through his mind:

> Two men of her crew alive
> What put to sea with seventy-five

and he felt that he was one of the lucky survivors of that unlucky crew.

During the following months, when remembering weeks spent on the peninsula, he often recalled 'small, queer things' like 'an ivory white mule's head lying in the sand with green beetles running through the eye-holes'. And it seemed to Hargrave that he would always remember the natural details: 'every blade of dead grass, every ripple of blue, every pink pebble, every stone of jagged rock'. He often imagined future archaeologists digging at Suvla Bay and discovering the skeletons of the 10th, which had sunk into the silver sand or the stony earth. What would they make of this layer of human bones?

He wrote numerous verses to articulate questions like this and to conjure up the strange life he had so recently led at Buccaneer Bivouac, including a poem inspired by one of Thomas Moore's famous *Irish Melodies*:

Oft in the stilly night
By yellow candle-light
With finger in the sand
We mapped and planned.
This is the Turkish well.
That's where the captain fell.
There's the great Salt Lake bed.
There's where the Munsters led.
Primitive man arose
With pre-historic pose.
Like dugout men of old
By signs our thought were told.

Every time he put pen to paper, disturbing Suvla memories would float into his mind: 'a dead man's hand sticking up out of the sand, the grit of sand in the mouth with every bite of food, the tattered, begrimed and sunken-eyed appearance of the men, the ingrained stale blood on my hands and arms …'.

Having heard that British forces had finally withdrawn from the Dardanelles by January 1916, Hargrave imagined the coastline of Gallipoli reclaiming its beautiful, bare character. That winter, he imagined that 'the stars still burn above the salt lake bed,' and 'the white breakers roll in each morning along the blue sea shore, sometimes washing up the bodies of the slain – just as they did when we camped near Lala Baba, but the guns are gone there now and the heavy silence of the waste places reigns supreme.'[37]

A casualty reaches the Gallipoli shoreline – a 'pilgrimage of pain' as one man called the journey.
Q 13449 IWM

Anzac Cove today – thousands of Irish soldiers were decanted here on the night of 5 August.
WILSON

Two Indian soldiers negotiate the cliff-paths of the
'Anzac' sector.
N/RUR

It was up gullies like these that Irish soldiers climbed when asked
to take the Turkish high ground at 'Anzac'.
WILSON

Irish officers find time to relax in the September sun at 'Anzac'.
Q 13433 IWM

Fragments from a British rum-jar still lie today in a field at Lala Baba.
WILSON

Gallons of water from Egypt – but too late for the first Irish soldiers who landed at Suvla.
Q 13448 IWM

Gallipoli fauna fascinated Irish soldiers.
WILSON

A Gallipoli sunset behind Imbros, 2004.
WILSON

VII
VICTIMS

You would not know me now if you saw me

While the soldiers went ashore at Anzac and Suvla, life in various corners of wartime Ireland continued much as before. In County Down on the weekend of 7 and 8 August, Chadwick's 'Big Circus' visited the small milltown of Killyleagh, bringing with it thirty 'artistes' and sixty horses. Children were allowed in for as little as 2*d.* to see the midday shows. On that same Saturday afternoon the board of guardians of the nearby Downpatrick Hospital met to discuss the fact that the portable boiler in the upper infirmary was beyond repair.

On the following day while the 10th Division counted its losses on Green Hill, Chunuk Bair and the Kiretch Tepe ridge, an intercessory service was held in Down Cathedral where, overlooking the flat marshland of the Quoile river, prayers were said for all those fighting in His Majesty's Forces and the beautiful anthem 'Father Omnipotent Protect Us' was sung by the cathedral choir. When Monday morning came, the pupils of the nearby Ballee National School gathered in their classrooms and were congratulated by their teachers for having brought 1378 eggs into school in recent months for the wounded soldiers who were now lying in hospitals and rest homes across the country. A violent and mysterious domestic tragedy also unfolded in the local community when a farmer from Portaferry, who had been married a few months before, was found dead in an upstairs bedroom having shot himself for no discernible reason.

The local paper, *The Down Recorder*, reported all of these stories but also cast its net farther, describing the removal of the body of the old Fenian O'Donovan Rossa to Dublin's Glasnevin Cemetery, with a crowd of 10,000 in attendance, including representatives of Patrick Pearse's militant wing of the Irish National Volunteers and James Connolly's Marxist Irish Citizen Army. The newspaper commented that there had been 'at least 3000 rifles in evidence' then noted with disapproval the presence of 'over 6000 young men of military age'. However, within a couple of weeks, news of the new phase of the campaign in Gallipoli found its way into the Irish papers, though it did not at first reveal the grimness of what was happening there.[1]

'I have returned', an *Irish Times* correspondent said, 'from a visit to our new position at Suvla Bay and it is charming farming country, dotted about with great trees.' The correspondent described the villages of 'Big Anafarta, the cottages of which are hidden behind a noble grove of cypresses ... and Little Anafarta, a picturesquely situated village with a shining white minaret'. After this he went on to describe how 'the Irishmen marched across the Salt Lake, wheeled into the plain and then came back at the hill with relatively few casualties' when they attacked Green Hill.

Such reports, written in the style of a tourist guide and prematurely putting together a light casualty list, were soon overtaken by sombre and voluminous records of those who were killed, often accompanied by photographs and personal details of those who were bereaved.[2]

Very soon, personal and graphic accounts of the fighting in Gallipoli emerged. By 6 September *The Irish Times* had carried a story by Robert Spence, a Methodist chaplain who had once ministered in Lisburn, County Down. He described in full and distressing detail how the lighter that he had come ashore on had ' run aground too soon' so that within moments he was 'shoulder-deep in the shell-swept waters, struggling to help wounded men keep their head above water'. He revealed the full horror of the landmines that the Turks had planted, describing how the troops went 'forward, nervous and white' despite the fact that 'the limbs and bodies of their comrades' that had been blown high into the air 'kept falling heavily upon them'. That night the men around him had had to sleep in wet clothes, their evening rations soaked in sea-water and blood.

Spence explained to his readers just how exasperated he felt at his inability to help his comrades, saying, 'never did I wish so much for medical knowledge and surgical skill'. He also spoke of the grief he had felt for the loss of a personal friend Joseph Lee, one of the three Lee brothers from Dublin who all joined the forces. Joseph had survived only a short while after leading his Munster Fusilier platoon onto the heights of the Kiretch Tepe ridge. He was, according to Spence, 'a young fellow whose successful college career promised a future of rare brilliance' but had been found 'lying face downwards, motion-less and lifeless'. Just twenty-four hours earlier, Spence and he had been 'laugh-ing and chatting together on the troopship' and now the chaplain was left 'looking through tears on his lifeless body' before the corpse was quickly committed for burial 'on a rocky slope overlooking the sea'. Spence went on to reassure his readers that 'by his very willingness to die for the cause of right' Joseph Lee had 'proven his title to that unending life where morn shall rise and shadows end'.[3]

The disturbing reports continued throughout September. One Inniskilling officer wrote to his relatives – 'you would not know me now if you saw me. I have not had a wash or a shave for a week ... it is a God-forsaken country here, mostly sandy scrub and anything that is green is prickly'. Trying to find things in the Turkish landscape that his family could relate to, he explained that there was a 'cottage' just in front of his trench and that it was 'just like an Irish cottage – an open hearth and pot hanging on it just like in Ireland. It is evacu-ated of course'. Then in an attempt to unburden himself about Suvla but also to reassure those waiting at home that not everything at the front line was bad, the young Irish officer explained:

> Since we came up here we have had to bury a lot of our poor fellows killed in the attack last week ... the swarms of flies are awful. In spite of everything we are all cheery and bright and all ready and willing to go on with the fight. We have no grudge against Johnny Turk. He is a clean, decent fighter who is putting up a great fight for his own country.

To illustrate his point, he mentioned two wounded Irishmen who had been lying out on the hillside for some days and said that 'a party of Turks came across them one night, took their money and papers but bandaged their wounds and left them water'.[4]

Another letter from the front to *The Irish Times* described in detail the injuries that Juvenis received on 15 August during an attack on the ridge. The author wrote: 'Lt MacWilliam asked me quite coolly to see how far the wound went into his head' and then explained to the paper's readers that though he was 'covered in blood and had no coat on and was cold', young MacWilliam had been 'very brave'.[5]

Is Ireland proud of you?

Another national daily paper, the *Irish Independent*, also gave its readers a powerful and detailed understanding of the human impact of the conflict at Suvla, adding to its already considerable coverage of Irish casualties and achievements in the 29th Division since its arrival at Gallipoli in April. Once news of the carnage became known in mid-August, the pages of the paper were filled every day with photographs of dead, wounded and missing officers, usually with a pen portrait that included information about their family, their peacetime career and – in guarded detail – the manner of their demise. Sometimes a complete group photograph of a battalion's officers was printed with a caption that explained who in the portrait had so far survived and who had become a casualty. One photograph printed on 23 August showed the officers of the 6th Royal Irish Fusiliers in the days when they were training in Ireland. The paper referred to the time when the battalion was stationed in the barracks at Portobello in Dublin and to local people who came along to the fine concerts that the men staged.

Like almost all papers of that era, the *Independent's* coverage of the casualties focussed on the officers, about whom there was ample information as well as an existing portraiture. Readers looking at the daily detail of grief and loss, must have felt that the ranks of Ireland's most talented sportsmen were being devastated. They read of the death of Frank Phillips, the well-known cyclist, R.W. Carter, the hockey international and R. Stephenson, the popular Irish rugby player. They must also have felt that even if they themselves were unscathed, huge damage was done to the ranks of Ireland's landed gentry. They read of the deaths of men like William Eastwood of the Royal Irish Rifles who, had he survived, would have been the future owner of Castletown House near Dundalk. They must also have sensed the intense family tragedy behind photographs of victims like Lieutenant F.J. Wisely, the young doctor from a Belfast Catholic family, who on 28 September was reported killed at the Dardanelles, leaving behind a widowed mother in a house on Belfast's Ravenhill Road.

The dead of Suvla, even when they were not known to the reader, were often described in their pre-war individuality through carefully captioned newspaper photos. Major Jephson, whose exploits on the Kiretch Tepe ridge made him such a legend at Gallipoli, stared confidently out of his photograph at all those who survived him, his face still bristling with a luxuriant and carefully waxed moustache.

The stories of the men in the ranks of the 10th Division who were casualties of Gallipoli were conveyed in the minimalist way determined not only by the social conventions of a hierarchical society but by the limited information available. Privates, lance corporals, corporals and sergeants were the most common Irish victims of the conflict, and their stories were reduced to their surname, the first initial of their Christian name and their regimental number. The lists of casualties of the 5th Connaught Rangers looked like this:

Carr 225 M.
Cosgrove 778 J.
Coyle 793 P.
Doughty 448 J.
Dunne 3177 M.
Ellis 3338 W.
Fahey 3851 M.
Farrell 352 T.
Feeney 875 M.
Flynn 2894 M.
Gannon 1099 D.
Gara 3806 D.

Some of the casualties in the ranks of the 7th Royal Dublin Fusiliers were represented as follows:

Byrne 15830 P.
Connolly 15825 R.
Deegan 12196 M.
Dehaney12491 P.
Doyle 17980 A.
Doyle 18344 T.
Elliott 18117 T.
Fallon 21922 J.
Gallogher 21924 N.

Newspapers could of course make mistakes or relay mistakes made by others. On 28 August Lieutenant Ernest Julien was reported as injured when he had in fact been dead for three weeks. On 1 September a letter from Father Stafford, the Catholic chaplain, indicated that Ivone Kirkpatrick was about to die – 'I fear it is all over with him' – but by early September Kirkpatrick was well on his way to recovery on board a hospital ship. On the other hand, the *Independent* informed its readers on 14 September that Captain F.C. Burke, reported killed at the Kabak Kuye wells, was in fact alive and making good recovery in a hospital in London.

Among the most distressing stories that the paper covered in the final week in August was that of a young man called Ewen Cameron, who was found shot dead in the lavatory of a train on the coastal route from Dublin. Just after the train left Greystones station the passengers heard a muffled shot, then found the toilet door bolted from inside. When railway officials forced the door open a few minutes later they discovered that the young man had died of a self-inflicted pistol shot to the brain. The *Independent* was given to understand that Cameron was motivated to join 7th Dublin Fusiliers by his soldier brother's drowning near Athlone, not many months before. He had been refused a place in the battalion as it was sent to the front, ostensibly because the positions for officers were all taken up, but quite possibly also because of the nervous behaviour he increasingly exhibited. Now as news came in of the terrible casualty list amongst the Fusiliers, he decided to bring his own life to a violent conclusion.

Despite the news of tragedy and articles about growing opposition to plans for conscription in Ireland, the *Independent* continued to carry a range of Irish recruitment advertisements, like the one that called out unashamedly:

> Young Man, is anyone proud of you?
> Is your mother proud of you?
> Is your sister proud of you?
> Is your sweetheart proud of you?
> Is your employer proud of you?
> Is Ireland proud of you?
> Join an Irish Regiment today and they will all be proud of you.[6]

Bright eyes burning for relief of tears

Once the telegram boy had knocked on the door, the official letter had been opened or the news had been delivered in another less formal way, bereaved families wanted to find out more about the circumstances in which their loved one had died. Mr Lee senior, grieving for his son Joe and aware that his other son Tennyson had been injured in recent fighting, wrote to the 6th Munster Fusiliers' commanding officer requesting information. Colonel Worship replied:

> Dear Mr Lee
>
> What can I say? I have no words that can express my sympathy with you and Mrs Lee and all your family. In the course of my 25 years' service I have met many men but I have never met more honourable, brave and conscientious than your two sons. I cannot say enough for them or tell you how deeply I feel their loss.
>
> Circumstances have prevented me getting any tidings of the younger one. I hope with all my heart that he is doing well.
>
> The body of the elder one was recovered and was buried by the chaplain where a cross marks the place. Forgive me if this scrawl is crude and ill expressed, there is a heavy bombardment going on and I am crouched under a rock. All I want is to express my very deepest sympathy.
>
> Yours V. Worship

Enclosed with this letter to the Lee family was another missive from one of Joe's colleagues in the battalion, presumably giving more intimate details of his death. Mr Lee, on reading both letters, appears to have held back the latter, at least until Mrs Lee had absorbed the full impact of the first.[7]

Sometimes news that came through from Gallipoli merely stated that the loved one was missing. Herbert Findlater in the Dublin Fusiliers had gone forward to follow the lead given by Poole Hickman, on the Kiretch Tepe ridge during the assault on 15 August. Herbert, along with some men from his platoon, had vanished by the time the Irish attack was repulsed. Whether he lay dead behind Turkish lines or had been taken prisoner, nobody knew. In a campaign where few prisoners were taken by the Turks and even fewer survived through the three remaining years of the conflict, there was little hope of good news either in 1915 or at the final armistice.

Weeks later, confirmation of their boy's fate still eluded the Findlaters even though Herbert's brother Alex, who was a doctor at Suvla, 'left no stone unturned to find out all about Herbert' and urged his parents not to give up hope. The family gained access to official statements made by Ernest Hamilton, a colleague from Herbert's platoon, indicating that the rocky ground from which the Pals had been forced to retreat had been so heavily shelled and raked with machine-gun fire that it was highly unlikely that Herbert Findlater or any of his fellow Fusiliers could have survived. The family still made strenuous attempts to find out if he had been captured by the Turks, although their hope dwindled rapidly as the months went by. Herbert left behind two young sons, Max and Godfrey, and a reputation as a good husband and father, a fine solicitor, skilful hockey player, yachtsman and amateur actor of some distinction.[8]

The personal letter that all relatives wished to receive was one that stated that a brother, father or son was still alive and well. One such letter was the scrappy, dirt-stained note from Suvla sent to his 'darling wife' by Major Armstrong of the 5th Inniskillings on 19 August. Clearly struggling to find something relevant but not worrying to say, he spent a lot of the letter talking about a recent battlefield trophy, a 'very fine new revolver with a long barrel' that he had gotten 'off a dead Turkish captain'. Then, more uncomfortably, he mentioned his friend Major Thompson who had 'gone home or away suffering from nerves or shock'.

The letter also mentioned the Gallipoli wind that made it 'next to impossible to write at all' because it blew the sand into his face. Finally he touched on the topic of casualties, the publication of which he felt must have given his wife 'something of a shock'. He then drew to a close and sent 'love and kisses' until he had the opportunity to see his wife again.[9]

The cruellest of letters were those that bred false hope in the recipient. Captain Tobin of the Dublin Pals wrote home speaking of his attempt to 'snipe' Turks just as he and his father had once tried to 'snipe rabbits at Aughnavagh' and claiming that 'the bigger the game, the finer the excitement'. Tobin reassured his parent that, so far, he had suffered only minor injuries, referring to a recent mission to fetch ammunition during which he and his men had had to dig themselves in under fire. He casually told his father: 'as I was digging, a bullet hit something in my bit of trench and a bit of it hopped up and hit me in the eye'. Two days later, well in advance of his cheery letter's arrival, Tobin was dead, shot down as he tried to assume control of the Pals after his senior officers were mown down in front of his eyes.[10]

By late summer of 1915 there were working-class Dublin streets where black ribbons adorned the handle of door after door and where blinds stayed pulled down.[11] At the other end of the social scale, the writer Katherine Tynan also found

Dublin to be a place of intense mourning. Arriving one day at the house of a friend for a midday reception she found that there were two new war widows at the luncheon table and one girl whose brother had been killed. She also noted that there were 'many black-veiled figures at morning masses in Newman's University Chapel' every day, a clear indication that among the Catholic intelligentsia of the capital there had also been losses at Suvla and Anzac.

As more names appeared on the Gallipoli casualty list, Tynan recorded how 'blow after blow fell on one's heart'. There was a lot of bitterness as there was little evidence that the sacrifices of the 10th Division at Suvla and Anzac or indeed at Cape Helles were appreciated by British politicians in terms of public commendations or medals awarded for gallantry on the field of action. All one could gather from newspapers was brief but horrific information about 'the burning beach and the blazing scrub' and hints from correspondents that many Irish troops were mutilated and dismembered, which according to Tynan did not bear thinking about. She soon became familiar with the 'look of the new widows – hard, bright eyes burning for the relief of tears, a high feverish flush in the cheeks, hands that trembled, and occasionally an uncertain movement of a young head'.[12]

The men were scarcely cold in their graves

Bitterness about the massacre of the Irish Division at Suvla Bay soon made it a strongly contested political issue. The nationalistically inclined *Irish Independent* was troubled by reports that commanders of the Mediterranean Expeditionary Force were unhappy with the quality of the new divisions fighting at Suvla and by similar criticisms that appeared in certain English papers. John Redmond, leader of the Irish Parliamentary Party, was horrified not only by the death and destruction at the Dardanelles but also by the way in which Irish bravery and sacrifice were being ignored by the British establishment. Where were the Suvla medals and decorations?

Perhaps Redmond was ignoring the degree to which the military establishment was embarrassed by the debacle and inclined to perceive the lack of praise for the Irish at Suvla as a deliberate cultural snub, while it was possibly a symptom of the deep unease about the whole Dardanelles campaign. There was evidence that Irish achievements with the 29th Division at Cape Helles were also ignored: the Dublin, Inniskilling and Munster Fusiliers who perished there received no mention in official dispatches.[13]

Redmond's political colleague, John Dillon, felt he had gained fresh insight into British bungling and incompetence. He spoke to the House of Commons during the winter of 1915–16, lamenting the tragedy of 'the officers who led our regiments at Suvla without artillery or a single gun, and who hurled themselves to death on the slopes of those hills, which they would have carried and which would have enabled them to get to Constantinople had they been decently led.' Dillon finished with the radical cry: 'we must democratize the British army' and complained that that organization still was 'as it has been in the past ... permeated with society interest ... as any man who has a good strong pull in London society may blunder and blunder again quite safely and spill the blood of gallant men owing to his incompetence'.[14]

However, the pro-Union *Northern Whig*, published in Belfast, was having none of this and replied to public claims being made by Irish nationalists that 90 per cent of the 10th Division was Catholic and nationalist stating that the numbers 'did not even reach one quarter of that ridiculous figure, but the lie has gone on ever since and it is now given as a reason why Home Rule should be granted to Ireland'. The *Northern Whig* rounded on all those it believed were making political capital out of the 10th Division and said that 'it is about time the Nationalists ceased claiming it as their own'. In a bitter newspaper campaign the Belfast paper asserted that at no time had the 10th ever been even 25 per cent Catholic or 50 per cent Irish. The paper used statistics supplied by a Protestant chaplain in the division whose involvement in the political argument does not reflect the cordial Suvla ecumenism spoken of elsewhere. A religious census had been conducted among the men of the division in November 1915. Not surprisingly, in the aftermath of Suvla and Anzac the survey registered 8734 Protestants and only 4874 Roman Catholics in the division, due to the way reinforcements had been drawn from Protestant-dominated British territorial areas immediately after the slaughter of so many of the Irish Catholic volunteers of 1914.

However, the *Whig* concluded that nationalists had no case to make for the political ownership of the 10th Division and that due to recruitment problems among Irish Catholics, most of the Irish regiments were in fact no longer Irish save in name. The paper suggested that this reluctance to serve in the army made nationalist Ireland 'the one black spot in the Empire today'.

The Irish Times, ardently pro-Union yet less entangled in the sectarian arguments of Belfast, was content to hope that Gallipoli might, despite all its sorrows, have a positive effect as 'the Unionists and Nationalists who stormed the hill at Suvla have sealed a new bond of patriotism and the spirits of our dead Irish soldiers will cry trumpet-tongued against the deep damnation of internecine strife in Ireland'. *The Irish Times* went on to claim that 'of those who never came home we can truly say, as the Spartans said of their dead, their tombs are altars, their lot glorious and beautiful'. Acknowledging that mistakes had been made in leadership and strategy, the newspaper forecast that 'the name of Gallipoli will be uttered with tears in hundreds of Irish homes for many years to come' but nonetheless hoped that 'the solution of many of her age-old problems will be found there', in a place where her citizens had learned to sink their differences and strive together for a ' united Ireland' as part of a 'mighty Empire'.[15]

So it was that the dead of the Great War instantly became a political football to be kicked around by Irish opinion-formers of various political colours in a way that seems strangely familiar ninety years later, when the sacrifice of the Ulster Division at the Somme and the martyrdom of the leaders of the Easter Rising in 1916 have long since occluded the battle of Gallipoli in Ireland's political consciousness as rival badges of identity. It is also interesting to see how, many decades before their reuse as prototypes of domestic reconciliation at the end of the Ulster 'Troubles', the nationalist and unionist dead of the Great War were used as an instance of exemplary fraternity. The men who died at Anzac and Suvla were scarcely cold in their graves before they became contested ideological property.

No song, no love, no memory

By the winter of 1915–16 the terrible news from Gallipoli, accompanied by reports of mounting casualties in France and Flanders, indicated that the struggle with Germany and her allies would be a long fight. Many more British soldiers would be required. Although it looked like conscription was ultimately on the cards, a renewed attempt to entice volunteers needed to be undertaken. In Ireland, as elsewhere, the process began.

A number of men who survived Gallipoli were involved in this, including Frank Laird who had been shipped back home to recover from his chest wound and had been placed in the 10th battalion of the Dublin Fusiliers, which functioned as a reserve unit, based in Ireland.

From the Dublin Fusilier depot in Naas, County Kildare, Laird and his fellow soldiers travelled into the surrounding countryside to search for new recruits. The usual procedure was to arrive into a town on a fair day after Mass when the band would parade up and down before speeches began, after which the band would get hold of likely converts and drink with them in adjacent public houses to fire their enthusiasm. In the company of Sergeant Devoy, a Clongowes College old boy and survivor of the Irish landing at Cape Helles, Laird made several appeals from the recruiting platform. The two Dardanelles veterans soon found that despite all the music, eloquence and good liquor, the recruitment drive produced almost no results. Laird later concluded that 'the youth of these parts reserved itself intact for our own "Irish" war'.[16]

By now the 10th Division, restocked with troops from British army reserve depots, had sailed to Salonika and become involved in a low-key but persistent war with the Bulgarian army in Serbia and Macedonia.[17] To one female observer who was already in the Balkans with a British hospital unit and who saw the men of the 10th arrive into Salonika, the men looked inappropriately clad in cotton shirts and shorts, with no warm clothing whatsoever. However, the troops appeared remarkably cheerful and regaled the nurses with songs while drinking their mugs of thick, sweet tea.[18]

In this campaign, the Gallipoli survivors faced very different conditions to those on the peninsula. They fought in the malarial Struma valley and on the wintry Balkan hills. At the battle of Kosturino, many men suffered from frostbite and their clothing became so frozen that greatcoats were as stiff as boards after a night on the mountains. It was here in Macedonia and Serbia that some men finally collapsed from strain.[19] Among those taken away from the battlefield were John Hargrave, suffering from malaria, Bryan Cooper,[20] suffering from prolonged gastro-intestinal illness, and Francis Ledwidge, wounded in action.[21]

Private Joe O'Leary from Skerries also began to feel the effects of his recent Gallipoli injuries, including a perforated and bleeding eardrum caused by exposure to Turkish shelling and the continuing infection of a shrapnel wound received at Suvla. O'Leary was also suffering from the onset of tuberculosis. The infectious risk posed by TB meant that Joe had to be placed on a hospital ship in Salonika harbour where he was operated on en route to Egypt to release septic fluid from his badly swollen leg. By November he had landed in Alexandria, and was feeling much healthier. He spent Christmas in Luxor in a hospital in the Winter Palace, in the care of an Irish matron called Murphy. The good food, the rest, the mild, dry air of an Egyptian winter and the attentions of the expert nursing staff all helped him to make a physical if not a psychological recovery. The nightmares of Suvla continued to haunt him.[22]

Other Irish troops were not as 'lucky' as Joe O'Leary. Charlie Martin from Monkstown, having been through the ordeal of Suvla, found himself enduring new torments on the Salonika campaign. On 9 December, in the vicinity of the cold peak known as the Crête Simonet, a burst of Bulgarian machine-gun fire riddled Charlie's company of Dublin Fusiliers and he was instantly killed. A few weeks later his brother Thomas, who had been wounded at Gallipoli, returned to active duty in the new theatre of operations and learned that Charlie had recently died.[23]

For some young men the strain of the new war in the Balkans was too much and their insubordination at the front line came with a heavy price. Private Patrick Downey of the Leinster Regiment was a twenty-year-old working-class boy from Limerick who refused to obey an officer's orders at Kosturino, was court-martialled, sentenced to death and shot by a firing squad two days after Christmas in 1915. His body was subsequently taken to the Mikra military cemetery in Salonika where he lies buried under a gravestone that does not reveal his particularly tragic and inglorious end.

This severe decision is indicative of attempts to deal with the problematic discipline and morale that afflicted the entire division in the Balkans. The 10th had to be rebuilt after Gallipoli and had received into its ranks many young and inexperienced troops from a variety of British regional backgrounds. The Gallipoli survivors were exhausted and the bleak Balkan conditions did not help them to recover. Long periods of boredom, continued problems with poor supplies and the widespread threat of malaria in the Struma sector all contributed to the malaise. The number of court martials for various offences in the 10th Division during their stay in the Balkans now considerably exceeded the Great War average, with the 5th Connaught Rangers under the draconian Colonel Savvy Jourdain reaching a grand total of 126, caused it seems, by his troops' persistent interest in selling their equipment to the locals, to get money for alcohol.[24]

Before he left Salonika for an Egyptian hospital, Francis Ledwidge had once again taken up the pen he had so rarely employed at Gallipoli, sending letters and poems to friends like Robert Christie, who had since been evacuated to Britain where, as a wounded ex-serviceman, he was able to leave the forces and with his family's financial support, prepare for a new career as a dentist in Belfast. Ledwidge revealed how his old, melancholy preoccupations had survived the horrors of Suvla saying: 'I get no rest from Ellie, even yet'. And in a letter to Lord Dunsany, written during the Serbian winter in late 1915, he had expressed his desolation by telling Dunsany how 'one awful night of thunder and rain, I was thinking of the end of the world as the bible predicts it and tried to imagine Love and Beauty leaving the world hand in hand, and we who not yet die standing on the edge of a great precipice, with no song, no love, no memory'.

Later, while lying in a hospital bed in Cairo, still far from home, he meditated on the life of a rootless wandering soldier that he had craved so much in the summer of 1914. In a few lines of poetry that he sent to his friend Lily Fogarty he gave vent to his feelings, animated by the resemblance between himself and the nomadic tribesmen of the Sahara:

> There is a distance calling in our hearts,
> We know not, wandering thro' so many lands
> The western side of day ...
>
> ... whatever way we roam
> In the four distances of Heaven's dome,
> A dream of strange lands gives us hope,
> The wild brown wastes a home.[25]

Other veterans of Suvla and Anzac survived their Balkan war more or less intact. Among them was John McIlwaine, his only physical problem being rheumatism in his left ankle, which on one occasion made him faint with pain on an overly long and hot route march.[26] William Knott also survived the Balkan campaign, but by the time it was over he was completely disillusioned with the army he had entered with such high hopes and principles in 1914: 'What a useless sacrifice of poor men's lives,' he wrote in his diary, 'it is as well people at home do not know the facts or they would certainly rise against the unnecessary waste of manpower.' He wrote scathingly of a religious service he attended that fell on the anniversary of the outbreak of the war and condemned the way in which the Army authorities were 'upholding England as a righteous nation fighting a holy war, demonizing Germany in all things, upholding our Christian nation'.

Eventually in September 1917, Knott, along with the rest of his 10th Division colleagues, made his way from Macedonia to a new sphere of engagement. He sailed over a stormy sea in the direction of Egypt on his way to Palestine and spent much of the voyage vomiting out of a porthole. On 16 September he saw the famous lighthouse of Alexandria in the distance as he had seen it when his ship pulled into the harbour on the way to the Dardanelles.[27]

This time, attacked by fellow Irishmen

But by the end of the 10th Division's stay in Macedonia, Ireland had experienced an armed uprising that made the country that the Gallipoli survivors eventually returned to a very different place from the one they had left with such bravado and hope. By Easter 1916 the secret plans of Patrick Pearse and James Connolly had come to a kind of fruition. Backed by a mere 1600 men of the Irish Citizens Army and the Irish National Volunteers, with a fading hope of German logistical support, the separatist leadership seized various key buildings throughout Dublin and issued their proclamation of an Irish Republic from the steps of their headquarters in the GPO in Sackville Street.

The proclamation declared the right of Irish people to the ownership of Ireland and deemed the position of England in Ireland to be that of an alien government that had divided the citizens of the island from one another in order to rule them more effectively. The proclamation invoked a history of periodic armed insurrection against England that they believed to be a more honourable and enduring Irish military tradition than that represented by Irishmen in the British army.

Patrick Pearse called on God to bless their endeavours. Then the fighting began.

For a week, the rebel troops held out against the police, British garrison troops and the reinforcements that were quickly sent to help them. By the time the leaders in the General Post Office surrendered, parts of central Dublin lay in ruins and there had been 450 deaths and over 2600 people wounded, including rebels, police, soldiers and ordinary civilians. Within a short space of time the British government asserted its authority with a curfew, house searches, the imprisonment in England of hundreds of suspected and actual rebels, and the court martial and execution of the leaders, including Pearse, Connolly and Francis Ledwidge's friend Thomas MacDonagh.

In the months that followed, instead of quelling the separatist spirit in Irish life, these British repressive measures only inflamed it. The 'martyrdom' of the Easter 1916 leaders created a huge amount of sympathy for the republican cause, and revived an old tradition of insurgent patriotism. There was the threat that military service, now compulsory in Britain, would be extended to Ireland. Thousands of young Irishmen were surely needed in the British army if the increasingly costly war with Germany was to be won. As the winter of 1916–17 went by, Sinn Féin, the radical party of anti-conscription and Irish political independence, began to grow in strength.[28]

Several men who had had a part in the story of the 10th Division were caught up in the bloodshed of Easter 1916. Perhaps the most tragic was Frank Browning, whose leadership had inspired many of the Dublin Pals to join up. Although deeply distressed by Gallipoli's appalling casualties, Browning continued to take part in the activities of the Home Defence Force volunteers who performed a variety of military training manoeuvres in the Dublin area in the hope that they might be of assistance, should the war ever spread to Ireland.

The volunteers gloried in the self-given name Georgius Rex but were known as the Gorgeous Wrecks because there were plenty of old, unfit, would-be heroes in the ranks. On Easter Monday they were in the middle of an exercise on the coast at Kingstown when they heard of the storming of the GPO in Sackville Street and made their way back towards the city centre to offer their assistance against the rebels, even though they had no ammunition for their guns. One half of the party made their way down Shelbourne Road towards Beggar's Bush Barracks, while Browning led the other half down Northumberland Road. A group of insurgents encamped on a nearby bridge opened fire when they saw the men marching towards them in military uniform. As one terrified observer later reported, the result was chaotic and bloody: 'A sharp report rings out and the man in the foremost rank falls forward, apparently dead, a ghastly stream of blood flowing from his head. His comrades make for cover – the shelter of the trees, the side of a flight of steps.' She watched as bullet after bullet was fired and then, when gunfire ceased, she saw a doctor drive up in a car and take the wounded members of the Georgius Rex into nearby houses for medical treatment. That help was of little use to one man. Frank Browning died of his injuries.[29]

Several Suvla veterans had already observed tensions building up in the capital in the days before the Rising, revolving around the vexed issue of conscription. One wounded Royal Irish Fusilier who had served with the 10th in Gallipoli wrote to *The Irish Times* at the end of March to say that he had been spat at, jostled and insulted by an anti-recruitment crowd outside the Mansion House in Dawson Street on the previous day.[30]

A number of soldiers then had to attempt to crush the rebellion. One was Francis Ledwidge's old mentor, Lord Dunsany, who was sent south from the Inniskilling Barracks in Derry to help put down the insurrection and promptly drove up to a barricade at Church Street bridge, where he saw military action for the first and very nearly the last time, as a bullet fired from a rebel position grazed his cheek.[31]

Another former 10th Division soldier to face danger was Frank Laird, who found himself under fire again for the first time since he had been wounded at Suvla Bay. This time, instead of facing Turkish gunmen, he was being attacked by fellow Irishmen. On Easter Monday he had gone to his new wife's family home to take a walk in the Dublin Mountains with some friends. The train that was to take them out of the city never turned up at the station so they started to walk southwards. On the route they encountered one of Frank Browning's volunteer soldiers who was making his way towards Beggar's Bush, having been informed that a rebellion had just broken out in the town centre. Scarcely knowing whether to believe this story, Laird had lunch with his friends and then decided to head back towards the city to investigate. At 5 pm he put on his uniform, mounted his bicycle and set off, but he soon discovered the seriousness of the situation when he encountered a group of British soldiers being fired on by rebel troops near the canal at Portobello Bridge. He soon headed for Wellington Barracks where he was made welcome by a small defending party of policemen and soldiers.

Laird remained there for the next ten days, 'listening to the roar of guns and the rattle of machine guns and watching Dublin burn'. During this period only one of the men from the barracks actually died, shot as he led a ration-party down a nearby street. Later one member of this ration party who had disappeared during the shooting returned to the barracks, handed in his uniform that had been made up in a neat parcel, and then left, quitting the ranks for good.

Cut off from all news, Laird and his colleagues were subject to all kinds of rumours, including the false news that the Germans had landed on the west coast. At last, with the rebellion suppressed, he emerged from the barracks. He was soon participating in a military clamp-down all across the city, in the course of which he acted as a guard at the captured rebel stronghold in the Four Courts. He could already see resentment being stoked up by British army units who were acting with such indiscriminate zeal in the aftermath of the violence. A friend and fellow soldier who was home on leave from France and dressed in 'civvies' was arrested on the street by an army patrol and lodged in Arbour Hill military prison on suspicion of being a rebel. He spent several anxious days there, during which his brother desperately searched for him, before he was located and his identity and political affiliations confirmed.

Laird was also a witness and participant as the gap widened between nationalist and unionist in the days that followed. A civil servant friend of Laird's who had been captured by the rebels and held in a cell in Bridewell police station during Easter Week was convinced that he had recognized one of his captors from his own workplace. Upon release, this friend was determined to effect the arrest of this rebel who had so far escaped the eye of the authorities.

With a determination made more steely by the news that his father had died during the rebellion, he marched into the office where he worked, accompanied by a posse of British soldiers, identified the 'traitor' and had him arrested at gunpoint. According to Laird, allegiances in the office were now divided between those who were 'loyal' and those who evinced some sympathy for the ideals if not the tactics of the rebels. Laird himself was in the party of soldiers that marched the man – 'a somewhat unsavoury ginger-haired gentleman' – to Royal Barracks, en route for Kilmainham Gaol and subsequently an English prison.[32]

The same green-coloured flag

The military action of Easter Week and the subsequent punishment of the rebel leadership took place in the precise geographical location where the 10th Division had so recently assembled to go off to the East. When Eammon Kent led his men to the South Dublin Union buildings to occupy them as a rebel base on Easter Monday, they could hear military music coming from the square in the nearby Richmond Barracks. In the same barracks, a short while later, the court-martial of Thomas MacDonagh and other revolutionary leaders was held in rooms not far from where MacDonagh's acquaintance and admirer Francis Ledwidge had once drilled, marched, looked after the battalion stores and then sat writing poetry at night.

Within hours, MacDonagh was to be shot by a firing squad made up of men from the British army's 59th Division, as he stood blindfolded with his hands tied behind his back. Along with other rebel leaders he was then buried in Arbour Hill cemetery, a short distance from the Royal Barracks from which the 7th Royal Dublin Fusiliers had marched so confidently a year earlier.[33]

Even if the nationalists who fought for an Irish Republic in 1916 chose a vastly different way of expressing their Irishness than the men who stormed the beaches at Gallipoli, there are striking similarities between the anthems and the banners they cherished. As the rebel contingent occupied the South Dublin Union, they kept their spirits up by singing 'A Nation Once Again', the same song that had been heard at Anzac as 29th Brigade faced death at the hands of the Turks. From upstairs windows the rebels unfurled the same green-coloured flag that Bryan Cooper noticed was cherished in the ranks of his own Connaught Ranger battalion.[34]

Later, as the occupants of the GPO were marched down Sackville Street between British soldiers they were heard singing 'God Save Ireland Say the Heroes', with the patriotic cry:

> Whether on the scaffold high
> Or the battlefield we die
> Oh, what matter if for Erin dear we fall!

This was exactly the same anthem heard on the streets of Basingstoke when some of the men of the 10th Division broke into song as they marched from their camp towards the railway station in the light of a July dawn on their way to the Dardanelles.[35]

Were they not one with Christ who strove and died?

In due course news of the Easter Rising reached Macedonia where the division was serving. Reactions to it were predictably negative among those from a unionist background, as in the case of one young officer who explained in a letter home that he was too disgusted to think about it, never mind write anything about it. [36] Noel Drury of the Dublin Fusiliers was equally disgusted and, as he wrote in his diary, felt concerned that all Irishmen in the British army would now be 'tarred with the same brush' despite their sufferings for the Empire – 'Isn't it awful?' he asked himself, 'It's a regular stab in the back for our fellows out here. I don't know how we will be able to hold our heads up here as we are sure to be looked on with suspicion. The men are mad about it all, but don't understand who is mixed up in the affair. I'm sure Germany is at the bottom of this somewhere.' [37]

However for those who were nationalists, news of the 1916 Easter Rising and its grim aftermath was greeted with ambivalence. One such soldier, Francis Ledwidge, was in England at the time of the rebellion. He had been sent back home from Cairo to make a further recovery and was staying with his sister in Manchester, where, despite the status accorded to him on various social occasions as a wounded soldier, he was dreaming of his imminent return to the Inniskilling Barracks in Derry. It was a feeling that he soon expressed in a poem:

> We went to where gay women danced and sang,
> And clever men were juggling with repartees,

And people pleased to see us rowed us down
To fête us at a dozen garden parties.
And as they laughed and talked of some new wonder
Perhaps they thought my coldness most unkind;
How could they know the lovely clock of Derry
Was striking every quarter in my mind.

Back in Derry, Ledwidge was soon haunted by the thought of his friends who were executed at Kilmainham Gaol. From this point on until the end of his short life he wrote on average one poem a month in memory of the martyrs of Easter 1916. He wrote to his old friend Robert Christie asking: 'Though I am not a Sinn Féiner and you are a Carsonite, do your sympathies not go out to Cathleen ni Houlihan? Poor MacDonagh and Pearse were two of my best friends and now they are dead, shot by England. McDonagh had a beautiful mind. Don't you know his poetry?'

Ledwidge eventually took leave from the barracks in Derry and visited his family in Slane, where he was found, morose and pensive, in the bar of the Conyngham Arms Hotel, saying, 'If I heard the Germans were coming in over our back wall, I wouldn't go out now to stop them.' He felt like an exile in his own environment, especially now that Lizzie was no longer there but living in Kingstown, many miles away. Visiting Richmond Barracks in the capital to ask for an extension of leave, he was horrified to enter the place where the Easter martyrs had been court-martialled. Arguing with an officer who poured contempt on the rebellion, Ledwidge tried to argue the rebels' case and when he was met with hostility he expounded his own credentials as a nationalist who had fought at Gallipoli in the British army for the rights and freedoms of small nations like Ireland.

Travelling north again, Ledwidge met with Robert Christie and talked to him at his Duncairn Gardens home in Belfast. His old friend claimed to have the medical expertise and status, in his new role as a trainee dentist, to help him apply for a medical discharge from the army. Ledwidge returned to Derry however and began to prepare for a return to the front. As Christie later explained, it was 'against his principles' for Ledwidge to take the easy route out of service, whether through unjustified medical discharge or the other option, desertion and disappearance into the remote Donegal hills until the war was over.

In Derry, Ledwidge also wrote about his memories of the voyage to Gallipoli and in particular of the days spent at Mitylene where, despite the beauty of the island, he had been constantly preoccupied with Ireland and the song of the Irish blackbird in particular. What disturbed him, now that he was home once more, was that he found no solace in the Irish landscape that had consoled him when he was many miles away in the Mediterranean:

> Nor Peace nor Love again I find,
> Nor anything of rest I know
> When south-east winds are blowing low.

And in another poem, addressed to his native land, he spoke of having 'deserted her' in order to travel abroad with the army:

> And then I left you, wandering the war
> Armed with will, from distant goal to goal
> It is my grief your voice I couldn't hear
> In such a distant clime.

Ledwidge's conflict of loyalties continued. Court-martialled for not returning from leave in time, he lost his lance corporal's stripe. Known to be a nationalist, he was taunted by his unionist fellow soldiers. Sometimes he was moody and withdrawn and at other times he treated all the men in his company to drinks when the weekly pay came in. Some men knew him as a poet who would point out a copy of his poems in a bookshop in Derry and who would retire to a room provided by Lord Dunsany to write. Other men were struck not so much by his literary interests as by his heavy drinking.

While still mentally distressed, Francis Ledwidge returned to the front line, although not to Salonika with his old division but to Flanders where he was involved in the infamous Third Battle of Ypres in 1917. He still wrote poetry and in some of his work tried to express his loyalty not just to the men of Easter 1916 but to the soldiers who had been his companions at Suvla. In a poem entitled 'The Irish in Gallipoli' he reiterated the reasons why he and so many other Irishmen had gone to war two and a half years ago and called for the sacredness of Irish soldiering to be reaffirmed:

> We but war when war
> Serves Liberty and Justice, Love and Peace …
> Who said that such an emprise could be in vain?
> Were they not one with Christ Who strove and died?
> Let Ireland weep but not for sorrow. Weep
> That by her sons a land is sanctified

On 6 January 1917 he wrote to Katherine Tynan, 'I may be dead by the time this reaches you, but I will have done my part. Death is as interesting to me as life ... I hear the roads calling and the hills, and the rivers wondering where I am ... It is a terrible thing to be always homesick.' Then in June, writing to an American academic, he struck a more positive note, hoping that 'a New Ireland will arise from her ashes in the ruins of Dublin, like The Phoenix ... with one purpose, one aim and one ambition.'

However, his sense of desperation surfaced when he lamented in a letter, 'What it is to me to be called a British soldier while my own country has no place among the nations but the place of Cinderella?' He also wrote to his old sweetheart: 'Dear Lizzie, send me a flower from the bog, plucked specially for me ... you have no idea how I suffer with this longing for the swish of the reeds at Slane ... the far night is loud with the sound of our guns bombarding the positions we must soon fight over.'

On 31 July, near a notorious location known as Hellfire Corner, the group of soldiers with whom Ledwidge was busy on road-building duties stopped for a break. A stray German shell landed at the roadside and blew the body of the young Irishman to pieces. The Catholic padre in the battalion was Father Devas, who had also been at Gallipoli in 1915, and he was on hand to say the last rites over the mangled remains, retrieve the identity disc and to attempt a letter home to the Ledwidge family. Consoling his mother, Devas spoke of how Francis had been to confession on the evening before his death and how, that very morning, he had been to Holy Communion. The padre then returned to his duties – the battle for Ypres continued and the war itself had more than a year still to run.[38]

Dynasties crumbled and empires fell apart

During that final year of war, Ledwidge's old division experienced the challenges of life in Palestine, where the war against the Ottoman Empire continued under the command of General Allenby. By now the 10th Division was not an Irish one in any meaningful sense and the men who had made it through unscathed from the Irish recruiting stations of 1914 were a select few. A number of the Irish regimental units that the division was composed of were amalgamated and while some men stayed in Palestine, others were sent to France. There they joined divisional units on the Western Front while the gaps in the 10th were filled by newly arrived Indian troops.

Among those who stayed in Palestine was the battle-hardened Noel Drury who participated in the British northward advance through a landscape filled with resonant biblical names. Having failed in 1915 to capture Constantinople, that great holy city of both Islamic and Christian tradition, the 10th Division was now a part of the army that did capture and conquer that most important and contested holy city of all, Jerusalem. After this success the troops pushed farther north and played a part in the battle of Megiddo, fighting in the Palestinian region that gives the world the linguistic origin of that sonorous and fateful word, 'Armageddon'.[39]

By early winter 1918 the German nation was economically and socially in turmoil and her troops facing defeat. In November an armistice was signed, preceded by a declaration of surrender from the Turks. Peace came at last to a European continent that was exhausted and deeply altered by the experience of four years' incessant war. In Germany, Russia, Austro-Hungary and Turkey, dynasties crumbled and empires fell apart. All across the continent, demobilized soldiers began to return to their homeland, and among those who made the journey were tens of thousands of Irishmen, among them the Irish survivors of Suvla and Anzac.

It is difficult to establish the number of Ireland's Great War dead, given that many died in non-Irish regiments and many non-Irishmen perished in divisions like the 10th. However, it may be assumed that a figure of approximately 35,000 is valid. It may also be assumed that there were no fewer than 9000 casualties in the 10th Division while at Gallipoli, of whom at least 4000 died.[40] Even if it is borne in mind that perhaps a third of these men had been drafted into the division from across the Irish Sea, it is still the case that at least 2700 native Irishmen perished at Anzac and Suvla, almost all of them in the three weeks of August when they fought most intensely. This amounts to the massacre of 900 Irishmen per week, a casualty rate that far exceeds Easter Week in Dublin in 1916. Understandably, many Irish families had little to celebrate when the ceasefire came on 11 November.

Of the three Lee brothers from County Dublin who had joined up in 1914, only Tennyson survived. Not only did Joseph die at Gallipoli, but his brother Ernest perished when the Irish mailship, *The Leinster*, was sunk in the Irish Sea by a German submarine on 10 October 1918, just a month before the end of the war and with the loss of over 500 lives.[41] The Findlater family also had little reason to celebrate: not only had their son Herbert been killed at Suvla but his brother Charles, on recovering from his Gallipoli injuries, was told to rejoin the front-line troops in France, where he was killed in action in November 1916.[42]

For some of Ireland's Suvla veterans making the return journey from the front in 1918, there was the added ignominy of being labelled by a number of English critics as 'Sinn Féiners' and Irish traitors. John Willis, a Dublin Fusilier who survived the horrors of Gallipoli, now underwent the painful experience of being billeted at an English seaside resort with an Irish regiment in the final days before full demobilization. The Fusiliers heard that a 'patriotic' play was showing at a local theatre and that the Irish were portrayed as treacherous cowards in it. When word got around they decided to attend the production and occupy front seats in the auditorium. When the worst anti-Irish lines were uttered, a senior officer stood up and loudly said 'That's a bloody lie!' after which 'all hell broke loose in the theatre'.[43]

Back in Dublin Bartholomew Hand, who had been injured at Suvla, had already returned to civilian life, trying to find a niche for himself as a gardener in one of the big houses and estates of south Dublin, despite one of his arms being considerably shorter and stiffer than the other due to injury. He was delighted, as a wounded Gallipoli hero, to have his picture taken for the local paper when he first returned home. He had a copy framed and placed above the fireplace in the family home.[44]

Joe O'Leary also returned to his home town of Skerries, having sailed to England on the *Dunluce Castle*, then completed the trip and found himself on a vessel with Harry Reynolds, a republican from his home town who had just been released from an English gaol following his participation in the Easter Rising. Despite continuing problems with anxiety and stress that the medical authorities labelled 'shell-shock', Joe's tuberculosis had gone into remission, his leg wound had healed and his perforated eardrum was not bothering him. He contemplated the possibility of running a small general grocery and hardware store in Skerries and hoped that the post-war years would be calm and easy ones in which he might recover his mental stability and, if possible, earn some much-needed money. [45]

Paddy Tobin – he had already died by the time his
letter home from Suvla arrived.
O'H/H

Joseph Lee, one of two Lee brothers to perish in
the Great War.
LEE

Irish women contribute to the war-effort.
Q 33216 IWM

Irish Great War recruitment poster.
IRISH ARCHIVE FOR THE WORLD WARS

Thomas MacDonagh, the Easter Rising martyr.
Another kind of war, another kind of patriot.
NATIONAL MUSEUM OF IRELAND

Frank Browning, founder of the Dublin Pals –
a casualty of the Easter Rising.
O'H/ H

The wounded of Gallipoli in a Cairo hospital.
DOWN MUSEUM

Macedonia, late 1915: an Irish battalion assembles to head for a new front-line.

Q531717 IWM

Peacetime memories helped many to endure the war; Joe O'Leary (back row) with his family.

FINGAL INDEPENDENT

Memories of Gallipoli stayed with its survivors all through the rest of the war. Often they were of simple 'domestic' rituals as well as the hideous things once witnessed.

Q13511 IWM

VIII
GHOSTS

NOVEMBER 1918–AUGUST 2006

An armed representative of an alien power?
Suddenly Ireland changed before the eyes of its Gallipoli veterans. In the 1918 elections Sinn Féin became the biggest political force on the island, replacing the Irish Parliamentary Party as the main voice of nationalists. As an expression of their unapologetic separatism, Sinn Féin representatives founded their own 'Dáil', or parliament, in the centre of Dublin. These political developments were accompanied by the creation of a self-styled 'Irish Republican Army', which the beleaguered Royal Irish Constabulary was given the task of suppressing. In the north of the country, meanwhile, where unionists were the dominant force and yet a substantial nationalist population also existed, civil unrest soon turned into sectarian blood-letting.

In 1919 Irish Republican Army volunteers attacked police and army barracks in an endeavour to obtain weapons. The War of Irish Independence began, which grew within a couple of years into a full-blooded conflict, the intensity of which had not been witnessed in Ireland for over a century. Britain's attempt to quell the disorder in Ireland was motivated by the knowledge that throughout her large empire, other subject nationalities were watching with keen interest. The local constabulary were reinforced with thousands of ex-soldiers from across the Irish Sea, among them the dreaded 'Black and Tans' whose policy of ferocious reprisals on those communities deemed to be sheltering gunmen was matched by the ruthless and accurate guerrilla warfare masterminded by the charismatic IRA leader Michael Collins.

Now the veterans of Suvla and Anzac found that they shared the same uncomfortable British army pedigree as the Black and Tans who were torching Irish towns and villages, shooting at crowds of Irish civilians and, on occasion, threatening to take their vengeance on places such as Athlone if they did not exhibit their loyalty by closing down their commercial premises to mark Remembrance Day. By the time that the War of Independence was at its height, many Irishmen felt that the enemies whom they had recently been asked to fight as Great War soldiers in British army uniforms, represented far less of a threat than those Englishmen who still laid violent claim to an ill-founded dominance of Ireland. The sentiments expressed in poetic form by one IRA prisoner, held in an internment camp in Ballykinler, County Down, began to hold true for many of his countrymen:

> God made the Irish
> He also made the Turk
> But the devil made the English
> To do his dirty work.

By 1921 a political solution, no matter how imperfect, was urgently required and on 6 December a constitutional agreement was hammered out that gave to the southern twenty-six counties of Ireland the title of 'Irish Free State' and the status of a dominion within the empire, while the six northern counties retained full British status and a unionist–dominated parliament of their own in Belfast. Of course this arrangement did not solve Ireland's problems. Within the northern state, civic calm was eventually achieved with the help of brutal policing measures, while in the Irish Free State a brief but bitter civil conflict broke out over the issue of whether to accept the compromises required by 'The Treaty'. In the course of this Michael Collins was killed by 'hard-liners' opposed to a 'sell-out' of their ideals for what appeared to them to be merely a territorially compromised revision of Ireland's Britishness. The traumas of Gallipoli and other Great War battles would now, for various reasons, take second place in the Irish nationalist memory to the pain and heroism of these wars, subsequently fought on Irish soil.

The British empire in southern Ireland was effectively at an end. A new green, white and orange flag flew over Dublin Castle, a new unarmed police force had replaced the old Royal Irish Constabulary, and parliamentary representatives in the new Dáil could make most of the decisions that mattered for Irish society, unhindered by their old imperial master.[1]

This was the environment that Suvla veterans returned to and in which the relatives of the Gallipoli dead endeavoured to mourn their loved ones. The position was one of real vulnerability. Some of the 10th Division's original volunteers in their peacetime careers had been members of the Royal Irish Constabulary or had been raised in police families. In 1919 they started to come under attack from the Irish Republican Army.[2] In addition, all of the demobilized soldiers in the 10th had recently worn a British army uniform, which since Easter 1916 made them potential targets in republican eyes, as armed representatives of an 'alien power'. To speak of an army career in France or at Gallipoli in southern Ireland in the early 1920s was to risk the premature death that a veteran thought he had eluded when the Great War came to an end.

In Northern Ireland a returned 10th Division soldier would possibly have found his position rather more comfortable within a society where army veterans were often encouraged to join the new pro-British Royal Ulster Constabulary, but this would be an unlikely route to take for a Gallipoli veteran from an Ulster Catholic and nationalist background. Indeed, for some Ulster Catholic veterans of the 10th Division, the IRA rather than the RUC was the 'militia' of choice and Seán McCartney, a former member of the 5th Connaught Rangers battalion, joined an active service unit where his ability as a marksman could be put to use. He did not have long to exhibit the military skills he had acquired as he was killed during a British ambush, training on Lappinduff Mountain in County Cavan in the early summer of 1921.[3]

We were far better off under the empire than this Free State

Bartholomew Hand, living in south Dublin as an ex-soldier, knew he must not talk too loudly about his wartime experiences, nor mention in public the disquiet he felt about the turn of events in Ireland. One fellow veteran, Frank Fox, would come round to Hand's house and the two men would grumble about the exploits of the hundreds of 'so-called soldiers' fighting for their country's freedom in the Ireland of the early 1920s, comparing them unfavourably with the men they had known in 'the 10th'. He would lament to his family and friends that they had been far better off under the empire than under this new 'Free State'. He frequently told them, 'The day they painted the lamp-posts and pillar-boxes green in this country was the worst day of our lives.' He never voted in any of the Irish Free State's elections, reserving his deepest distaste for the country's emerging political master, Eamon de Valera. He retained the picture of himself as a returned Suvla hero dressed in British army uniform, and placed it above his fireplace, continuing to treasure his military medals. During difficult times, Hand relied on the British army disability pension which he cashed at Donnybrook post-office.[4]

Joe O'Leary, having worked hard at his small shop in the centre of Skerries, soon found fresh sorrows to add to the legacy of illness and injury that he had carried since his days at Suvla. His wife's death left him unable to cope with business pressures and the rearing of children. The younger boy was sent to an uncle and aunt while Joe exchanged his role as shop-owner for that of local cobbler. Suffering periodically from shell-shock, he would lose self-control and become deeply angry, distressed and isolated. In calmer periods, when probed by one of his sons for tales of his wartime experiences, Joe would at first talk quite calmly about the journey to Gallipoli then become increasingly emotional as the narrative went on. Eventually he would place his head in his hands, unable to continue, proclaiming that he had had enough and wanted to be left alone.[5]

It was not just among the ranks of former privates such as Bartholomew Hand and Joe O'Leary that distress manifested itself. Lieutenant Ernest Hamilton who travelled to Suvla with the Dublin Pals had been injured in action and sent back to Ireland to recover. On being told to return to the front line with another division in the summer of 1916, he found himself in France in the latter days of the Somme offensive. The young and handsome medical student who had posed confidently for the camera in every photo taken of his battalion during the early days of the 10th Division, now became a 'shell-shocked' Suvla veteran whose addiction to 'the bottle' soon prevented him from making any further serious attempt at soldiering in France. Court-martialled for drunkenness, he was dismissed from the army and after the war was unable to settle domestically in Ireland. He never resumed his medical studies, had a brief and unhappy marriage and died as a result of alcoholism a few years later.[6]

What is of course remarkable is that so many men did manage to rebuild a life. Another former officer in the 10th Division, Tennyson Lee, returned from a war in which he had been injured and had lost two brothers. Yet during the 1920s and 1930s he dealt with the anguish of memory as best he could and provided a stable and happy domestic environment for his wife and children.[7]

One officer who seemed to make something useful out of his post-war years was Bryan Cooper, formerly of the 5th Connaught Rangers, who had resumed his political interests and become an independent member of the Dáil at the start of an extraordinary political evolution that would eventually take him into the ranks of Eamon de Valera's party, Fianna Fáil. He had had to witness the despoliation of his beautiful County Sligo home, Markree Castle, vandalized by Free State soldiers when they removed the priceless furniture for distribution around the cottages of the district, ransacked bedrooms and nursery and scrawled obscenities on the library walls, tearing up illustrations in rare ornithological books. Added to this material damage were his family difficulties, including the personal distress of a rapidly failing marriage.

However, by 1927 Markree had been restored to its former beauty; the swans had returned to the lake, the sound of children's laughter could be heard in the corridors and Cooper was busy writing plays, essays and poems. Unfortunately the remembered traumas of wartime and the tensions of the immediate post-war years meant that Cooper drank heavily throughout the 1920s. By 1930 an alcohol-related illness had killed him while he was still in his forties and seemingly destined for greater things. At Cooper's funeral his coffin was covered by both a Union Jack and an Irish Tricolour.[8]

Other men, who at the psychological level had survived their Gallipoli experiences, found that the physical damage they sustained cut short their peacetime existence. Damage to his lungs caused by Turkish bullets at Gallipoli left Frank Laird susceptible to serious respiratory illness and he died in 1925, just seven years after the end of the war.[9]

General Bryan Mahon, commander of the Irish troops at Suvla, survived until 1930, adapting to the new political environment. He became a senator in the Upper House of the Free State parliament although this left him vulnerable to attack by republican gunmen who attempted to destroy one of his family homes in County Kildare during the Civil War. He was active in establishing a memorial for the Irish Great War dead and in the affairs of his beloved Punchestown racecourse until his death. His funeral was attended by numerous dignitaries, including the Irish President.[10]

Treacherous remnants of the ancien régime

In a post-war nation going through such military, economic and social turmoil while renewing its identity, it is scarcely surprising that the needs of Ireland's British ex-servicemen should be neglected. However, innovative attempts were made by Britain during these post-war years to cater for Great War veterans who lived in Ireland. One scheme involved the creation of 7000 new homes for old soldiers across the island. Conscious that demobilized Irish troops might return to an environment where their fighting expertise would make them welcome recruits in the fledgling IRA, the British were determined to secure the loyalty of many such men, offering the incentive of a fine new cottage, possibly with a few acres of land attached. After the Anglo-Irish Treaty of 1921 and the arrival of independence, a 'Sailors and Soldiers Land Trust' was set up to continue this task on behalf of the British government, albeit with limited funds and curtailed objectives.

The high-quality housing developments created in the 1920s included one at Shantallow in Derry, another at Cregagh in Belfast, and the most impressive of them all, at Killester in Dublin, where the low housing density of just four cottages to an acre would, it was hoped, make the development suitable for retired officers as well as men from the ranks.

This innovative housing policy, designed to cater for the welfare of Irishmen who had endured Gallipoli and the Somme, increased the hostility of fellow-countrymen who felt that British army veterans were now being handed out too many privileges. Some parts of Dublin, where old Dublin Fusiliers were being granted new housing, became known to the locals, somewhat laconically, as 'the Dardanelles', while the development in Killester was known as 'Little Britain'. In classrooms in several schools close to such enclaves, the boys would often divide into two factions, those whose fathers had reputedly been nationalist combatants and those whose fathers had been in the British army.

Vocal Irish nationalists soon classified this attempt to build colonies of houses for soldiers as a new plantation of Ireland aimed to 'bribe and divide them from their fellow countrymen'. One angry politician claimed 'the attempt to settle ex-soldiers on our lands is an invasion of our sovereign rights which should be resisted by every means at our disposal right up to the use of force'. Another political representative elected to the Dáil, spoke of 'a most undesirable class of soldiers getting these lands while IRA soldiers are walking about unemployed' and called for a complete end to the housing scheme. However, building work continued and by 1933 the housing trust had met its reformulated target of 3700 dwellings, including houses both north and south of the Irish border.[11]

In one part of the midlands county of Westmeath, the land trust provided houses for three returning Gallipoli veterans named Foley, Poynton and Neade. Each cottage, situated in the vicinity of Battstown, not far from Delvin, was built to modern specifications and was accompanied by a few acres of farmland. All three men had joined up in 1914, under the influence of a member of the local gentry. In what seemed to some local people like an unfair acquisition of property in the heart of their own townland, the three ex-soldiers settled down to their new lives. None of the Gallipoli veterans was truly a 'local' from this particular townland and one came from as far away as County Tipperary. What is more, one of the ex-servicemen had been a member of the Royal Irish Constabulary.

The difficulties of once belonging to a family with military connections in this part of rural Westmeath are all too apparent in anecdotes handed down of young boys whose fathers had been in the British forces and then had the temerity to turn up at school displaying their poppy on the anniversary of the November Armistice. According to one local, a particular boy was 'beaten around the room' by a hostile lady schoolteacher who insisted he never appear again in her school-room wearing such a 'British' symbol. However, the three Gallipoli veterans who lived with their families in Battstown all survived these years of Irish civil conflict and stayed put in 'the Dardanelles'. [12]

Many famous veterans, such as Emmet Dalton and Tom Barry, returned to Ireland only to join the IRA. There seemed to be good reason for the British authorities to be rather wary of all Irish veterans of the Great War in the years between the Armistice and the advent of Irish independence. After the 1921 Treaty all Irishmen, whether or not they had fought for Britain in Gallipoli and Flanders, were in danger of being 'tarred by the same brush'. When they travelled to England, Suvla veterans were indistinguishable from those other Irishmen who had 'treacherously' killed British troops on the streets of Dublin in order to pull Ireland away from the empire.[13]

The striking absence of public endorsement and the confusion of political identity undoubtedly contributed to the high levels of psychiatric disorder at the Leopardstown ex-serviceman's hospital in Dublin in the years just after the war. In 1917 the historic mansion house and beautiful tree-lined grounds at Leopardstown were loaned to the British Ministry of Pensions as a site for the care of Irish ex-servicemen by a former member of the wealthy Power family, famous throughout the world for their whiskey business. The hospital opened in March 1918 and immediately focused on the care of patients suffering from 'neurasthenia'. After Irish independence a British trust fund continued to run the hospital and by 1924 there were 136 beds for psychiatric cases although two years later the institution also started to admit general nursing and surgical cases.[14]

A huge number of Irish ex-soldiers were soon waiting at Leopardstown for psychiatric treatment. In 1921, 120 officers and 1200 men from the ranks awaited medical care, a number far higher than at any equivalent hospital in the British Isles. The long waiting-list was due in part to the scarcity of such care in a country enduring civil conflict. The only other comparable psychiatric care provided in Ireland was at Craigavon Hospital near Belfast. But a high incidence of mental and emotional illness was to be expected in a country where there was an absence of social reintegration and national affirmation to heal the emotionally wounded soldier and bring meaning to the suffering endured or inflicted on others.[15]

There would be no need for this memorial

Among the features of social inclusion for most returning armies is the creation of public rituals and sacred sites of commemoration. In Ireland, this too would be difficult and contested. Those who wished to remember the men in shallow graves at Suvla Bay were faced with volatile remembrance services and parades. The November 1919 'victory parade' in Dublin appeared to many like a disproportionately huge display of armed might designed to intimidate Sinn Féin. Scenes of wild disorder were provoked on the streets of the city when unionist students from Trinity College, singing 'God Save the Queen', clashed with young Catholics from the National University singing 'The Soldiers' Song'.

The annual Remembrance Day ceremony in the city centre allowed the sizeable Protestant and unionist population of the region to assert itself and make a continued show of Britishness, even after the inauguration of the new Free State administration. In 1924, with the new Free State now entering a period of relative calm, 70,000 people gathered in central Dublin and the event included a march-past by thousands of veterans. Unionist citizens used the opportunity to unfurl Union Jacks and wear their poppies. This practice gave rise to 'poppy-snatchers' who would tear the offending flower from the wearer's lapel or pull down, carry away and burn any British flags that they could seize. In turn, the custom developed of concealing a razor blade to thwart the aspiring 'poppy-snatcher'.

By 1926 the Free State government had decided to remove the annual service of commemoration to Phoenix Park on the western outskirts of Dublin. Aware of the fragility of the young regime and conscious of the power of the public, quasi-militaristic displays of the pro-British Orange Order on each 12th of July in Northern Ireland, Irish government minister Kevin O'Higgins declared that he wished to discourage 'the mentality that would make of 11th November, a 12th July' and insisted that any plans for a Great War cenotaph to be placed in the heart of the capital city, were not appropriate, as 'it was not on their sacrifice that this state is based'.[16]

The least controversial memorials were those positioned many miles away on the former battlefields of Europe. A committee set up by generals Mahon, Hickie and others in the Free State during the 1920s to create Irish commemorative sites, devised a monument for the 10th Division. A Celtic cross was sculpted, inscribed in Gaelic with the motto 'For the Glory of God and the honour of Ireland', and transported not to the still volatile post-war republic of Turkey but to the southern border region of the new nation of Yugoslavia, where it was erected on a hillside not far from the location of the 10th Division's headquarters during the Salonika campaign.[17]

By the end of the decade agreement was reached on a substantial Irish memorial site – a large area of parkland at Islandbridge on the western edge of the city, in the vicinity of Kilmainham, long associated with Irish soldiering. The complex monumental sculpture envisaged for Islandbridge was built by a team of Irish and British ex-servicemen to a design given by Edward Lutyens, whose powerful memorial to the missing of the Somme was unveiled in 1932. The design at Islandbridge focused on traditional commemorative sculptural emblems such as an altar, a fountain, a pergola and a sword-shaped 'cross of sacrifice'. It aimed to put on public display a copy of the beautiful book illustrated by Harry Clarke known as 'Ireland's Memorial Records', commissioned after the war and purporting to carry the name of every single Irish soldier killed in the conflict.

However, Islandbridge was to contain no other visual hints of the tradition of British military allegiance in Ireland and the names of particular army units such as the 10th Division and of specific battles such as Gallipoli were to be omitted. Although the park was ready for opening by 1938, Europe was lurching once more into war and so, keen to preserve a visible Irish neutrality in the ensuing conflict, Prime Minister Eamon de Valera postponed the opening of Islandbridge until the new war between Britain and Germany would finally be over.

Several attempts were made to create smaller local memorial sites during the 1920s and 1930s, amid considerable opposition. In August 1925, on the anniversary of the landings at Suvla Bay and Anzac Cove, the Gallipoli veteran Bryan Cooper, ever to the fore in promoting the memorial process, stood in the midlands town of Longford in front of a crowd of 1000 people, many of whom were holding Union Jacks. He announced the opening and dedication of the town's new war memorial, then thinking back to the men he had known and loved in the 10th Division, explained that 'these acts of commemoration … are the last and most loving tribute we can pay to our comrades'. He stressed 'memorials like this are to be found all over France, Italy and Great Britain but in the Free State they are very rare …' and spoke respectfully about that lost generation of men who in 1914 had 'of their own free will, left home and fireside, and all that makes life dear, to sacrifice their lives for a great cause'. He concluded by asserting, as he had first done in 1915, when sailing away from Gallipoli, that 'they and their deeds are immortal'.

However, the flag-waving, loud singing of the British national anthem and Cooper's eloquent speech forewarned those in his home town of Sligo who were anticipating a similar unveiling ceremony at the new war memorial during the days to come. One local politician insisted that the Royal British Legion, the ex-servicemens' organization primarily responsible for the event, should not 'make propaganda out of the unveiling' and then, referring to some of Ireland's most well-known Great War British army officers and the British monarchy in the same breath, went on to say that 'we don't want bands playing God Save the King … God gave me brains to think and I have come to the conclusion that if there were less Kings and Queens, Coopers and Hickies … there would be less men dead and there would be no need for this memorial'.[18]

Nonetheless, at a number of locations across the island, several inclusive memorial rituals were enacted after the war, allowing space for an un-controversial public show of grief and remembrance on the part of local families who had lost sons, brothers or fathers, whether at Gallipoli or during other battles. In the strongly republican city of Cork in the early 1920s, two memorial services were held, one after the other, on Remembrance Sunday, before the unveiling of the town's war memorial. The British Legion's Protestant service was followed by Catholic worship, organized by ex-servicemen, before the two groups met for a joint ceremony. A considerable degree of ecumenism also existed at various commemorative events in Northern Ireland. The opening of the Enniskillen war-memorial saw a parade of Catholic and Protestant war orphans laying wreaths together at the cenotaph while bands from both Orange and Catholic backgrounds played music.

In the Orange citadel of Portadown in 1925 a Catholic soldier who had been in the Connaught Rangers spoke at the dedication of the new cenotaph, and claimed that his inclusion in the event was 'emblematic of the brotherhood that was born in the gullies of Gallipoli and cemented on the firing steps of Flanders'.[19]

However, the generally favourable, and sometimes politically generous climate for Great War remembrance in the North did not always lead to a greater visibility for the minority of servicemen there who had fought at Gallipoli with the 10th. The memorial process in Northern Ireland increasingly centred on deeds of the largely Protestant 36th (Ulster) Division and in particular on their slaughter on the banks of the river Ancre at the opening of the Somme offensive, almost a year after the 10th Division's debacle at Gallipoli. 'Somme Day' on 1 July became a crucial part of the Ulster commemorative calendar and a memorial tower was built at Thiepval in France on the site of Ulster's great 'sacrifice for the Empire'. Other Irish aspects of the Great War became marginalized in public memory. Among these omissions was the story of the deaths of Irishmen at Suvla Bay, whose allegiances and social backgrounds were highly varied and more difficult to categorize and whose destruction had been occluded on a sunny July morning in 1916 by the accurate and deadly fire of the German machine-guns of the Somme.

Throughout the 1920s and early 1930s Great War commemoration always had the potential to be contentious in the Free State. The IRA continued to exist, albeit in covert and reduced form, reluctant to accept the compromises of the Treaty and incensed by memorial services such as the one at Longford. The British Legion came under attack and its premises at Inchicore were twice subjected to arson attacks during the late 1920s, with militant republicans being seen as the likely culprits.

In 1932 a rally in Dublin's College Green was organized by a group called The League against Imperialism. The event took place on the eve of Remembrance

Day and speakers included Peadar O'Donnell and Maud Gonne-McBride. A British flag was burned and a resolution was passed calling on the government to seek the 'complete independence of Ireland'. Alarmed by the continued capacity of the Great War heritage to stir up dangerous antagonisms from Civil War years, the new and vulnerable Fianna Fáil government enacted legislation permitting public commemoration of the war but prohibiting the display of Union Jacks and seeking the replacement of quasi-military parades with 'processions'. The sale of poppies would still be allowed although it would be carefully monitored. Thus did Eamon de Valera's government seek to allow commemorative space for those who publicly wished to mourn the dead of the Somme and Gallipoli whilst striving to rid the remembrance process of its pro-British aura.[20]

It was often in other more socially focused semi-public venues across the south of Ireland, at workplaces, schools, sporting institutions and church interiors, that plaques, stained-glass windows and other memorials to the Gallipoli soldiers of 1915 were to be found. A memorial in Dublin's Four Courts to lawyers who died in the war included former Dublin Pals such as Poole Hickman, whose name was also to be seen on a memorial at Lansdowne Road international rugby ground.[21]

Southern venues that offered the most distinctive acts of remembrance usually belonged to traditionally Protestant and unionist institutions; at Trinity College names of former students and academics were inscribed on the walls of the new 1937 Reading Room.[22] In independent Protestant educational establishments such as the Wilson's Hospital near Mullingar, County Westmeath, a roll of honour was displayed in a prominent place after the war was over, listing those ninety 'old boys' who had enlisted in the armed forces, as well as three members of staff who had volunteered. Out of these numbers, twenty had 'paid the supreme sacrifice'.

The boys of Wilson's Hospital were often of a humble and unprivileged Protestant background and received monetary assistance to help with their schooling. One such pupil was Thomas Hall from Ballanboyne in County Meath who entered the school in 1904 as a boy of nine on an educational scholarship. He enlisted in the 10th Division in 1915 and was injured at the Dardanelles, then evacuated to Ireland for recuperation before returning to the front line in France where he would be wounded once more. Out of the lives and deaths of such ordinary young Irishmen were the rolls of honour composed.[23]

A file of clippings from the obituary columns

In the 1940s and 1950s the memory of Suvla faded still further and the few rituals and sites of public Irish Great War remembrance began to lose some of their power. Those who had been soldiers at Gallipoli were an ageing, diminishing band and the Irish Protestant community that had done so much to keep their memory alive was a much reduced force in a fully independent republic. Although Islandbridge Memorial Park was still the site of yearly commemorative services, it was developing an uncared-for and overgrown look.

Individual acts of commemoration continued to occur. For the Lee family, there would be a quiet and dignified yearly act of remembrance. Accompanied by members of his workforce, Mr Lee senior walked down to the War Memorial in Bray, County Wicklow, each November, carrying a wreath that he placed there in memory of his two dead sons. After the old man's death in 1927 the family tried to continue the tradition. At no time was the wreath disturbed or damaged, which seemed like a token of the good relations that the family had always had with those who differed from them on matters of political and religious allegiance.[24]

Many men who had been to Gallipoli with the 10th created their own personal means of remembrance and so handed down the story of Suvla to succeeding generations. Bartholomew Hand would bring his son Paddy on bike rides around Dublin when the boy was growing up. On several occasions he took him to the memorial gardens at Islandbridge although they never felt able to attend the Protestant service held there on Remembrance Day. Paddy was taken to see a number of churchyards where his father would point out the graves of old comrades. Only in later years did Paddy fully understand that his father was taking him on a personal pilgrimage. Later, when hearing the bugle call for Reveille at a Remembrance Day service, Paddy began to understand his father's behaviour when he stood at the back of their Dublin house and sang:

> Boys, if you're able
> Come into the stable
> And feed your horses some hay

– words that traditionally accompanied the Reveille. His father had heard the bugle call sounded every morning of his training as a soldier, first in Ireland, then at Basingstoke, and afterwards on board ship before arriving on a Greek island in preparation for departure to Gallipoli. Despite the horrors of Suvla

Bay, affection for the army in which he had found both adventure and comradeship had been retained in Bartholomew Hand's mind as a much older man. When Paddy and his brother went to England to find work and ended up enlisting in the British armed forces, their Irish father approved.[25]

Suvla veterans like Hand, who depended on their British disability pension, were soon part of dwindling number. In the early 1950s some 10,500 Irish Great War veterans were still receiving a pension; by the start of the 1960s the number had halved and by the beginning of the 1970s it was a quarter of that figure.[26] For some of these old soldiers the British Legion provided a crucial support network. Others were involved in regimental Old Comrades Associations although these began to dwindle because the southern-based Irish regiments from which much of the 10th had been formed were disbanded in 1922. On this occasion the regimental 'colours' had been handed to King George V at Windsor Castle for 'safe keeping' in a scene in which both monarch and generals wept openly together.[27]

Throughout the decades, many old soldiers kept an eye on the fortunes of their former Gallipoli comrades. Those who read English newspapers would occasionally have been aware of John Hargrave who, bearing the self-chosen name 'the White Fox', became a prolific writer and the dynamic leader of an organization that began as an offshoot of the scouting movement and eventually was known by a Kentish dialect name as 'the Kibbo Kift'. Its members were expected to have a second 'animal name', to live close to nature and to create and decorate their own totem pole. At one stage several thousand of the group marched through the streets of London in semi-military formation wearing green shirts and berets. While resembling Oswald Mosley's fascists, their policies were, however, very different and their manifesto focused on world peace, meditation, woodcraft and a minimum wage or 'social credit' for all citizens.[28]

Few old soldiers of the 10th lived so colourfully. For many came the news of the deaths of former comrades. Noel Drury kept a file of clippings from the obituary columns. In February 1943 he noted the death in County Carlow of the Gallipoli padre Father Murphy. Six years later he learnt of the death at Rostrevor in County Down of another old Suvla comrade, Bill Whyte, brought out of retirement in 1939 to help organize the South Down branch of the Home Guard.[29]

In a number of former battalions of the 10th, officers would meet for commemorative dinners, having long since picked up the threads of civilian life, survived the rigours of another World War and in many cases established a home outside Ireland. On 5 October 1954, to mark the fortieth anniversary of the founding of the 5th Inniskilling Fusiliers, ten former officers from the battalion met for a celebratory meal at The Savoy Hotel in London, the food a far cry from the bully beef and dry biscuits on offer at Suvla. After a sumptuous repast, toasts were proposed to the Inniskilling Regiment and to the British monarch, Queen Elizabeth II.[30]

Ivone Kirkpatrick was among those present. He had had an interesting career working for the Intelligence Services in the latter part of the Great War, then becoming a diplomat in the 1920s. He had accompanied Chamberlain to Munich and can still be seen in several famous photographs, looking carefully at the map of the central European region that Adolf Hitler was about to make his own. During the Second World War the unexpected flight of Rudolf Hess to Britain presented Kirkpatrick with a chance to exercise his knowledge of German culture when he was sent to 'debrief' the eccentric Nazi leader. In the late 1940s, Kirkpatrick ended up as British High Commissioner to Germany and eventually became Under Secretary at the Foreign Office.

Among other former Inniskilling officers included at The Savoy in 1954 was Lord Dunsany who, despite never having been at the front in 1915, seemed to relish his role as an old comrade of the Inniskillings four decades after the death of his gifted young protégé, Francis Ledwidge.[31]

There was no mention of the Irish at Gallipoli

Survivors who read extensively would have been aware of the increasing volumes that since the 1920s attempted to analyse and describe Gallipoli. These included an official history, volumes of reminiscences by officers such as Sir Ian Hamilton, critical accounts by journalists who had covered the campaign and other vivid narratives by men who had fought there. They would also have been aware of how the public remembrance of Gallipoli had become a feature of Australian culture, where an annual 'Anzac Day' was devoted to the anniversary of the first Gallipoli landings on 25 April 1915.

By contrast, the specific experience of the Irish at Gallipoli, both in the 10th Division and in other units, was not only meagrely commemorated but was, before long, a little known part of the modern Irish historical narrative, despite the existence of some powerful accounts of the battle. The able Dublin barrister, Henry Hanna, had written a history of the Dublin Pals, published in pre-independence Dublin. Articulate veterans such as 'Juvenis', John Hargrave and Bryan Cooper also wrote careful accounts of their experiences. Others such as Noel Drury and William Knott committed their extensive diaries to the archives of the Imperial War Museum and the National Army Museum in London for safe-keeping. However, most of Ireland's twentieth century historians were selective in their use of such accounts and had nothing of significance to say about Ireland's participation in the Great War and the death of thousands of their countrymen at Gallipoli.[32]

Writers generating the new Irish history textbooks for use in schools and colleges in the new 'Irish Free State' faced immense problems. The Civil War wounds of the 1920s and the still contested issue of partition meant that in the early decades Irish history lessons stopped in August 1914.[33]

For several Irish historians striving to give an account of Ireland that spanned the centuries, Irish volunteer soldiers in the First World War clearly had little role to play in the unfolding drama whose denouement was independence. Edmund Curtis, in his *History of Ireland* in 1936, limited his commentary to the inaccurate observation that 'some 100,000 Irishmen altogether served in the British ranks' and that 'to outward seeming Ireland was for the Allies'.[34] Dorothy McArdle, in *The Irish Republic* in 1937, took more careful note of the wartime years and spoke briefly of the contrasting backgrounds and experiences of the 16th and 36th divisions but failed to mention the 10th.[35] T.W. Moody and F.X. Martin in their 1967 collection of essays *The Course of Irish History*, reprinted regularly until 1984, covered the Great War in a couple of lines about John Redmond's call for Irishmen to fight for Britain and a photograph of an anti-conscription rally. There was no mention of the Irish at Gallipoli.[36]

The painful legacy of Suvla nonetheless flowed quietly under the surface for much of the century. Those who ran the new country and stamped their image upon it were far from ignorant of the Gallipoli story nor should we suppose they felt anything other than compassion for those who were its victims. The Lee family owned a house in Blackrock named Bellview that the de Valera family temporarily leased from them during the 1930s. On several occasions Mrs de Valera and Mrs Lee would converse about family matters and Mrs Lee often spoke of her two dead sons, Joseph and Ernest, and of how she still felt their presence around the house and in Bellview's beautiful garden. Thus did the ghosts of Gallipoli haunt the home of a politician whom one might assume to have been troubled by spectres from other more recent Irish blood-lettings.[37]

In 1966, on the advent of the fiftieth anniversary of the Easter Rising, the Irish Republic celebrated its origins and it seemed a new era was opening when the complexities of the recent past could be reconciled with the present. Taoiseach Seán Lemass spoke positively of those who had, in 1914 'volunteered enthusiastically to fight, as they believed, for the liberty of Belgium' and regretted how he personally had once been prone to 'question the motives of those men who joined the British armies'. He could see that they were 'motivated by the highest purpose and died in their tens of thousands in Flanders and Gallipoli, believing they were giving their lives in the cause of human liberty, everywhere, not excluding Ireland'. There was even talk in some governmental circles of building a commemorative bridge across the river Liffey to pay renewed homage to 'the fallen'.[38]

The flower that labelled him an inauthentic Irishman

Sadly, the renewal of civil strife in Northern Ireland changed all that. Widespread unrest and sectarian rioting led to the arrival yet again of British troops as 'peacekeepers' onto the streets of Ulster towns; by the early 1970s their relationship with local nationalists had deteriorated and a reconstructed Irish Republican Army was soon locked in conflict with the Royal Ulster Constabulary and British army. Soon new 'Loyalist' paramilitaries added to the violence and brought their own retaliatory bombing campaign to the streets of the Irish Republic.

Although southern Ireland remained stable and was tolerant of its own Protestant minority, the continued involvement of British Crown Forces in the six counties to which the Irish Republic still felt it had a territorial claim made it hard for further recognition to be given to the long tradition of Irish involvement in the British army,[39] so that many old soldiers were offered nothing but silence in their declining years.

Irish stories of Gallipoli and the Western Front were only rarely articulated in the media or sought out by local historians, as they were elsewhere in an era of renewed interest in the Great War and its oral history. And so the experiences of those working-class soldiers, many of them Catholic and nationalist, who had little taste for writing diaries or journals, became lost forever.

Indeed the Irish branches of such purely benevolent military organizations as the Royal British Legion were wary of attack from the IRA. Even Leopardstown Hospital, which provided generously for the welfare of many hundreds of former British servicemen was not immune from a number of explicit threats of violence. To the handful of Gallipoli veterans among the 350 Great War disability pensioners left in the Irish Republic at the end of the 1970s, it must have seemed as if the animosity that had first greeted them on their demobilization and return to Ireland had been rekindled.[40]

A nadir was reached with the bombing by the IRA in 1987 of the War Memorial in Enniskillen during a Remembrance service. The 'no-warning' attack resulted in several deaths and terrible injuries, but the bombing caused intense outrage throughout the island of Ireland, indicating that enlistment in the British army, while indicative of centuries of iniquitous political and cultural domination, was nonetheless considered a meaningful and far from universally shameful part of Ireland's long and complex history. It was felt that Irish remembrance of those who once fought with Britain's armed forces should not be violated.[41]

However, a belated recognition of the 10th Division's war experiences in Gallipoli still looked bleak. In the north new stirrings of interest in the First World War were still focused on the Ulster Division, whose martial prowess and calamitous fate had emblematic force for Northern Ireland's beleaguered Protestant population who feared cultural extinction and believed that they must fight hard to prevent it. The poppy retained its politically negative connotations for northern nationalists, who were alienated by the tendency for Remembrance Day services to connect the dead of the World Wars with the more recent, controversial roll of honour drawn from Northern Ireland's security forces.

Furthermore, many respected historians had still not spoken in any meaningful way about the Irish experience of Gallipoli. Among those guilty of omission were J.C. Beckett in *The Making of Modern Ireland* (1965), F.S.L. Lyons in *Ireland since the Famine* (1972) and Roy Foster in *Modern Ireland 1600–1972* (1989).[42]

In the Republic, most remaining public war memorials lay abandoned. At Islandbridge, itinerants grazed their horses in a park dominated by litter, weeds and broken bottles. Michael Lee, grand-nephew of the Lee brothers, now wore his poppy only on 11 November and in the confines of his church. He did not want to exhibit a flower that, while it might not have provoked a display of explicit hostility, nonetheless would have labelled him an inauthentic, anglified Irishman, for whom the derisory term 'West Brit' had been invented.[43]

I can think of no more eloquent symbol of reconciliation

In the late 1980s and the 1990s Ireland was to change rapidly in ways that favoured the rediscovery of its role in the Great War. In the north, a sustained if imperfect peace process gradually brought an end to the war between republicans and British Crown Forces, while the Belfast Agreement of 1998 involved both governments in new relationships aimed to broaden and relax antagonistic definitions of identity that had so bedevilled the country throughout the twentieth century. Ireland's 'tiger' economy and position as an independent-minded and respected member of the European Community eased old fears that a fresh focus on Ireland's British military past might facilitate a cultural if not a territorial re-assimilation into the United Kingdom. Thousands of immigrants arrived in Ireland from across the world seeking asylum, work, and a measure of prosperity or freedom unknown in their own homeland. Ireland had to embrace multi-culturalism overnight and a broader national narrative became a much more desirable project. Perhaps the story of Ireland's British war-dead could at last be seen as a valid if deeply tragic part of the national history. Indeed its recognition might even serve a reconciliatory function.[44]

At Messines in Belgium 1998, on the site of the battlefield where the 16th and 36th divisions had fought side by side, the Irish President and the British monarch participated in a joint ceremony to commemorate the Irish war-dead, during which a memorial tower was opened to the public, the culmination of a cross-border volunteer project involving local political representatives and young people from within each of the Irish jurisdictions, north and south. In the course of the opening of this Messines 'Peace Park', the hope was expressed that Irish people could more readily understand and move on from a complex and antagonistic past. One commentator spoke of 'the laying of troubled spirits to rest and of the hope for a peaceful future' with 'the president of Ireland ... the British Queen and the Belgian monarch, representing our common European past and future'.[45]

In the north the work of a new Somme Heritage Centre and related interest groups such as the Somme Association stressed the need to remember all those who had left Ireland for whatever motive and from whatever background, to fight and die on foreign soil. By the early years of the new century, a number of Ulster's nationalist politicians, including those associated with the IRA, were prepared to attend memorial services and lay wreaths to commemorate the dead and those who had sought work, adventure or comradeship in the ranks of the British army.[46]

In the south a national Day of Commemoration also offered public ceremonies of respect for those Irish men and women who died in the World Wars and a range of other international conflicts. The Irish Army provided a guard of honour, the Irish President and Taoiseach were invariably present, the Irish tricolour was flown at half-mast, and the Last Post and Reveille were sounded. An archive devoted to Ireland's involvement in the two conflicts was officially opened within the National Museum.[47] The Islandbridge Memorial Gardens were also carefully restored and reopened. No flags of national allegiance were to be unfurled there and the park was designated a 'neutral' commemorative space. Few inscriptions had been planned by Edward Lutyens for the Islandbridge monuments but engraved on one is a fragment of muted lyricism by Rupert Brooke, who in 1915, on his way to Gallipoli as a volunteer soldier, died from an unexpected illness:

> We have found safety with all things undying,
> The winds, and morning, tears of men and mirth,
> The deep night, and birds singing, and clouds flying,
> And sleep and freedom, and the autumnal earth

While in its hard-won state of renewal, Islandbridge offered a place to remember the dead without recourse to political statement, elsewhere local communities endeavoured to restore their war-memorials, in Limerick and in small towns such as Bandon in County Cork.[48] Newspaper articles recognizing Ireland's Great War experiences regularly appeared, scholarly books were written, early accounts by Irish soldiers of their wartime adventures were republished, and regimental traditions of old British army units were once again cherished by organizations such as the Royal Dublin Fusiliers Association, whose existence would have been unthinkable twenty years previously. However, gaps and absences still remained.[49]

One such gap surfaced in an otherwise sensitive, detailed RTÉ television documentary, 'Sown in Tears and Blood', shown in 1998. While Irish soldiering on the Western Front was carefully described, the 10th (Irish) Division received no mention whatsoever. The programme-makers paid close attention to the Messines memorial project, reconciling the traditions of nationalist and unionist, as represented by the 16th and 36th divisions; the less politically homogeneous, more culturally elusive, yet equally tragic 10th Division slipped through the net.

Gallipoli was the Australian battle

The neglect and indeed disparagement of the Irish Gallipoli story can be seen in one of the key genres of Irish popular culture. Only a handful of traditional songs ever touched on the battle, of which the most well-known is the republican anthem 'The Foggy Dew', written immediately after the Easter Rising and celebrating the 'fearless men' who had 'flung out the flag of war' in Dublin under the command of Pearse and Connolly. The song referred explicitly both to the battle fought at Suvla Bay by the 10th Division and the attempt by the Irish troops in the 29th Division to take a small Turkish coastal town at Cape Helles. In a memorable phrase, the song-writer claimed that

'twas better to die beneath an Irish sky than at Suvla or Sud El Bar

and went on to endorse the supersession of such 'unpatriotic' foreign soldiering:

'Twas England bade our Wild Geese go that small nations might be free
But their lonely graves are by Suvla's waves or the fringes of the Great
     North Sea.
O, had they died by Pearse's side, or had fought with Cathal Brugha,
Their names we'd keep where the Fenians sleep, 'neath the shroud of
     the Foggy Dew.

The song predicted that the names of the Gallipoli dead, because they had no place in an iconography of Irish separatist martyrs, would be forgotten as subjects for Ireland's musicians. The recovery of the 'fourth green field' of Ulster from British hands was more likely to be the topic of patriot singers than the Turkish field of bones where Irish Great War dead still lay. The only Gallipoli veteran whose name had been cherished in the Irish folk-song repertoire was Seán McCartney, Connaught Ranger turned IRA man. His name had appeared in 'Belfast Graves' which had caught the imagination of Brendan Behan, who heard it performed in pubs along the Falls Road in the 1940s:

On Cavan's Mountain, Lappinduff
Fought one with bravery,
Until the English soldiers killed
Brave Seán McCartney

But of McCartney's earlier bravery at Anzac Cove as an 'English soldier' there was, perhaps understandably, no mention.

Yet what must be acknowledged in Ireland's Gallipoli story is that McCartney's career had followed a not uncommon military trajectory. Born in Norfolk Street in the lower Falls area of Belfast, he had worked, like many of his family, in one of the local mills. And like many other Irish National Volunteers, he had been recruited to the 10th Division after John Redmond's call for young nationalists to join the British Army. Posted to a battalion of the Connaught Rangers, he found himself aboard the *Mauretania*, heading for a futile and bloody war against the Turks. Both at Gallipoli and elsewhere, he witnessed the slaughter and despair of the Great War at first hand. Then he returned to a Belfast riven with sectarian strife, as an unemployed ex-service-man, disillusioned with John Redmond's outdated version of the Home Rule dream. Joining the local unit of the IRA he swiftly rose to become commander of B Company in the 1st battalion.

After his death in County Cavan, McCartney was interred in Belfast's Milltown cemetery, in a plot that would soon bear testimony to the enduring complexities of Irish soldiering. In the same grave was placed the body of IRA general Joe McKelvey, executed by a Free State firing squad during the Irish Civil War. Volunteer Terrence Perry was later buried there, having died on hunger strike in Parkhurst goal during a brief IRA campaign in the 1940s. Also inscribed on the same gravestone is the name of the nineteenth-century Fenian, William Harbinson, who shared with McCartney and so many other Irish patriots an experience of service in the British army.

For Sean McCartney, and for those who revere his memory, the Great War was indeed a mere prelude to the 'greatest war' – the war for Irish independence, which would not be fought at Gallipoli but 'at home'. [50]

Yet new kinds of music were being created in the 1980s. The London-Irish band The Pogues, fronted by song-writer and lead singer Shane McGowan, performed abrasive, unsentimental songs about aspects of life placed in 'soft focus' within traditional musical culture. Shane McGowan sang of alcoholism, penury and homelessness, of men and women whose experiences are always at the margins of any national narrative, including those who emigrate, only to find work as ill-paid labourers in far-off continents, down-and-outs in foreign cities or those who find no alternative to the dangerous, rootless life of a merce-nary soldier. Yet in their coverage of one deeply painful aspect of the twentieth century narrative of so many nations, The Pogues could neither find nor invent an 'Irish song'. The song they chose to speak for marginalized and traumatized survivors of the Great War was Eric Bogle's bitter ballad about a young

Australian who sails to Gallipoli, only to be injured at Suvla Bay, after which he returns to his homeland, mutilated, isolated and deeply disillusioned.

McGowan's version of this intense Gallipoli ballad recounted with pain and clarity the very agonies that thousands of Irish soldiers had once experienced but for which there was in Ireland no significant memorial framework and no song of lament: He sang of how 'in that hell that they call Suvla Bay we were butchered like lambs at the slaughter'. He painted a musical portrait of a shoreline where 'the blood stained the sand and the water' and he conveyed to thousands of young Irish listeners the 'mad world of blood, dust and fire' in which the men at Gallipoli had had to fight. The song dwelt on the isolation of 'the crippled, the wounded and maimed, the legless, the armless, the blind and insane' – and then concluded with a bleak and apt reference to the returned veterans of Suvla: 'forgotten heroes of a forgotten war'.

Almost no one in Ireland who sang along with the words of this ballad knew that thousands of young men had once sailed from this island towards the very place called Suvla, to experience suffering, death and then cultural oblivion. In truth, Gallipoli was now the 'Australian' battle. Anyone who had seen Peter Weir's film thought they knew that fact. In this powerful, deeply Australocentric film, Anzac soldiers are shown being slaughtered at a notorious location known as the Nek, while British troops at Suvla are rumoured to be sitting on the beaches drinking cups of tea. However, several thousand of the troops on the Suvla Beach at this moment were in fact Irish. As well as drinking tea they fought, they bled and they died.

Just as Irish casualties were eliminated from this cinematic Gallipoli myth, buried amongst the 21,000 non-Anzac British war-dead, so too were Indians and other colonial soldiers. Nor did the film mention the more than 10,000 Frenchmen who died at Gallipoli, a figure exceeding the number of Australians who perished. Indeed the French cemetery at Morto Bay is a testament to an earlier and equally profound forgetting. Many of the French colonial troops buried there shared the Islamic faith of their Turkish enemies. Each soldier was 'remembered' beneath a memorial cross, the symbol of an alien religion.[51]

Sailing to Byzantium

Part of the reason for the rapid disappearance of Suvla Bay and Anzac Cove from Irish consciousness was the sheer geographical inaccessibility of Gallipoli throughout much of the twentieth century. Turkey was at the other end of

Europe from Ireland and few could contemplate the journey, least of all those who had served in the ranks and whose families could never afford the luxury of foreign travel. Throughout the early 1920s Turkey was still immersed in conflict, conducting a fierce war against Greece. Not until after the Treaty of Lausanne in 1923 was it possible for the British War Graves Commission to finish gathering the remains of the dead from various isolated graves and place them in a number of larger cemeteries. A vast number of the British dead had no known resting place, so cemeteries at locations such as Lala Baba and Green Hill contained not graves but memorial stones laid out in neat rows, each with a personalized inscription, many chosen by the bereaved family.

However, distance was no obstacle to the Australian representatives who arrived on the tenth anniversary of the Gallipoli landings to unveil memorials to the heroes of Anzac, nor to the increasing number of well-heeled but grief-stricken pilgrims who travelled to the peninsula from Britain throughout this period. However, from 1935 onwards, Gallipoli was once again difficult to visit, when it resumed its role as a strategic military location, fortified by the Turks against the military threat posed by Fascism and Nazism, then after 1945 against the might of the Soviet armed forces. Turkey's conflict with Greece over the fate of Cyprus and her continuing internal struggle to achieve a stable democracy also made Gallipoli a difficult place of pilgrimage until very recent times. Since the 1950s the battlefields of the Western Front have been accessible to anyone with an interest in the Great War and a family connection. Now, in the twenty-first century, with the Cold War consigned to the dustbin of history, and cheap aeroplane flights to Turkish Mediterranean seaside resorts available for all, there is little reason for any interested Irish citizen to feel that he or she cannot go there.[52]

There have been other reasons for a continued lack of focus on the 10th Division. In recent years, to remember how Irishmen died at the Somme, Ypres and Messines has been to recall Ireland's involvement in a fierce military enmity between powerful European neighbours such as France, Germany, Britain and Russia that in the 'new Europe' seems to have vanished forever, offering 'comfortable' suggestion that Ireland's divisions can also be transcended within a new European, post-bellum modernity. The sites of memory connected to the 10th Division offer little of this kind of hope.

The most distinctive divisional memorial is the Celtic cross erected in the 1920s on the site of the division's Great War engagements at Rabrovo in Macedonia, in a part of the Balkans where territoriality, ethnicity, religion and the political uses of violence continue to matter in a very 'pre-modern' and enduring way. The Balkans continued to be a 'powder-keg' at the start of the twenty-first century as they had been in 1914, when an assassination in Sarajevo had signalled the start of the four-year war. In the Balkans, Irishmen in British army uniforms and in the blue berets of the United Nations peace-keeping force have recently attempted to resolve the bitter conflicts of an imploding Yugoslavia. The Balkans is not a place where those who wish to rename the unacknowledged war-dead of Ireland can feel a sense of catharsis or of closure. Travelling into Macedonia from Greece, the visitor to Rabrovo may well have to wait several hours at a border-crossing, aware of the fraught transition from Christian Greek culture to the Islamic environment of this part of Macedonia, with which it has often been at odds.

Nor can it escape one's attention that the 10th Division's memorial cross is a blatantly Christian emblem within this Islamic region.[53]

At the Dardanelles, the Turks welcome their visitors with warmth and generosity. The past is remembered with little bitterness. However, Turkey contains numerous potent cultural forces which throughout much of today's world are deeply at odds with one another. It is a country attempting to recon-cile both Europe and the East, both secularism and Islam, and both modernity and tradition. It holds onto a proud veneration of the founding father of modern Turkish nationalism, Kemal Ataturk, yet also struggles in its eastern regions with the unresolved problem of Kurdish nationalism.

An Irish observer at Gallipoli can perceive how the battlefield has become a source of national founding-myths, not just for the thousands of Australians who now travel as pilgrims to Anzac Cove each year, believing it a testament to the emergence of a distinctive 'Aussie' spirit, but for the Turks who also travel to Gallipoli to stand where Atatürk once stood on the Chunuk Bair as the master of the heights, at the beginning of his project of Turkish national renewal.

To gaze on the inscriptions on the Turkish and Australian monuments is to recognize that the alternative to a national amnesia about one's war-dead may be the transformation of thousands of ordinary men into martyrs, exalted heroes or, at the least, exponents of a perceived national virtue. It is thought-provoking to read one Turkish inscription on the heights above the Gallipoli shoreline that states, 'Every second which passed, every instant and every fallen soldier changed the destiny of Turkey and its people', and, nearby, to see another offering a quotation from the Koran, telling us that martyrs in paradise request only one thing of Allah:

> For the sake of You, O Lord
> Send us back to the world again
> That we may be martyred once more

In re-acknowledging fellow Irishmen who fought at Gallipoli, are we unintentionally situating ourselves on one corner of the ancient, lamentable, newly relevant map of conflict between Christian and Islamic peoples?[54]

But it is for other reasons that, out of all the Great War experiences, Suvla vanished most swiftly and completely after 1915. As Ireland's own journey towards modern national identity gathered pace in the post-war era, the religious views, sense of ethnicity and political inclinations of its inhabitants were assimilated into two opposed, increasingly homogeneous national camps. The 36th Division and, to a slightly lesser extent, the 16th, were created to cater for these intensifying, oppositional Irish nationalist and unionist affiliations. The divisional 'categories' made sense in a partitioned post-war island.

The 10th Division, however, had not been created with political antagonism in mind. Those who joined up did so from motives less easily ascribed to national identity and more easily connected to peer-group affiliation, class, the ethos of a family circle, personal hardships or ambitions. and the place an individual felt they inhabited in the divinely ordained scheme of things.

For unionists the 'Britishness' of the division lacked the 'purity' of the Ulster Volunteer Force ethos of the Somme, while the 'Irishness' of the division looked to nationalist eyes more diluted and miscellaneous than that of the 16th, its variegated hue deepened by the addition of so many recruits from across the Irish Sea, among them Englishmen such as John Hargrave and William Knott, on whom we have to rely to fill out any definitive and complete divisional narrative. The 10th Division was victim of the binary approach to twentieth-century Irish political construction, just as in the more recent years of reclamation. Meanwhile, newly-independent Ireland was busily establishing its own 'founding narrative' based on what had unfolded in the General Post Office in Dublin in 1916. The blood-sacrifice of Pearse and Connolly was inspirationally anchored to the Christian calendar's Easter rituals of death and rebirth. It offered to future generations a dramatic martyrdom of young patriotic poets, academics, seers and idealists. It contrasted with the 'impersonal', seemingly passive deaths of the thousands 'hoodwinked' by Britain into filling the mud-brown trenches of the Western Front, in a mechanized, soulless and elongated war.

However, the destruction of the 10th Division at Gallipoli had the potential to stand out from the bleak carnage in France and Flanders. Here, as in Dublin at Eastertide, was the stuff of drama and epic, and of swift, bloody closure. As powerful accounts published by Henry Hanna, Juvenis and Bryan Cooper showed, Irish poets, professors, and artists had fought at Gallipoli with pathetic, blood-soaked dignity. Cultured sons of gentry and illiterate sons of peasants died side by side and domestic political differences were transcended. They had perished in a heartbreakingly beautiful landscape after voyaging to a part of Europe redolent with the apostolic charisma of St Paul, the chivalric heroism of the Crusaders, the mythic swagger of the Argonauts and the epic glamour of Homer's Trojan warriors. A public retrieval of the Irish Suvla legacy in the 1920s and 1930s had potential as a high tragedy of costly patriotism as bloody, personal and stirring as the story of Easter 1916.

There was therefore good reason for Suvla to be banished from public memory in the fragile years of the new Free State's bid for mythopoeic autonomy. The frontispiece to an alternative twentieth-century national story, it offered a potential alternative founding myth for a misplaced version of the Irish future.

In this 'other future', the Easter Rising had been called off by Connolly and Pearse. Wartime sufferings instead brought unionist and nationalist closer together and post-war Ireland, deeply proud of its new 'Home Rule', possessed an imperial parliament in Dublin. This was an Ireland with its pre-war social hierarchies still relatively intact, flourishing within a modernizing British empire in an attempted reprise of the illustrious eighteenth-century era of 'Grattan's parliament'. Under the influence of the many Trinity College and National University 'old boys' who were so powerful in the running of the state, the Gallipoli sacrifice had become the ultimate national emblem of the shared Irish wartime losses that had been the context for the founding of the state. Remembering the deep peer-bereavement of 1915 and a map of the Aegean, hanging on the wall of their boyhood classics classrooms, these leaders could see a particular fittingness in the Suvla motif, with Gallipoli grief something they knew was shared in thousands of ordinary homes from Limerick to Dundalk.

This strange counter-factual scenario not only suggests why Gallipoli was so readily forgotten but helps us recognize afresh that all battles can be represented as ideology, even those whose actual fate was historical marginalization.

Gallipoli might have been a modern Irish founding myth only if Ireland had stayed true to the empire, but this should not blind us to the potential of the sufferings at Suvla Bay, Cape Helles and Anzac Cove to function as a marker of identity and as a tool of social power.[55]

Despite the post-war banishment from public memory of Ireland's sufferings at Gallipoli, it is interesting to note that the two greatest Irish writers of their era would summon up archetypal power generated on the south-eastern edge of Europe in their quest for the new forms of literary achievement that we know as modernism. In *Ulysses* James Joyce gave to the everyday lives of the troubled, wandering pre-war Dubliners, Stephen Daedalus and Leopold Bloom, the mythic licence once offered only to gods and heroes such as Odysseus, who had been, after all, a soldier making an unhappy post-war journey to his island home from a bloody battle at the mouth of straits we know as the Dardanelles. And in one of his most eloquent attempts to postulate a transcendence of the pain of mortality by purely human means, W.B. Yeats composed 'Sailing to Byzantium', which tells of an old man on a boat-journey from an Ireland full of youth, fertility and energy, across the Mediterranean to 'the holy city' of Constantinople, the 10th Division's ultimate military goal.

The potential of the Aegean and the Bosphorus as force-fields for political and literary Irish mythology, at one of the great turning-points in the nation's history, is a fascinating subject for debate. Gallipoli forces us to think of what might have been and counter-factual speculations are in keeping with the spell that this ill-fated campaign casts on all who study it, contemplating a twentieth-century Europe that might have been the Gallipoli legacy had Constantinople been captured, Russia supported and stabilized, the Bolshevik Revolution prevented, Communism nipped in the bud and the 'anti-bolshevism' that engendered Nazism rendered historically void.

Time passes, shadows fall

The Irish commemorative presence at Suvla may become more visible in the future when the Ulster-based Somme Association aims to provide a specific, lasting tribute to Irishmen who died at the Dardanelles with a memorial stone, on which is discretely inscribed, in relief, the Christian symbol of a Celtic cross.[56] The memorial would be situated at Green Hill Cemetery and those who go there would discover much that is eerily familiar as they travel around the peninsula.

They will smell the wild flowers and herbs whose fragrance once masked the stench of so many dead British and Turkish soldiers; they will recognize the sharp branches of the tangled brush-wood that fed a conflagration started by shellfire and fanned by the Mediterranean breeze; they will recognize the stony landmarks of the Kiretch Tepe skyline and see the almond-trees, the tomato-plants and the lush green stretches of earth, indicating where the Gallipoli springs still are. They will see the salt lake reincarnated as a fish farm of mixed economic fortunes. The Cut, which the men of the 10th once leapt across in a game of chance with Turkish shells and bullets, is safe and silent now. Fishing boats are moored there in a channel to the sea, which rolls ashore at A Beach, much as Irish veterans always remembered it. The distant outlines of Samothrace and Imbros can still be seen, behind which sunsets still glow.

Out of the soil at Lala Baba or Green Hill, the shards of old rum jars may still be retrieved, thin scraps of shrapnel, pieces of old barbed wire, the rusted 'keys' for opening bully beef tins, and an occasional Mauser or Lee Enfield bullet. More rarely, identity discs can still be found or the fragments of a rib-cage or a piece of broken human femur, in the place that when the British Graves Registration Unit first came, was still a headland of wooden crosses, unexploded shells and thousands of human bones.

Gazing out to sea from the lofty pinnacle of Chunuk Bair it is impossible not to visualize how, nine decades ago, volunteer Irish soldiers, having crossed a continent to fight for what their fellow-countrymen would eventually deem to be the 'wrong cause', sailed towards the Gallipoli coastline, crammed below decks on boats with names such as *Snaefell* and *Honeysuckle*, as they made their way through the darkness of an August night towards their Gallipoli 'undertaking'.

In the graveyards of the peninsula a full sense of the tragic folly of Gallipoli begins to unfold. Irish names are there in abundance: the Barrys, Fitzmaurices, Walshes, Lennons, Toomeys, Droys, Ryans, Leonards and many others. The inscriptions on the memorial stones still bear the weight of human suffering:

More dear to memory than words can tell

My darling very precious boy from his ever broken-hearted mother

Safe in God's keeping till we meet again

No one in Ireland can any longer say that it is impossible or inappropriate to discover the full story behind these faraway memorial stones or trace precisely how they came to be inscribed. To embrace the Suvla legacy is not to flirt with bizarre revisionism or to install a pro-imperial counter-myth about the era of Ireland's search for independence. Most of all, the writing on the memorial stones of Gallipoli leads us towards the enduring and universal human realities of courage and endurance, of loss and pain.

One such inscription is found on the stone of 'adopted' Irishman, Charles Frederick Ball, commemorated at Lala Baba in a small, verdant cemetery that overlooks the sea in a picturesque manner which this professional gardener might well have loved. Ball's memorial stone states simply, in the words used on so many Great War gravestones: 'Greater love hath no man than this.'

On C Beach, in mid-September, Ball had been waiting for a boat to take him away from Suvla to the Greek islands where he might recover from the severe dysentery that by now had crippled and enfeebled him and where he might write a letter once again to his young Irish wife. Awaiting embarkation with Ball stood a number of other sick and injured soldiers. A Turkish shell exploded close to one of the men who had been standing by the water's edge. Instead of taking cover, Ball went to the aid of the badly wounded man. Within moments a second shell had arrived, causing him a serious injury. Transported to a hospital ship, he died within hours. His body was committed, after a short Christian service, into the depths of Suvla Bay. The inscription on his memorial stone at Lala Baba Cemetery bears witness to the death of a man Frank Laird once described as 'a friend on whom one might count for a lifetime'.

Saddest by far are those memorial stones that contain inscriptions invoking the power of memory to preserve the realities of Gallipoli:

> Time passes, shadows fall,
> Loving remembrance outlasts all

> Their glory shall not be blotted out

During the lifetime of the Gallipoli veterans, the 10th Division was indeed 'blotted out' of the Irish national record. No attempt to write it back into the historical narrative can ever entirely atone for that inglorious fact.

In the course of modern European history, oblivion was the fate of many millions who died as conquering armies trampled across the continent and brutal regimes annihilated their own unwanted citizens. For many of the victims there will never be an act of retrieval because the blotting out was too calculated and much too widespread. Yet despite disappearing from Ireland's public consciousness for such an extended period, stories of the Irish Great War dead can still be retrieved in powerful if incomplete detail.[57]

This retrieval was possible because of the courageous men whom we have met on these pages, who decided to act as the chroniclers of human fortitude and suffering. It was also possible because of the formidable historical archives that exist in the British Isles and Ireland, and the enduring commemorative spaces of Gallipoli itself. Equally important in Ireland is the fact that local stories of participation in global events do not entirely disappear and the local landscape may often be imbued with a remarkable degree of fragmented or refracted historical meaning.

It was into such a local landscape of bog-lands, bungalows, laneways and open fields that I travelled south some years ago, to visit a friend who had moved from Belfast to live in the heart of the Irish midlands. I knew little, at that stage, as a northerner, either of this part of Ireland or of the story of the 10th (Irish) Division, but my curiosity was instantly aroused on hearing one of my friend's new neighbours refer to the road down which we walked as 'the Dardanelles'.

And so the quest began.

Rabrovo, Macedonia. The 10th Division's official memorial.

Laying up the colours of the disbanded regiments at Windsor Castle, after the creation of the Irish Free State.

Leopardstown Hospital, Dublin, where Great War veterans were treated for 'shell-shock'.
O'HANLON

John Hargrave, Suvl vetran and
political activist.
www.kibbokift.org

Bryan Cooper, Gallipoli veteran –
in the 1920s he served in the Free State parliament.
At his funeral the coffin was draped with Irish
tricolour and Union Jack.
LENNOX ROBINSON

Joe O'Leary with his wife outside his new shop in Skerries.
Coping with business pressures soon proved too much for the
'shell-shocked' veteran.

FI

Charles Frederick Ball. The
words 'Greater Love Hath No
Man Than This' on his
memorial stone are no empty
cliché.

O'H/H

Graves registration units still gathered in the
Gallipoli bones in the 1920s.

Q14338 IWM

Sean McCartney's Belfast grave – IRA man and Gallipoli veteran.
WHITE

An Islamic shrine at Gallipoli.
WILSON

The author searches for the grave of Charles Frederick Ball at Lala Baba cemetery, 2004.
WILSON

One of the monuments at Islandbridge Memorial Gardens in Dublin.
O'H

'The Dardanelles', County Westmeath, Ireland, 2005.

O'H

PHOTOGRAPHIC SOURCES

John Boyd, Ballymena, County Antrim

*Alice Curtayne, *Francis Ledwidge: a Life of the Poet* (Martin, Brian and O'Keeffe 1972)

Fergus d'Arcy, Dublin.

Down Museum, Downpatrick, County Down.

The Arthur J. England collection, Irish Archive for the World Wars, Irish National Museum, Dublin.

The Fingal Independent

The Getty collection, London.

Hampshire County Council Museums service

*Henry Hanna, *The Pals at Suvla Bay*, (E. Ponsonby 1916)

Imperial War Museum, London

Irish Archive for the World Wars, Irish National Museum, Dublin

Irish National Museum, London

Keith Jeffery, Belfast

Michael Lee, Dublin

Edwin Mitchell, Saintfield, County Down.

Royal Ulster Rifles Museum, Belfast.

Sinead O'Hanlon, Dublin.

*Lennox Robinson, *Bryan Cooper* (Constable 1931)

Somme Heritage Centre, Bangor, County Down

Jonathan White, Oxford

Brian Wilson, Killyleagh, County Down.

www. kibbokift.org

* published books containing photographs of key figures in the 10th Division.

NOTES

I. THE QUEST

1. R. Ayliffe et al, *The Rough Guide to Turkey*, 5th edn (Rough Guides 2003), p.241.
2. From the song 'Gallipoli' by Pete St. John.

II. VOLUNTEERS

1. T.Bartlett and K. Jeffery (eds), *A Military History of Ireland* (Cambridge University Press 1996), p.337.
2. M. Dungan, *They Shall Grow Not Old* (Four Courts Press 1997), p.25.
3. P. .Simkins, *Kitchener's Army* (Manchester University Press 1988), pp. 1–80
4. H. Harris, *The Irish Regiments In The Great War* (Mercier 1968), pp.11–12 and Lennox Robinson, *Bryan Cooper* (Constable 1931), p.90
5. The war-diary of J. McIlwaine, 5–6 August 1914 IWM 96/29/1
6. *The Irish News*, 6 and 7 August 1914.
7 *The Down Recorder*, 15 August 1914.
8. For information on the Home Rule crisis see A.T.Q. Stewart, *The Ulster Crisis* (Faber and Faber 1967).
9. For further detail see *The Irish Times* and the *Irish Independent*, June, July and August 1914
10. B. Cooper, *The Tenth (Irish) Division in Gallipoli* (Irish Academic Press 1993), pp.19–33
11. H. Hanna KC, *The Pals at Suvla Bay* (E. Ponsonby 1916), pp.13–17
12. Interview with Paddy Hand, Killyleagh, County Down.
13. Interview with Joe O'Leary Jun., Lusk, County Fingal.
14. *The Blue Cap*, vol. 9, September 2002 and vol. 10, December 2003.
15. Interview with Michael Lee, Dublin; A. Findlater, *Findlaters – The Story of a Dublin Merchant Family* (A&A Farmar 2001), pp.251–67
16. Cooper, p.58; *The Irish Times*, 16 and 23 August 1915.
17. Hanna, pp.13–17
18. T. Johnstone, *Orange, Green and Khaki* (Gill and Macmillan 1992), pp.87–8
19. Harris, pp.16–17
20. War-diary of N.E.Drury, pp.1–9, NAM 7607-69-1
21. A. Curtayne, *Francis Ledwidge: A Life of the Poet* (Martin, Brian and O'Keeffe 1972), pp.1–84. The quotation is from the poem 'After My Last Song'.
22. Cooper, pp.9–37; Robinson, pp.36–82.
23. Hanna, pp.15–17.
24. John Hargrave wrote two versions of the Suvla story, published several decades apart. For the information given here, see J. Hargrave, *At Suvla Bay* (Constable 1916), pp.1–32. See also the

biographical material at www.kibbokift.org

25. The war-diary of William Knott, IWM P305.

26. T. Denman, *Ireland's Unknown Soldiers* (Irish Academic Press 1992), p.23.; Eric Mercer, 'For King, country and a shilling a day', *History Ireland*, Winter 2003.

27. Simkins, pp.59–66, 112–15.

28. G. Drage, *From Chindwin to Criccieth* (Evans 1956), pp.98–103.

29. See the following sources: Simkins, pp.112–15; PRO WO 162/20,24; N.Perry, 'Nationality in the Irish Infantry Regiments in The First World War', *War and Society*, XI, 1, 1994, p.78; Denman, p.24.

30. Simkins, pp.32–50.

31. T. Dooley, *Irishmen or English Soldiers?* (Liverpool University Press 1995), pp.8, 124–6; see also the 1911 census, held in The Public Record Office of Northern Ireland, Belfast.

32. Drury, pp.8–14.

33. Cooper, pp.16–22 and Robinson, p.91.

34. F. Laird, *Personal Experiences of The Great War* (Eason & Son 1925), pp.10–11.

35. Hanna, p.20.

36. J. Hargrave, *The Suvla Bay Landing* (Macdonald 1964), pp.46–8.

37. The war-diary of Sir Ivone Kirkpatrick, pp.1–5, IWM 79/50/1; I. Kirkpatrick, *The Inner Circle* (Macmillan 1959), pp.1–8.

38. Curtayn, pp.85–101.

39. Drage, pp.102–3.

40. *The Blue Cap*, vol. 9, September 2002; Hanna, pp.17–31; Cooper, pp.19–29.

41. Laird, pp.1–6.

42. Harris, p.18.

43. *The Irish News*, 25 December 1914.

44. N.Steele and P.Harte, *Defeat at Gallipoli* (Macmillan 1994), pp.1–70.

45. Drury, pp.15–25.

46. Robinson, pp.100–1.

47. War diary of McIlwaine: November 1914, December 1914, March 1915.

48. Curtayn, pp.102–6.

49. Drury, pp.29–31.

50. Hanna, pp.28–31; *The Irish Times*, 1 and 2 May 1915; Knott, 28 April–1 May 1915.

51. Hargrave (1964) pp.49–50.

52. S. Parnell Kerr, *What The Irish Regiments Have Done* (Unwin 1916), pp.150–60.

III. VOYAGERS

1. Cooper, pp.28–33.

2. Hanna, pp.33–44; T. Bowman, *Irish Regiments in The Great War* (Manchester University Press 2003) pp. 81–82; Denman, p.55.

3. Laird, pp.22–6.

4. Hargrave (1964), pp.50–2.

5. Kirkpatrick (IWM), p.8.

6. Drury, pp.31–6.

7. Curtayn, pp.107–17.

8. Knott, 30 April–11 July 1915.

9. The war-diary of Reginald Ford, IWM 97/16/1.

10. Drury, pp.37–44.

11. Hanna, pp.43–45; Cooper, pp.32–40; Knott, 13–14 July; Kirkpatrick (IWM), pp.8–9; McIlwaine, 3–9 July 1915; Drage, p.104. Also referred to here are the official war-diaries of 10th Division HQ staff, 31st Brigade HQ staff, 54th, 55th and 56th Royal Field Artillery, 5th battalion of the Royal Irish Regiment, 5th and 6th battalions of the Royal Irish Fusiliers, 10th battalion of the Hampshire Regiment, 5th battalion of the Royal Irish Rifles, 6th battalion of the Royal Inniskilling Fusiliers, 65th, 66th and 85th companies of Royal Engineers, the Cyclists Corps, the Veterinary Service and the divisional Medical Service, for the period 27 June –13 July 1915. PRO WO95 4294-6.

12. P. Orr, *The Road to the Somme* (Blackstaff Press,1987), pp. 30–75.

13. The Brett papers, p.5, PRONI T 2967.

14. Drury, pp.45–52.

15. Hanna, pp.43–8, pp.135–140; Laird, p.31.

16. Knott, 17–19 July 1915.

17. McIlwaine, 10–16 July 1915; war-diary of 5th Connaught Rangers , 18 July 1915, PRO WO 95 4294-6.

18. 56th Field Artillery war-diary, 11 July 1915 and 10th Division Veterinary Service war-diary, 10–18 July 1915, PRO WO 95 4294-6; Hargrave (1916), p.35.

19. Curtayn, pp. 118–121 and Kirkpatrick (IWM), pp.9–10.

20. War-diary of 6th Royal Irish Fusiliers, 10–24 July 1915, PRO WO95 4294-6; Drury, p.54; Hanna, p.49.

21. Knott, 24 July 1915.

22. Drury, pp.59–62.

23. Hanna, pp.49–51; McIlwaine, 23–25 July 1915; Interview with Joe o'Leary Jnr.

24. T. Travers, *Gallipoli 1915* (Tempus 2001), pp.97–147.

25. Drury, p.62; Hargrave (1964), p.36.

26. Hanna, pp.51–55; McIlwaine, 25 July 1915.

27. 10th Division HQ war-diary, (Adjutant and Quartermaster's section), the 5th Royal Irish Regiment war-diary, 30th Field Ambulance war-diary and 10th Division Medical Service war-diary, 17 July to 4 August, PRO WO 95 4294-6.

28. Cooper, pp.39–47.

29. Kirkpatrick, pp.11–12; Hargrave (1916), pp.52–5.

30. Juvenis, *Suvla Bay and After* (Hodder and Stoughton 1916), pp.1–5.

31. Hanna, pp.51–7.

32. Drury, pp.63–79.

33. Cooper, pp.48–9.

34. Pearse's speech is given in Sean McMahon, *Rich and Rare* (Poolbeg 1984), p.77–9.

IV. INVADERS

1. J. McIlwaine, 5–6 August 1915; War-diary of 5th Connaught Rangers, 4–7 August 1915, PRO WO95 4294-6.

2. 10th Divisional HQ and 30th Field Ambulance Brigade war-diaries, 4–7 August 1915, PRO WO95 4294-6.

3. Cooper, pp.48–51; Robinson, p.97; Hanna, p.55.

4. Travers, pp. 1–40.

5. *The Dardanelles Commission*, H.M.S.O., 1919.

6. 10th Division HQ war-diary, 6 August 1915, PRO WO 95 4294-6.

7. 10th Division HQ war-diary (Adjutant and Quartermaster's section) 4–6 August 1915, PRO WO 95 4294-6.

8. Drage, pp.104–5.

9. Juvenis, pp.12–16.

10. War-diaries of 5th and 6th Royal Irish Fusiliers, 6–7 August 1915, PRO WO95 4294-6.

11. Kirkpatrick (IWM), pp.14–15.

12. Hanna, pp.59–60.

13. War-diaries of 65th, 66th and 85th Companies of The Royal Engineers, 6–7 August 1915, PRO Wo 95 4294-6.

14. Drury, pp.79–80.

15. Travers, pp.137–47.

16. Drury, pp.80–1.

17. Hanna, pp.59–65; Laird, p.33.

18. Knott, 7 August 1915.

19. Hargrave., (1916), pp.59–74.

20. Drage, p.105.

21. Kirkpatrick (IWM), pp.15–16.

22. Juvenis, pp.16–25.

23. Travers, pp.146–149.

24. Steele and Hart, pp.247–249.

25. Drury, pp.23–25.

26. Hanna, pp.61–81. Tippett and Julien are both seen leading C Company in photos in the Arthur J. England collection, in the Irish National Archive for the World Wars.

27. Laird, pp.34–42; Hanna pp.61–81.

28. Drury, pp.23–25.

29. 30th Brigade HQ war-diary, 7–9 August 1915, PRO WO 95 4294-6. Godfrey Drage's letter to the author of the Official History of The Gallipoli Campaign, Cecil Aspinall-Oglander, is inserted into the war-diary of 7th Munster Fusiliers, PRO Wo 95 4294-6.

30. 5th Royal Irish Regiment and 30th Field Ambulance war-diaries, 7–8 August 1915, PRO WO 95 4294-6.

31. War–diaries of 65th, 66th and 85th companies of The Royal Engineers, 7–8 August, PRO Wo95 4294-6.

32. Kirkpatrick (IWM), pp.16–17.

33. Juvenis, p.26.

34. Drage, pp. 105–6 *and* S. McCance, *History of The Royal Munster Fusiliers*, vol. 2, (Gale and Polden 1927), p.178.

35. *Handbook of The Turkish Army* (Stationery Office, February 1915); K. Fewster, V. Basarin and H.H. Basarin, *Gallipoli – the Turkish story* (Allen and Unwin 2003), pp.95–101, p.106, pp.113–23; Travers, pp.149–151.

36. Travers, pp. 137–162.

37. C.F. Aspinall-Oglander, *Military Operations:Gallipoli* (William Heineman 1932), p.238.

38. H. Kannengiesser, *The Campaign in Gallipoli* (Hutchinson 1927), p.203.

39. Drury, pp.83–86.

40. Juvenis, pp.33–46.

41. War-diary of 31st Field Ambulance Brigade, 8–9 August 1915, PRO Wo 95 4294-6.

42. War-diary of 5th Royal Irish Fusiliers, 8–9 August 1915, PRO WO 95 4294-6.

43. Hanna, pp.83–5.

44. Hargrave (1916), pp.68–91.

45. Kirkpatrick (IWM), pp.17–22.

46. Juvenis, pp.26–33.

47. Drage, pp.102, 106–8.

48. Travers, pp.153–60.

49. Drury, pp.87–92. For details of Jennings' family origins and a church memorial tablet commemorating him in East Bergholt, Suffolk, see *The Blue Cap*, vol. 10, Dec 2003.

50. Laird, pp.43–9.

51. Drury, pp.87-92.

52. Knott, 9 August 1915.

53. 31st Brigade HQ war-diary, 8–10 August 1915, PRO WO95 4294-6.

54. War-diaries of 5th & 6th Royal Irish Fusiliers, 9–10 August 1915, PRO Wo95 4294-6.

55. Juvenis, pp.34–7.

56. Drage, pp.105–10. See also the letter from Drage to C.F. Aspinall written during the process of compiling the Official History of Gallipoli, inserted into the war-diary of 7th Royal Irish Fusiliers PRO Wo 95 4294-6 .

57. Hargrave (1916), pp.110–25.

58. Travers, pp.138–62.

59. Dungan, p.116; Curtayn, pp.121–5.

60. Captain J.J. Kennedy, 'With the 5th Service Battalion During The Great War' in *Sprig of Shillelagh* magazine (Book no. 102 in the Royal Inniskillings Regimental Museum); *The Story of the 6th Service Battalion of The Inniskilling Fusiliers in The Great War* (Book no. 100A in the Inniskillings museum).

V. WARRIORS

1. For the ongoing struggle at 9th Corps HQ see R.R. James, *Gallipoli* (Pimlico 1999).

2. For the mysterious disappearance of the 'Sandringham' Company of a battalion of The Norfolk Regiment, see N. McCrery, *All the King's Men* (Pocket Books 1992).

3. The war-diary of 5th Royal Irish Regiment, 7–10 August 1915, PRO WO 95 4294-6.

4. 30th Field Ambulance Brigade war-diary, 7–10 August 1915, PRO WO 95 4294-6.

5. War-diaries of 65th, 66th and 85th companies of Royal Engineers, 7–10 August 1915, PRO WO95 4294-6.

6. 10th Division HQ war-diary (Adjutant and Quartermaster's section), 7–10 August 1915, PRO WO 95 4294-6.

7. War-diaries of 5th and 6th Battalions, Royal Irish Fusiliers, 10 August 1915, PRO WO 95 4294-6.

8. The Inniskilling officer, J.A.Armstrong, wrote to Captain Cecil Aspinall-Oglander in the mid-1920's. The letter is to be found inserted into the war-diary of 5th Royal Inniskilling Fusiliers PRO WO 95 4294-6.

9. 10th Division Medical Service war-diary, 8–11 August 1915' PRO WO 95 4294-6.

10. Hanna, pp.86–102.

11. Hargrave (1916), p.98.

12. Juvenis, pp.38–60.

13. Drury, pp. 93–102.

14. T. Holt and V. Holt, *Battlefield Guide to Gallipoli* (Leo Cooper 2000), p.226.

15. M. Dungan, *Irish Voices from The Great War* (Irish Academic Press 1995), pp.66–73; Hargrave (1916), pp.66–78.

16. Knott, 12 August 1915.

17. Kirkpatrick (IWM), p.24.

18. War-diary of 30th Field Ambulance Brigade, 14–16 August 1915, PRO WO 95 4294-6.

19. Statistics were hard for the command staff to obtain in the midst of battle but the figures cited here are offered by Lieutenant Colonel The Earl of Granard, the commander of The 5th Royal Irish Regiment, as mentioned in Johnstone, p.138.

20. Johnstone, pp.134–140; MacDonagh, pp.162–6.

21. Drury, 15–16 August 1915 (page references are no longer used by Drury at this stage in the diary).

22. Hanna, pp.98–112; Drury, 15–16 August 1915.

23. Knott, 15–17 August 1915.

24. Ford.

25. Drury, 16–18 August 1915.

26. Knott, 17 August 1915; 31st Field Ambulance Brigade war-diary, 17 August 1915, PRO WO 95 4294-6.

27. The letter, from Inniskilling officer. V.H. Scott, may be found inserted into the official war-diary of 5th Inniskilling Fusiliers. PRO WO 95 4294-6.

28. 10th Division Medical Service war-diary, August 1915, PRO WO 95 4294-6.

29. Hargrave (1916), pp.128–9.

30. Kirkpatrick (IWM), pp.25–40.

31. Juvenis, pp.60–80.

32. The war-diary of 5th Royal Irish Regiment, 17–20 August 1915, PRO WO 95 4294-6.

33. War-diaries of 5th & 6th Royal Irish Fusiliers, 17–20 August 1915, PRO WO 95 4294-6.

34. Hargrave (1964), pp.207, 230.

VI. CASUALTIES

1. PRO 30/57/55 and PRO 30/57/63; 10th Division HQ war-diary, PRO WO 95 4294-6.

2. For a detailed study of The Australasian campaign see L.A.Carlyon, *Gallipoli* (Bantam 2003).

3. Cooper, pp.48–61; the war-diary of 5th Connaught Rangers, 5–12 August 1915, PRO WO 95 4294-6.

4. McIlwaine 6–31 Aug 1915; Cooper, pp.48–75; Robinson, pp.99–101.

5. McIlwaine, 7 Aug to 29 September 1915; Cooper, pp.103–14; Jeremy Stanley, *Ireland's Forgotten Tenth* (Impact 2003), p.48.

6. Jourdain's and Eastwood's letters to Captain Cecil Aspinall-Oglander, during the course of the latter's researches into the campaign, may be found inserted into the 29th Brigade HQ war-diary, PRO WO 95 4294-6.

7. Cooper, pp.133–9.

8. Kerr, pp.170–4.

9. For the larger strategy, co-ordinating the Anzac and Suvla attacks, see Travers, pp.113–76.

10. Drury, 17–22 August 1915.

11. Curtayn, p.129.

12. Drury, 17–22 Aug 1915; Hanna, pp.117–24.

13. Knott, 17–22 Aug 1915.

14. The war-diaries of 56th and 57th Brigades of Royal Field Artillery, 66th Company Royal Engineers and 5th Royal Irish Fusiliers, 19–25 Aug 1915. PRO WO 95 4294-6.

15. C.F.Aspinall-Oglander, *Military Operations: Gallipoli*, vol. 2 (Heineman 1929), p.344; Hans Kannengeiser, *The Campaign in Gallipoli* (Hutchinson 1927), pp.225–6.

16. Drury, 29 September 1915.

17. Rev. Denis Jones, *The Diary of a Padre at Suvla Bay* (Faith Press 1916), pp.67–83.

18. Hargrave (1916), pp. 96–171.

19. Knott, 27 August to 17 September 1915.

20. The war-diary of 30th Brigade HQ and 30th Field Ambulance Brigade, September 1915, PRO WO 95 4294-6.

21. The war-diary of the 10th Division Cyclists' Corps, August-September 1915, PRO WO 95 4294-6.

22. The war-diaries of 30th Field Ambulance Brigade, the three divisional companies of Royal Engineers, the 10th Division's Medical Service and Veterinary Service and 10th Division HQ (Adjutant and quartermaster's section), September 1915, PRO WO 95 4294-6.

23. Laird, pp.49–62.

24. Ford

25. E. Sutton, *The Fitting Out And Administration Of A Hospital Ship* (John Wright and Sons 1918), pp.20–63.

26. Kirkpatrick, (IWM), pp.37–45, 148–63.

27. Juvenis, pp.80–163.

28. 'The Padre', *50,000 miles on a Hospital Ship* (London 1917), pp.44–70.

29. For the changing dynamics of the campaign in The East, see J. Keegan, *The Face of Battle* (Hutchinson 1998).

30. Cooper, pp. 93–131.

31. Drury, 1 Oct 1915.

32. Knott, 28 September to 1 October 1915.

33. The war–diaries of the division's three companies of Royal Engineers, September-December 1915, PRO WO95 4294-6.

34. War-diaries of 5th and 6th Royal Irish Fusiliers, 25 September to 3 October 1915, PRO WO95 4294-6.

35. Cooper, pp.133–9.

36. Hanna, pp.76, 125–7.

37. Hargrave (1916), pp.138–81.

VII. VICTIMS

1. *The Down Recorder*, August 1915.

2. *The Irish Times*, 25 August 1915.

3. *The Irish Times*, 6 September 1915.

4. *The Irish Times*, 18 September 1915.

5. *The Irish Times*, 21 September 1915.

6. *The Irish Independent*, 20 August to 30 September 1915.

7. This letter is in the possession of Michael Lee, Dublin.

8. Findlater, pp.251–64.

9. Major J.A. Armstrong papers IWM P 405.

10. Dungan (1997), p.79; Hanna, p.87.

11. Michael Lee.

12. K. Tynan, *The Years of The Shadow* (Constable 1919), pp.177–8, and *The Wandering Years* (Constable 1922), pp.10–11.

13. *Hansard*, LXXVII, column 221, 21 December 1915; D. Gwynn, *The Life of John Redmond* (Harrap 1932), p.62.

14. *Hansard* Volume LXXVII, columns 1050-1051, 5 January, 1916.

15. *The Northern Whig*, 29 March and 16 April 1916; *The Irish Times*, 4 September, 25 September, 21 December 1915 and 10 January 1916; T. Hennessey, *Dividing Ireland* (Routledge 1998), pp.115–8.

16. Laird, pp.74–6.

17. P. Orr, 'The Road to Belgrade' in A. Gregory and S. Paseta (eds), *Ireland and The Great War* (Manchester University Press 2002), pp.171–89.

18. I. Hutton, *With a Woman's Unit in Serbia, Salonika and Sebastopol* (London 1928), p.44.

19. Orr (2002), p.173.

20. Robinson, p.107.

21. See the preface to Francis Ledwidge, *The Complete Poems* (Goldsmith 1997).

22. Joe O'Leary Jun.

23. *The Blue Cap*, vol. 9, September 2002 and vol. 10, December 2003.

24. Bowman, pp.107–8; Orr (2002), pp.175–6. For the issue of courts–martial and execution in the war see J.Putowski and J. Sykes, *Shot At Dawn* (Leo Cooper 1993).

25. Curtayn, pp.130–46. See the preface and supplementary notes in The Collected Poems for other biographical material mentioned here. The excerpt from Ledwidge's poetry is taken from *Wander Song*.

26. McIlwaine, 28 October 1915.

27. Knott, 28 October 1915; 7 June and 5 August 1916; 15–16 September 1917.

28. For an account of the rising see M. Caulfield, *The Easter Rebellion* (Frederick Muller 1964)

29. Caulfield, p.137; *The Sinn Féin Rebellion Handbook* (Weekly Irish Times 1916), pp.18, 56, 270.

30. *The Rebellion Handbook*, p.2.

31. Caulfield, p.184.

32. Laird, pp.77–87.

33. *The Rebellion Handbook*, pp. 60–166.

34. Caulfield, pp. 77, 185.

35. Caulfield, p.354.

36. Orr (2002), p.183.

37. Quoted in Dungan (1997), p.30.

38. Curtayn, pp.150–97. See the preface and supplementary notes in The Collected Poems for further biographical detail mentioned here. The quotations are taken from the following poems: *Manchester, The Lure, Ireland,* and *The Irish In Gallipoli.*

39. Stanley, pp.78–92.

40. Those sources that suggest 50,000 to 60,000 Irish Great War fatalities (including the figure engraved on the Irish War Memorial at Islandbridge, Dublin) are probably choosing to record the numbers who died in Irish Regiments, although by the end of the war the majority of these troops were in fact full of non-Irish soldiers. On the other hand Irishmen died in a great number of other non-Irish regiments and indeed tens of thousands of emigrant Irishmen were to be found not just in British divisions but in ANZAC, American and Canadian ranks. The current consensus among scholars is that up to 35,000 Irishmen died. A similar consensus exists concerning the (approx.) 200,000 demobilized Irish soldiers. My estimate of 4,000 deaths among 9,000 Gallipoli casualties is based on the assumption that the common estimate that one in three Great War casualties was a fatality would be too conservative, in a campaign where medical care was particularly limited and where few prisoners were taken by the Turks.

41. Michael Lee; *The Bluecap*, vol.10, December 2003.

42. Findlater, p.263.

43. *The Blue Cap*, vol. 9, September 2002.

44. Paddy Hand.

45. Joe O'Leary Jun.

VIII. GHOSTS

1. For an account of Irish from 1918 to 1923 see F.S.L. Lyons, *Ireland Since The Famine* (William Collins 1974), pp. 381–470. The poem quoted here is in a POW diary held in Down Museum, Downpatrick.

2. Cooper, p.23; Dungan (1997), p.41. The RTÉ documentary 'Sown in Tears and Blood' suggests that 100 Irish ex-soldiers were killed by the IRA during the War of Independence.

3. J.McDermott, *Northern Divisions – the old IRA and the Belfast Pogroms 1920–22* (Beyond the Pale Publications 2001), pp.70–1. McCartney is identified as a Gallipoli veteran by Barry McCaffery in *The Irish News,* 12 November 2003.

4. Paddy Hand.

5. Joe O'Leary Jnr; *The Fingal Independent,* 7 & 14 May 2004.

6. Findlater, p.260; Interview with Kevin Myers, Dublin.

7. Michael Lee.

8. Robinson, pp. 117–83.

9. Laird (1925), preface.

10. Interview with Martin Staunton, Geneva; K. Jeffery, *Ireland and the Great War* (Cambridge University Press 2000), p.112.

11. M. Fraser, *John Bull's Other Homes – state housing and British policy in Ireland 1883-1922* (Liverpool University Press 1996) pp.240–71.

12. Information on this example of a local 'Dardanelles' through conversations with a number of local people in the vicinity of Delvin, Co. Westmeath, 2002–3.

13. RTÉ documentary, 'Sown in Tears and Blood', 1998.

14. J.W. Todd, *A Short History Of The Leopardstown Park Hospital Trust 1917-1987* (n.p., n.d.).

15. J. Bourke, 'Shell-shock, psychiatry and the Irish soldier during the First World War' in Gregory, pp.155–70.

16. Jeffery, pp.107–33.

17. Interview with Tom Burke, Dublin.

18. N.C. Johnson, *Ireland, the Great War and the Geography of Remembrance* (Cambridge University Press 2003) pp.80–111.

19. Jeffery, pp.107–33.

20. J. Loughrin, 'Mobilising the sacred dead: Ulster Unionism, the Great War and the politics of remembrance' in Gregory, pp.133–50; Interview with Mr Tom Burke, Dublin.

21. For further details see Jane Leonard, *The culture of war commemoration* (Cultures of Ireland 1996).

22. Michael Lee.

23. For further information see D. Robertson, *Deeds Not Words* (n.p., 1998).

24. Michael Lee.

25. Paddy Hand.

26. Todd, p.25.

27. Harris, p.209.

28. For information on Hargrave see website www.kibbokift.org

29. Drury's clippings can be found, in loose leaf form, inserted throughout his war-diary.

30. A copy of a signed menu card from this reunion dinner can be located in The Royal Inniskillings Museum in Enniskillen, Co. Fermanagh. (no file reference no. offered).

31. For further details on Kirkpatrick's career see I. Kirkpatrick, *The Inner Circle* (Macmillan 1959).

32. See bibliography for a list of relevant publications.

33. Interview with Michael Gill, Dublin.

34. E. Curtis, *A History of Ireland* (Methuen 1936), p.406.

35. D. McArdle, *The Irish Republic* (The Irish Press 1951), pp.116–21.

36. See Professor Donal McCartney's chapter on the period of Irish history from 1891 to 1921 in T.W. Moody and F.X. Martin (eds), *The Course of Irish History* (Mercier 1984).

37. Michael Lee.

38. Harris, p.211; C.S. Andrews, *Dublin Made Me* (Mercier 1979), p.78.

39. For further detail on 'the Troubles', which erupted in Northern Ireland in 1969, see W.D. Flackes and S. Elliot, *Northern Ireland: A Political Directory 1968-1999* (Blackstaff 1999).

40. Todd, p.22.

41. For the 'poppy day' bomb and its aftermath see *The Irish Times* and the *Irish Independent*, 8–18 November 1987.

42. For a sense of Ulster's annual remembrance culture see a range of Northern Ireland's local newspapers during November of any year.

43. Michael Lee.

44. For a study of the northern peace process see D. de Breadun, *The Far Side Of Revenge – making peace in Northern Ireland* (Collins 2001).

45. Orr (2002) pp.185–7.

46. B. McCaffery, 'The fighting race respects its dead', *The Irish News*, 12 November 2003.

47. The ceremony for The National Day of Commemoration, held on 11 July 2004 at the Royal Hospital, Kilmainham, was a multi-faith event and included prayers by a Jewish Rabbi and an Islamic cleric.

48. The RTÉ documentary 'Sown in Tears and Blood' offers detail about the rebirth of Islandbridge and the restorations in Bandon and Limerick. The Royal Dublin Fusiliers Association publish a magazine entitled *The Blue Cap* whilst other Irish Regimental Associations have now been formed, including The Leinster Regiment Association, The Connaught Rangers Association and The Royal Munster Fusiliers Association.

49. Extended, scholarly work on the regional impact of The Great War in Ireland had an early and accomplished exponent in David Fitzpatrick. See D. Fitzpatrick, *Politics and Irish Life 1913-1921* (Gill and Macmillan 1977). A detailed coverage of the 16th and 36th Divisions appeared towards the end of the 1980s and in the early 1990s. See T. Denman, *Ireland's Unknown Soldiers* (Irish Academic Press 1992) and P. Orr, *The Road to the Somme* (Blackstaff Press 1987). In subsequent years, see T. Johnstone, *Orange, Green and Khaki* (Gill and Macmillan 1992), T. Dooley, *Irishmen or English Soldiers?* (Liverpool University Press 1995), M. Dungan, *Irish Voices from The Great War* (Four Courts Press 1995) and *They Shall Grow Not Old* (Four Courts Press 1997), K. Jeffery, *Ireland and the Great War* (Cambridge University Press 2000), T. Bowman, *Irish Regiments in the Great War* (Manchester University Press 2003) and A. Gregory and S. Paseta (eds), *Ireland and the Great War* (Manchester University Press 2002). Special study of the 10th Division has been represented by J. Stanley, *Ireland's Forgotten 10th* (Impact 2003).

50. The lyrics of the Irish folk-song called 'The Foggy Dew' are quoted here. The song heard by Behan is noted in McDermott, p.71. For information on McCartney's grave see also interview with Bobby Devlin, Belfast.

51. The song 'The Band Played Waltzing Matilda' by Eric Bogle appeared on the CD *Rum, Sodomy and The Lash* by The Pogues, 1985. The film *Gallipoli,* directed by Peter Weir and starring Mel Gibson, was released in the early 1982. See also B. Gammage, *The Story of Gallipoli: the Film about the men who made the legend* (Ringwood, Victoria 1981) p.144.

52. T. Holt and V. Holt, *Battlefield Guide to Gallipoli* (Leo Cooper 2000) pp.249–52.

53. Tom Burke.

54. Information on the Gallipoli peninsula today was gained during a visit to Turkey in 2004, in the company of Brian Wilson, Killyleagh, County Down.

55. For further information on the culture of commemoration see N. C. Johnson, *Ireland, the Great War and the Geography of Remembrance* (Cambridge University Press 2003); F. Brearton, *The Great War in Irish Poetry* (Oxford University Press 2000) and J. Winter, *Sites of Memory, Sites of Mourning* (Cambridge University Press 1995).

56. Information courtesy of Somme Heritage Centre, Newtownards, Co. Down.

57. Laird, p.61.

BIBLIOGRAPHY AND SOURCES

PUBLISHED AND RECORDED WORKS

Andrews, C.S., *Dublin Made Me* (Mercier 1979).

Aspinall-Oglander, C.F., *Military Operations:Gallipoli*, vol. 2 (William Heinemann 1932).

Ayliffe, R. et al., *The Rough Guide to Turkey*, 5th edn (Rough Guides 2003).

Bartlett, T. and K. Jeffery (eds), *A Military History of Ireland* (Cambridge University Press 1996).

Beckett, F.C., *The Making of Modern Ireland* (Faber and Faber 1966).

Bence-Jones, M., *Twilight of the Ascendency* (Mercier 1967).

Bowman, T., *Irish Regiments in the Great War* (Manchester University Press 2003).

Brearton, F., *The Great War in Irish Poetry* (Oxford University Press 2000).

Carlyon, L.A., *Gallipoli* (Doubleday, 2002).

Caulfield, M., *The Easter Rebellion* (Frederick Muller 1964).

Cooper, B., *The Tenth (Irish) Division in Gallipoli* (Irish Academic Press 1993).

Curtayne, A., *Francis Ledwidge: A Life of the Poet* (Martin, Brian and O'Keeffe 1972).

Curtis, E., *A History of Ireland* (Methuen 1936).

Dardanelles Commission, *Final Report of the Dardanelles Commission* (HMSO 1919).

Denman, T., *Ireland's Unknown Soldiers:The 16th(Irish)Division in the Great War 1914-1918* (Irish Academic Press 1992).

Dooley, T.P., *Irishmen or English Soldiers?* (Liverpool University Press 1995).

Drage, G., *From Chindwin to Criccieth* (Evans 1956).

Dungan, M., *They Shall Grow Not Old: Irish Soldiers and the Great War* (Four Courts Press 1997).

Dungan, M., *Irish Voices form the Great War* (Irish Academic Press 1995).

Ferguson, N., *The Pity Of War* (Penguin 1999).

Fewster, K., V. Basarin and H.H. Basarin, *Gallipoli – the Turkish Story* (Allen and Unwin 2003).

Findlater, A., *Findlaters – The Story of a Dublin Merchant Family 1774-2001* (A&A Farmar 2001).

Fitzpatrick, D., *Politics and Irish Life 1913-1921* (Gill and Macmillan 1977).

Flackes, W.D. and S. Elliot, *Northern Ireland: A Political Directory 1968–1999* (Blackstaff 1999).

Foster, R., *Modern Ireland 1600-1972* (Allen Lane, Penguin 1988).

Fraser, M., *John Bull's Other Homes – State Housing and British Policy in Ireland, 1883-1922* (Liverpool University Press 1996).

Fussell, P., *The Great War and Modern Memory* (Oxford University Press 1975).

Gammage, B., D. Williamson and P. Weir, *The Story of Gallipoli: The Film About The Men who Made a Legend* (Ringwood, Victoria 1981).

Gregory, A. and S. Paseta (eds), *Ireland and the Great War* (Manchester University Press 2002).

Gwynn, D., *The Life of John Redmond* (George C.Harrap 1932).

Handbook of the Turkish Army (Stationery Office Feb. 1915).

Hanna, H., KC, *The Pals at Suvla Bay* (E.Ponsonby 1916).

Hargrave, J., *At Suvla Bay* (Constable 1916).

Hargrave, J., *The Suvla Bay Landing* (Macdonald 1964).

Harris, H., *The Irish Regiments in the First World War* (Mercier 1968).

Haythornthwaite, P., *Gallipoli 1915 – Frontal Assault on Turkey* (Osprey 1991).

Hennessy, T., *Dividing Ireland* (Routledge 1998).

Holt, T. and V. Holt, *Battlefield Guide to Gallipoli* (Leo Cooper 2000).

Hutton, I., *With a Womens' Unit in Serbia, Salonica and Sebastopol* (London 1928).

James, R.R., *Gallipoli* (Pimlico 1999).

Johnson, N.C., *Ireland, The Great War and the Geography of Remembrance* (Cambridge University Press 2003).

Jones, D (Rev.), *The Diary of a Padre at Suvla Bay* (Faith Press 1916).

Juvenis, *Suvla Bay and After* (Hodder and Stoughton 1916).

Kannengiesser, H., *The Campaign in Gallipoli* (Hutchinson 1927).

Keegan, J., *The First World War* (Hutchinson 1998).

Kirkpatrick, I., *The Inner Circle* (Macmillan 1959).

Laird, F., *Personal Experiences of the Great War* (Eason & Son 1925).

Ledwidge, F., *The Complete Poems* (The Goldsmith Press 1997).

Leonard, J., *The Culture of War Commemoration* (Cultures of Ireland 1996).

Lyons, F.S.L., *Ireland Since the Famine* (William Collins 1974).

MacArdle, D., *The Irish Republic* (The Irish Press 1951).

MacLeod, J., *Remembering Gallipoli* (Manchester University Press 2004).

McCance, S.,*The History of the Royal Munster Fusiliers*, vol. 2 (Gale and Polden 1927).

McCrery, N., *All the King's Men* (Pocket Books 1992).

McDermott, J., *Northern Divisions – the Old IRA and the Belfast Pogroms 1920-22* (Beyond the Pale Publications 2001).

McMahon, S., *Rich and Rare* (Poolbeg Press 1984).

Moody, T.W. and F.X. Martin, *The Course of Irish History* (Mercier 1984).

Moorehead, A., *Gallipoli* (Hamish Hamilton 1956).

Orr, P., *The Road to the Somme* (Blackstaff Press 1987).

Parnell Kerr, S., *What the Irish Regiments Have Done* (Unwin 1916).

Padre, the, *50,000 Miles on a Hospital Ship* (Religious Tract Society 1917).

Putowski J. and J.Sykes, *Shot at Dawn* (Leo Cooper 1993).

Robinson, L., *Bryan Cooper* (Constable 1931).

Robertson, D., *Deeds not Words* (n.p. 1998).

Simkins, P., *Kitchener's Army: The Raising of the New Armies 1914-1916* (Manchester University Press 1988).

Sinn Féin Rebellion Handbook (The Weekly Irish Times 1916).

Stanley, J., *Ireland's Forgotten 10th* (Impact 2003).

Steele, N. and P.Hart, *Defeat at Gallipoli* (Macmillan 1985).

Stewart, A.T.Q., *The Ulster Crisis* (Faber and Faber 1967).

The Story of the 6th Service Battalion of the Inniskilling Fusiliers in the Great War (Enniskillen 1919).

Sutton, E., *The Fitting Out and Administration of a Hospital Ship* (John Wright and Sons 1918).

Todd, J.W., *A Short History Of The Leopardstown Park Hospital Trust 1917-1987* (n.p., n.d.).

Travers, T., *Gallipoli 1915* (Tempus 2001).

Tynan, K., *The Years of the Shadow* (Constable 1919).

Tynan, K., *The Wandering Years* (Constable 1922).

Winter, J., *Sites of Memory, Sites of Mourning: the Great War in European Cultural History* (Cambridge University Press 1995).

MANUSCRIPT SOURCES

Imperial War Museum, London –

War-diary of William Knott IWM P305,

War-diary of Jim McIlwaine IWM 96/29/1,

War-diary of Ivone Kirkpatrick IWM79/50/1,

War-diary of Reginald Ford IWM 97/16/1,

Armstrong Papers IWM P405,

The National Army Museum, London –

The Drury Papers NAM 7607-69-1

The National Archive, London –

Papers found at PRO WO 162/20, PRO WO162/24, PRO 30/57/55, PRO 30/57/63, and PRo WO95 4294-4296

Public Record Office for Northern Ireland –

Charles Brett Papers PRONI T2067

NEWSPAPERS, MAGAZINES AND OFFICIAL PUBLICATIONS

The Irish News

The Irish Times

The Down Recorder

The Blue Cap

History Ireland

War and Society

The Fingal Independent

The Northern Whig

The Irish Independent

Sprig of Shillelagh

Hansard Vol LXXVII

INTERVIEWS

Paddy Hand, Joe O'Leary, Michael Lee, Tom Egginton, Kevin Myers, Michael Gill, Tom Burke, Bobby Devlin.

INDEX

A Beach 68, 72–3, 79, 84, 85, 91, 98,
101, 107, 112–14, 116, 119, 139,
150, 158, 159, 172, 236
A Beach West 73, 76–8, 84, 92, 111,
126, 133, 151, 172
Abbey Theatre 24
Abbiseyah, S.S. 170
Achi Baba 70
Aegean, The 120, 151, 234, 235
Africa 10, 45, 46, 47, 48
Agamemnon 77, 172
Aghyll Dere 140, 147, 148
Aisne Canal 29
Alaunia, S.S. 41, 44–6, 52, 56, 57, 71,
151
Alexander, Major 27
Alexandra Basin 30
Alexandria 45, 46, 48, 52, 64, 159,
163, 164, 191, 193
Algeria 47
Allah 125, 233
Allenby, General 201
America 9, 16, 20, 201
Amiens Street 15
Anafarta 86, 157, 159, 171, 181
Ancre, River 218
Anglo–Irish Treaty 213
Anzac 4, 54, 87, 94, 121, 140–1,
142–3, 145–6, 147–9, 150, 167–8,
178, 180, 188–90, 193, 197, 202,
209, 230–1
Anzac Cove 4, 54, 58, 66–7, 68, 70,
74, 139, 140, 145–6, 166, 167, 168,
176, 217, 228, 230, 232, 235
Anzac Day 222
Anzac Sector 49, 105, 140, 142, 145,
148, 149, 177
Aquitania, S.S. 163–4
Arabian Nights, The 48
Arbour Hill 196, 197
Argonauts 166, 168, 234
Ariel 172
Armagh 15
Armenia 55, 86
Armistice 3, 186, 202, 214
Armstrong, Major 187
Asia 54, 55
Asmak Dere 140
Athlone 168, 185, 209
Atlantic 1, 10, 25, 42
Atlas Mountains 47
Aughavanagh 187
Australia 5, 16, 49, 58, 66, 96, 140–1,

142, 149, 161, 164, 172, 222, 228,
230–2
Austro–Hungary 166, 202

B Beach 72–3, 75, 79, 90–1, 113,
115, 153
Bachelor's Walk 12, 25
Baldoyle 40
Balkans 57, 140, 191–2, 231–2
Ball, C.F. 14, 82, 96, 237, 242, 244
Ballanboyne 219
Ballee 180
Ballina 168
Ballykinler 209
Ballymena 14
Bandon 44, 227
Barry, Tom 214
Basingstoke 36–40, 42–3, 48, 60, 80,
119, 198, 220
Bavaria 9
Beard, Paddy 126
Beckett, J.C. 225
Beggar's Bush 195, 196
Behan, Brendan 228
Belfast 11, 13, 19, 24, 43, 101, 183,
189, 192, 199, 209, 213, 215, 226,
228, 229, 238, 243
Belfast Agreement, The 226
Belgium 22, 224, 226
Belgrade 170
Bellview 223
Birr 26
Biscay, Bay of 44, 46, 163
Black and Tans 209
Black Sea 57
Blackrock 162, 223
Bloom, Leopold 235
Boers 41
Bogle, Eric 229
Bornu, S.S. 46
Bosphorus 235
Bournemouth 39
Brady, Joseph 16, 33
Bray 220
Brett, C. 43–4
Brian Boru 48
Bridewell 196
Bristol 20
Britain 3, 8–10, 21, 27, 46, 48, 56,
110, 111, 192, 194, 208, 213, 214,
127, 222–5, 233
British Expeditionary Force 29

British Graves Registration Unit 236
British War Graves Commission 231
Brooke, Rupert 227
Broussa Gendarmerie 86
Browning, Frank (or Browning, F.E.)
13, 30, 195–6, 206
Bryan, Corporal 126
Buckinghamshire 162
Bulgaria 166–7, 191, 192
Burke, Captain F.C. 185
Byng, Sir Julian 50, 139
Byrne, P. 184
Byrne, Stuffer 28, 150, 169
Byzantium 230, 235

C Beach 72, 75, 79, 112–13, 118,
157, 237
Cairo 193, 198, 206
California 20
Camberley 24
Camberwell 29
Cameron, Ewen 185
Cape Helles 49, 55, 70, 87, 138, 150,
160, 170, 188, 191, 228, 235
Carlow 26
Carlow, Co. 221
Carpathia, S.S. 44
Carr, M. 184
Carson, Sir Edward 12, 21–2
Carter Family 39–40, 62
Carter, Second Lieutenant R.W. 117
Castlebar 14
Castletown House 183
Cathleen ni Houlihan 199
Cavan 228
Cavan, Co. 210, 229
Celtic F.C. 101
Chadwick's Big Circus 180
Charak Chesme 113–14
Chocolate Hill 72, 79–80, 81–3, 87,
88–90, 114, 156, 158, 160
Christie, Robert 24, 29, 39, 47, 101,
192, 199
Chunuk Bair 107, 142, 144, 180,
232, 236
Church Street Bridge 195
Churchill, Winston 6, 26
Churchtown Road 171
Civil War 212, 219, 223, 229
Clacton, S.S. 66
Clare 19
Clarke, Harry 216

Clarke, Sergeant 56
Clery, Lieutenant 117
Clones 16
Clongowes Wood College 14, 191
Coldwell, Ernest 16
College Green 218
Collins, Michael 209
Colt Automatic Pistol 118
Commons, House of 189
Communism 235
Connaught 10, 19, 38
Connaught Rangers (or The
   Connaughts) 10, 11, 13, 16, 17,
   23, 28–9, 40, 41, 52, 66, 67, 104,
   141, 144–7, 149, 150, 168, 184,
   192, 210, 212, 218, 229
Connolly, James 12, 31, 181, 194
Connolly, R. 184
Constantinople 7, 49, 154, 189, 202,
   235
Conyngham Arms Hotel 199
Cooney, John 17
Cooper, Bryan 18, 19, 23, 28, 36, 42,
   54, 67, 141, 142, 144, 145, 149,
   167, 170, 191, 197, 212, 217, 223,
   234, 241
Cooper, Brigadier R.J. 13, 58
Cork 23, 155, 217
Cork, Co. 43, 44, 227
Cosgrove, J. 184
Cowley Barracks 20
Cox, Colonel Paddy 27, 95, 124, 151
Coyle, P. 184
Craigavon Hospital 215
Cregagh 213
Crete 51
Crête Simonet 192
Cromwell's Fort 10
Crusaders 168, 234
Cuchulain 8
Cullen, 'Fritz' 122
Cullinan, Captain 93
Cunard 1, 41, 164
Curragh 18, 21, 23, 25, 26, 27, 30
Curtis, Edmund 223
Curzon, Lord 59
Cut, The 80, 88, 108, 236
Cyclists Corps 159
Cyprus 231

Daedalus, Stephen 235
Dáil, The 208, 210, 212, 213
Dalton, Emmet 214
Dame Street 18
Danube, River 57
Dardanelles, The 1–4, 7, 27, 37, 49,
   70, 150, 152, 167, 174, 183, 188,
   191, 193, 198, 213, 214, 219, 232,
   235, 238, 245

Dardanelles, The (Ireland) 5,
   213–14, 238
Darius 172
Davis, Thomas 149, 170
Dawson Street 195
De Lisle, Maj. General Beauvoir
   138–9
de Valera, Eamon 211, 212, 217, 219,
   223
Dead Man's Gully 146
Deegan, M. 184
Dehaney, P. 184
Delvin 214
Devas, Father Charles Henry 152,
   201
Devon 14
Devonport 41, 42, 43
Devoy, Sergeant 191
Dillon, John 189
Dollymount 28, 74
Donegal 14, 199
Donnybrook 211
Doughty, J. 184
Down Hunt Hotel 11
Down Recorder 181
Down, Co. 11, 180, 181, 209, 221
Downey, Private Patrick 192
Downpatrick 11
Downpatrick Hospital 180
Downside 24
Doyle, A. 184
Doyle, Father 20
Doyle, T. 184
Drage, Captain Godfrey 20–1, 25,
   42, 69–70, 76, 83, 84–5, 93, 99
Drury, Noel 17, 23, 27–8, 30, 38–9,
   41, 44–5, 47–8, 50, 56–7, 71, 73–4,
   79–80, 83, 88–9, 94–7, 117–19,
   122, 123–7, 150–2, 154, 169, 198,
   201, 221, 223
Dublin 2, 9, 11, 12, 14, 16, 17, 18,
   20, 21, 24, 25, 27, 28, 29–31, 32,
   40, 54, 64, 65, 70, 74, 80, 81, 82,
   94, 95, 97, 115, 122, 124, 125, 126,
   127, 133, 165, 171, 181, 182, 183,
   185, 187, 188, 194, 195, 196, 197,
   201, 202, 203, 208, 210, 213, 214,
   215, 216, 218, 219, 220, 222, 228,
   233, 234, 241, 244
Dublin, Co. 15, 18, 162, 202
Duncairn Gardens 199
Dundalk 26, 183, 234
Dunluce Castle, S.S. 203
Dunne, M. 184
Dunphy's Corner 80, 119
Dunsany, Lord 17, 24, 39, 61, 193,
   195, 200, 222

11th Division 58, 68, 71–2, 74–5, 76,
   79–80, 81, 82, 85, 88, 89, 93, 94,
   95, 96, 100, 110, 118, 150, 152, 172
88th Field Company, Royal
   Engineers 170
East Anglia 20, 110
East Lancashire Regiment 144
Easter Rising (or Easter 1916) 190,
   194–5, 198, 199, 200, 203, 206,
   210, 224, 228, 234
Eastwood, F.E. 148
Eastwood, Colonel William 143, 183
Egerdir 86
Egypt 46, 47, 48, 50, 51, 52, 54, 84,
   92, 101, 102, 125, 150, 159, 160,
   162, 163, 179, 191, 192, 193
Elector, S.S. 66
Ellesmere Avenue 29
Elliott, T.C.M. 123, 136, 184
Ellis, W. 184
Elvery, Private 45
England 2, 10, 11, 16, 19, 20, 24, 26,
   28, 29, 39, 42, 77, 162, 163, 168,
   193, 194, 198, 199, 203, 214, 221,
   228
English Channel 42, 43
Enniskerry 14
Enniskillen 218, 225
Essex Regiment 112
Eton 18
Europe 2, 5, 9, 10, 26, 27, 31, 48, 59,
   70, 167, 202, 216, 217, 222, 231,
   232, 234, 235, 237
European Community 226
Everett, Lieutenant 111
Exeter 41

53rd Division 110, 112, 114, 117,
   150
54th Division 110, 111, 112, 150
59th Division 197
5th Battalion Leinster Regiment 141
5th Battalion Royal Inniskilling
   Fusiliers 17, 24, 29, 76, 83, 91,
   101, 113, 187, 222
5th Battalion Royal Irish Regiment
   52, 90, 97, 112, 133, 161
Fahey, M. 184
Fallon, J. 184
Falls Road 228
Farm, The 144, 147
Farrell, T. 184
Fashum, J.L.G. 33
Feeney, M. 184
Fenian (or Fenian Brotherhood) 59,
   181, 228, 229
Fianna Fáil 212, 219
Findlater Family 15, 186–7, 202
Findlater, Alex 15, 186

Findlater, Charles 202
Findlater, Herbet 186–7
First World War *see* Great War
Fitzgibbon, J. 14
Fitzgibbon, M. 14, 34, 123, 136
Flanders 26, 44, 50, 190, 200, 214, 218, 224, 234
Flynn, M. 184
Fogarty, Lily 193
Ford, Reginald 14, 40–1, 124–5, 137, 162
Fortnum and Mason 117
Foster, Roy 225
Four Courts 30, 196, 219
Fox, Frank 210
Foxhound, H.M.S. 124, 151
France 9, 25, 26, 29, 44, 50, 139, 165, 168, 190, 196, 201, 202, 210, 211, 217, 218, 219, 231, 234
Franz Ferdinand, Archduke 10

Gallipoli 1–5, 6–7, 22, 41, 43, 49, 52, 54, 55, 65, 67, 68, 70–1, 76, 84, 85, 89, 102, 104–05, 115, 116, 118, 119, 120, 122, 127, 129, 130, 134, 138, 139, 140, 141, 143, 145, 146, 147, 148, 149, 150, 151, 153, 154, 156, 158, 160, 162, 164, 165, 167–8, 169, 170, 171, 172, 174, 176, 179, 181, 183, 184, 186, 187, 188, 189, 190, 191–2, 194, 195, 197, 199, 200, 201, 202, 203, 206–07, 208, 209, 210, 211, 212, 213, 214, 217, 218, 219, 220–1, 222–4, 225, 227, 228–9, 230, 231–3, 234–5, 236–8, 241–3
Gallogher, N. 184
Galway 10, 11, 23, 28, 29
Galway, Co. 10, 16, 17
Gannon, D. 184
Gara, D. 184
General Post Office (or GPO) 194, 195, 198, 223
Georgian, S.S. 43
Georgius Rex 195
Gibraltar 1, 43, 44–6, 166
Giza 162
Gladstone, W.E. 85
Glasgow 24
Glasnevin 80, 181
Glavey, Private 168
Glencoe 41
Godley, General Sir Alex 140
Gordon, General 12
Gore, Colonel 99
Grafton Street 14
Great War 1, 4, 5, 190, 192, 202, 204–05, 209, 210, 212, 213, 214, 216, 217, 218, 219, 220, 221, 222, 223, 223, 224, 225, 226, 227, 228,

229, 231, 233, 237, 238, 241
Greece 149, 231, 232
Greek Islands 52, 54, 56, 66, 111, 112, 115, 119, 168, 237
Green Hill 72, 79, 82, 85, 87, 90, 97, 100, 112, 115, 143, 153–4, 180, 181, 231, 235–6
Gulf of Saros 154
Gurkhas 142, 147

Hackwood 36, 38
Hall, Thomas 219
Hamersley, General 79
Hamilton, Ernest 34
Hamilton, Sir Ian 27, 50, 57, 58, 87, 93, 111, 138–9, 167, 186, 211, 222
Hampshire 36–7, 39, 62
Hampshire Regiment 13, 41, 67, 142, 143–4
Hand, Bartholomew 14, 203, 210–11, 220–1
Hand, Paddy (or 'Paddy') 220–1
Hanna, Henry 222, 234
Harbinson Family 57
Harbinson, William 229
Harrison, Major 122
Harrison, W. 40
Hickie, General 216, 217
Hickman, Poole 16, 34, 122, 135, 186, 219
Hill 10 79–81, 88
Hill 60 145, 168
Hill, Brigadier General F.F. 13, 79
Hitler, Adolf 222
Holland 9
Holyhead 20, 30, 31
Home Counties 21
Home Defence Force Volunteers 195
Home Guard 221
Homer 3, 234
Honeysuckle, S.S. 70, 236
Howth 25

Iberia 146
Imbros 51–2, 58, 67, 68, 71, 151, 155, 157, 179, 236
Imperial War Museum 223
India 8, 10, 13, 25, 101, 115, 156, 201, 230, 177
Indian Supply and Transport Corps 113, 128, 156
Ipswich 42
Ireland 2, 4, 5, 8–10, 11, 14, 16, 17, 19, 20, 21, 22, 24, 26, 27, 29, 31, 35, 38, 39, 42, 43, 57, 58, 59, 70, 115, 117, 123, 133, 139, 149–50, 165, 167, 168, 170, 180, 182, 183, 185, 189–90, 194, 195, 198, 199,

200, 201, 202, 203, 208, 209, 210, 211, 213, 214, 215, 216, 217, 219, 220, 222, 223, 224, 225, 226, 227, 228, 229, 230, 231, 232, 233, 234, 235, 237, 238
Irish Brigade 9, 67, 141, 160, 170
Irish Citizens' Army 194
Irish Free State 3, 4, 209, 211, 223, 240
Irish Gardening 14
Irish Guards 13
Irish Independent (or *The Independent*) 183, 185, 188
Irish National Museum 227
Irish National Volunteers 12, 17, 40, 181, 194, 229
Irish News, The 11, 26
Irish Parliamentary Party 9, 14, 188, 208
Irish Republic 194, 197, 223, 224, 225
Irish Republican Army (or IRA) 208, 209, 210, 213, 214, 218, 224–5, 226, 228, 229, 243
Irish Rugby Football Union 13, 30
Irish Sea 1, 11, 19, 30, 31, 202, 209, 233
Irish Times, The 19, 30, 181–2, 189, 190, 195
Islam 85, 86, 202, 230, 232–3, 243
Islandbridge 216–17, 220, 225, 227, 244
Isle of Man 70
Ismail Oglu Tepe 94, 96
Italy 217

Jammet's Restaurant 27
Jennings, Major 95, 117
Jephson, Major 122, 184
Jephson's Post 84, 119
Johnson, Lieutenant 168
Jones, Rev. Davis 155
Jonquil 69, 79
Jourdain, Colonel H.F.N. 10, 16–17, 19, 144, 147–8, 192
Joyce, James 235
Julien, Lieutenant Ernest 16, 81, 82, 185
Juvenis *see also* MacWilliams, Lieutenant O.G.E. 55–6, 70, 77–8, 84, 89, 92, 98–9, 116–17, 130–3, 163–5, 183, 223, 234

Kabak Kuye Wells 145–6, 185
Kannengiesser, Hans 87–8
Karakol Dagh 151
Kelly, Private 171
Kemikli Burnu 1, 3

Kenny, Sergeant 123
Kent, Eammon 197
Kerr, Parnell 31
Kerry, Co. 20, 25
Keyham 41, 43
Khandahar 17
Khartoum 12
Kibbo Kift 221
Kidney Hill 93, 98–9, 122–3, 128, 130
Kilcullen 23
Kildare 23, 25, 26
Kildare, Co. 18, 21, 24, 27, 30, 190, 212
Killaloe 48
Killester 213
Killiney 74
Killyleagh 180
Kilmainham 197, 199, 216
King George V 37–8, 43, 221
King's Own Scottish Borderers 12, 25, 95
Kingstown 20, 195, 199
Kinsale 14, 43
Kiretch Tepe 68, 72–3, 76, 79, 83, 85, 91–3, 98, 101, 109, 111, 112, 113, 115, 118, 121, 127, 128, 130, 133, 134, 143, 151, 162, 180, 182, 184, 186, 236
Kirkpatrick, Ivone 24, 38, 42, 47, 55, 70, 76–7, 84, 91–2, 120, 128–9, 163, 185, 222
Kitchener, Lord 2, 9, 37, 38, 55, 138–9, 156, 167
Kitchener's Army 12, 14, 16, 21, 22, 37, 42, 49, 50, 54, 110
Knott, Private William 19, 30, 40, 41–2, 46, 48, 75, 76, 97, 120, 124, 127, 153, 157, 169, 193, 223, 233
Koran 232
Kosturino 191, 192
Krini, S.S. 91–2

Laird, Frank 14, 25–6, 37, 46, 75, 82, 95–6, 109, 161–2, 190–1, 196–7, 212, 237
Lake District 19
Lala Baba 72, 74, 78, 80, 102, 112, 151, 159, 174, 178, 231, 236, 237, 244
Lansdowne Road 13, 14, 16, 32, 81, 219
Lappinduff 210, 228
Larkin, James 16
Lausanne, Treaty of 231
League Against Imperialism, The 218
Ledwidge, Francis 17, 24, 29, 39–40, 47, 62, 101, 191, 192, 194, 195,

197, 198–201, 222
Lee Enfield Rifles 22
Lee Family 15, 186, 220, 223
Lee Senior, Mr 186, 220
Lee, Ernest 202, 223
Lee, Joseph 33, 182, 186, 202, 223
Lee, Michael 225
Lee, Tennyson 186, 202, 203, 211
Leinster Regiment (also The Leinsters) 13, 16, 20, 22, 26, 66, 67, 141–2, 143, 192
Leinster, S.S. 202
Lemass, Seán 224
Lemnos 43, 51, 52–3, 54, 55, 59, 65, 68, 69, 70, 73, 96, 104, 139, 149, 159, 160, 162, 169, 170
Leopardstown Hospital 214–15, 224, 241
Liffey, River 18, 30, 224
Limerick 14, 19, 24, 192, 227, 234
Linenhall Buildings 12
Linfield, F.C. 101
Lisburn 181
Little Britain 213
Liverpool 2, 41, 42, 43, 101
London 16, 19, 21, 23, 29, 38, 117, 163, 165, 185, 189, 221, 222, 223, 229
Londonderry (or Derry) 14, 29, 195, 198–200, 213
Longford 26, 217, 218
Lough Tay 57
Loughborough 14
Lughnasa 133
Luke, Captain 94
Lusitania 1, 44, 163
Lutyens, Edward 216, 227
Luxor 191
Lyons, F.S.L. 225

Macedonia 150, 166–7, 191, 193, 194, 198, 207, 231–2, 240
MacDonagh, Thomas 194, 197, 199
MacWilliam, Lieutenant O.G.E. *see also* Juvenis 55, 183
Mafeking 12
Mahon, General Bryan 12, 25, 27, 35, 38, 50, 51–2, 54, 58, 67, 69, 73, 79, 84, 85, 93, 110, 111, 121, 133, 138–40, 157, 160, 212, 216
Malta 46, 47, 57, 63, 163, 166
Manchester 21, 198
Manchester Regiment 75, 154
Mansion House 195
Maoris 142
Markievicz, Constance 15, 31
Markree 18, 212
Marmara, Sea of 49
Marne, River 29

'Marseillaise', 'The' 56
Martin Family 15
Martin, Charles (or Charlie) 15, 192
Martin, F.X. 223
Martin, Marie 15
Martin, Ross 148
Martin, Tommy (or Thomas) 15
Marylebone 19
Mauretania 1–2, 42, 43, 51, 60, 163, 229
Mauser 86, 236
Maxwell, General 94
Mayo, Co. 168
Meath, Co. 17, 24, 29, 219
Mediterranean 1, 4, 27, 40, 41, 42–3, 45–6, 47, 49, 50, 51, 54, 63, 66, 68, 115, 116, 119, 138, 142, 144, 161, 162, 163, 166–7, 170, 171, 172, 200, 231, 235, 236
Mediterranean Expeditionary Force 27, 50, 51, 188
Megiddo 202
Melville, S.S. 46
Messines 226, 227, 231
Mikra Military Cemetery 192
Mitylene 51–2, 53, 54, 55, 56–7, 59, 65, 68, 70, 150, 160, 199
Monaghan, Co. 16
Money, Major 147
Monkstown 15, 192
Moody, T.W. 223
Morocco 47
Morris, Bert 40
Mortimer, Lieutenant 117
Morto Bay 230
Mosley, Oswald 221
Moulin Rouge 48
Mourne Mountains 11, 19
Mudros 51, 52, 53, 54, 56, 65, 69, 71, 111, 112, 121, 145, 161, 163, 166, 168, 170
Mullingar 25, 219
Munster 20, 21, 38, 84, 133
Murphy, Father 28, 117, 167, 171, 221
Murray, Cecil 14, 123, 135
Mustafa Kemal (or Kemal Atatürk) 87, 94, 97, 100, 107, 111, 125, 142, 153, 157, 232

1937 Reading Room 219
9th Army Corps (or 9th Corps) 50, 51, 52, 53, 58, 68–9, 71, 85, 86, 87, 100, 110, 138, 154, 157
Naas 190
Naples 163
Napoleon 145
National Army Museum 223
National University 215, 234

Nazism 231, 235
Nealon, Sergeant 168
Nek, The 230
New Jersey 20
New Zealand 49, 58, 66, 140–2
Newbridge 26
Newbury 38
Newcastle, Co. Down 11
Newcastle-on-Tyne 10
Nibrunesi Point 74, 76, 79, 102, 115
Nicholl, Brigadier L.J. 13, 68, 124, 127, 158
Nile, River 162
Nitonian, S.S. 43, 46
Norfolk Street 229
North Irish Horse 11
Northern Ireland 210, 216, 218, 224, 225
Northern Whig 189
Northumberland Road 195
Novian, S.S. 42, 47
Nugent, Captain 143, 146

O'Carroll, Lieutenant 117
O'Connor, Father 149, 167
O'Donnell, Peadar 219
O'Farrell, Father 167
O'Higgins, Kevin 216
O'Leary, Joe 14, 48, 191–2, 203, 207, 211, 242
Odiham 40
Odysseus 235
Offaly, Co. 26
Orange Order 216, 218
Osmanieh, S.S. 169
Ottoman Empire 85, 201
Oxford 20

Palestine 166, 193, 201
Pals 16, 18, 23, 30, 32–3, 37, 45, 48, 51, 56, 70–1, 74–5, 80–2, 90, 114–15, 122–3, 187, 195, 206, 211, 219, 222
Parke, J.C. 16, 168
Parkhurst Goal 229
Patmos 166
Pearse, Patrick 12, 17, 31, 59, 181, 194, 199, 228, 233, 234
Perdita, S.S. 170
Perry, Terence 229
Phillips, Frank 183
Phoenix Park 24, 25, 27, 216
Piccadilly Tea Rooms 48
Pimple, The 83, 123
Pisparaghon 52, 54
Plymouth 41, 163
Pogues, The 229
Pontefract 20

Port Iero 52, 54, 57, 65
Portadown 14, 218
Portaferry 181
Portobello 183, 196
Powerscourt 14
Presentation College, Glasthule 14
Preston, Johnny 122, 126
Punchestown 212

Queen Elizabeth II 22, 226
Queen Mary 37
Quinn Family 29
Quoile, River 180

Rabrovo 231, 232, 240
Rawlinson, Sir Henry 50
Red Branch Knights 9
Red Cross 98, 113, 115, 131, 132, 159, 163, 167
Redmond, John 9, 14, 21–2, 37, 188–9, 223, 229
Remembrance Day 209, 215, 220, 225
Renvyle 10, 17
Reynolds, Harry 203
Rhododendron Ridge 6
Rhododendron Spur 142, 149
Richards, Lieutenant (or Richards, Billy) 122, 125–6
Richmond Barracks 24, 197, 199
Roberts, Lord 17
Rossa, O'Donovan 59, 181
Rostrevor 221
Roundwood 57
Royal Army Medical Corps (or Medical Corps) 15, 19, 38, 161
Royal Barracks 33–5, 197
Royal Botanic Gardens 14
Royal British Legion 217, 218, 221, 224
Royal College of Surgeons 30
Royal Dublin Fusiliers (or Dublin Fusiliers or Dublins) 8, 13, 15, 16, 18, 23, 26, 27, 30, 34–5, 38, 40, 41, 45, 48, 56, 71, 73, 81, 82, 83, 94, 96, 97, 115, 117, 118, 122–5, 140, 145, 150, 151, 152, 158, 169, 184, 185, 186, 190, 192, 197, 198, 213, 227
Royal Engineers 43, 52, 71, 84, 111, 151, 160, 169
Royal Inniskilling Fusiliers (or Inniskillings) 8, 13, 17, 24, 29, 52, 55, 70, 73, 76–7, 83, 84, 91–2, 93, 99, 101, 102, 113, 116, 121, 165, 187, 222
Royal Irish Constabulary 18, 208, 210, 214

Royal Irish Fusiliers (or Irish Fusiliers) 13, 15, 48, 70, 82, 87, 90, 97, 112, 118, 121, 128, 133, 170, 183
Royal Irish Regiment 8, 13, 43, 52, 83, 111, 133, 161
Royal Irish Rifles (or Irish Rifles or Rifles) 11, 13, 19, 41, 67, 115, 142, 143, 144, 148, 183
Royal Marines 47
Royal Munster Fusiliers (or Munsters) 13, 15, 20, 25, 33, 80, 92, 93, 122, 174

2nd Mounted Division 150, 153
6th Battalion Lincolns 94
6th Battalion Royal Dublin Fusiliers 23, 27, 38, 41, 45, 71, 83, 94, 97, 117, 118, 124, 150, 151, 169
6th Battalion Royal Inniskilling Fusiliers 102
7th Battalion Royal Munster Fusiliers 25
7th Division (Turkish) 86–7
16th Division 21–22, 37, 43, 223, 226, 227, 233
Sackville Bridge 30
Sackville Street 28, 194, 195, 198
Sahara 193
Sailors and Soldiers Land Trust 213
Salisbury 39
Sally Gap 57
Salonika 167, 191–2, 200, 216
Salvation Army 19
Samothrace 77, 78, 117, 120, 155, 236
Sandy Row 101
Sari Bair 121, 140, 144
Savoy Hotel 222
Scimitar Hill 94, 96, 97, 119, 152–3
Scotland 21, 117, 160
Second World War 222
Serbia 191, 193
Shanahan, Colonel 117
Shantallow 213
Shelbourne Road 195
Shrapnel Gully 140–1
Sikhs 142
Sinn Féin 194, 199, 203, 208, 215
Sitwell, General 79–80, 87
Skerries 14, 191, 203, 211, 242
Skibbereen 14
Skye 117
Slane 17, 24, 39, 199, 201
Sligo 68, 145, 217
Sligo, Co. 18, 20, 212
Smyrna 52, 56, 70, 86
Snaefell 70, 236
Somme 3, 190, 211, 213, 216, 218,

219, 231, 233
Somme Association 226, 235
Somme Heritage Centre 226
South Africa 12, 25, 140, 156
South America 9
South Dublin Union 197
Southampton 29
Spartans 190
Spence, Robert 181–2
St John 166
St Paul 46, 234
Stafford, Father 120, 167, 172, 185
Stanley Bay 48, 64
Stephenson, R. 183
Stopford, Lt. General Sir Frederick
    50, 51, 58, 66–7, 69, 72, 79, 85, 87,
    110, 138–9
Strabane 123
Struma Valley 191, 192
Suffolk Street 27
Sussex Lodge Hospital 163
Suvla 4, 58, 66, 68, 71, 72, 73, 78, 79,
    80, 82, 85, 86, 87, 88, 89, 90, 91, 93,
    94, 96, 98, 100, 102, 105–09, 110,
    111, 112, 113, 114, 115, 116, 117,
    119, 120, 120, 123, 127, 129, 131,
    133, 135, 137, 139, 140, 141, 143,
    145, 150, 153, 154, 155, 156, 157,
    158, 159, 160, 163, 164, 165, 169,
    171, 172–3, 174, 179, 180, 182, 183,
    184, 186, 187, 188, 189, 190, 191–2,
    193, 195, 200, 202, 203, 204, 209,
    210, 211, 212, 214, 220, 221, 222,
    223, 228, 230, 233, 234, 235, 237
Suvla Bay 1, 4, 48, 49–50, 52, 68,
    71–3, 76, 77, 78, 80, 83, 86, 87–8,
    89, 90, 93, 100, 101, 133, 138, 139,
    140, 151, 152, 154, 155, 159, 160,
    161, 165, 169, 173, 181, 188, 196,
    215, 217, 218, 228, 230, 235, 237
Suvla Plain 72, 78, 81, 90, 99, 116,
    121
Suvla Point 113, 115, 127, 134, 151

10th (Irish) Division (or 10th
    Division) 1, 2–4, 10, 12, 13, 14,
    15, 18, 19–20, 22, 24, 25, 26, 29,
    31, 35, 37, 38, 40, 41, 42, 46, 47,
    48, 50, 51, 54, 56, 58, 59, 61, 68–9,
    71, 72–3, 75, 78, 79, 80, 85, 87–8,
    89, 93, 96, 97, 98, 100, 110, 112,
    113, 114, 120, 125, 127, 130, 132,
    133, 138, 139, 145, 149, 150, 151,
    152, 153, 155, 159, 161, 166, 167,
    168, 170, 172, 173, 180, 184, 188,
    189, 191, 192, 193, 194, 195, 196,

197, 198, 201–02, 210, 211,
    216–17, 218, 219, 220, 221, 222,
    223, 225, 227, 228, 229, 231, 232,
    233, 234, 235, 236, 237, 238, 240
12th Division (Irish) 20
12th Division (Turkish) 86–7
12th Lancers 30
13th Division 38, 148, 150
29th Brigade 13, 58, 66, 140–1, 143,
    145, 148, 149, 167, 168, 197
29th Division 138, 150, 152, 183,
    188, 228
29th Field Ambulance Brigade 67
30th Brigade 13, 52, 67, 99, 121,
    124–5, 127, 128, 159, 169
30th Field Ambulance Brigade 53,
    84, 111, 114, 159
31st Brigade 13, 52, 84, 121, 128
31st Field Ambulance Brigade 89,
    127, 132
33rd Brigade 95
36th Division or (36th Ulster
    Division) 21–2, 43, 190, 218, 223,
    226, 227, 233
Tadley 40
Tangier 47
Tekke Tepe 86, 87, 88, 100, 112, 121
Temple Hill 162
Tennyson, Lord Alfred 15
Thomas, G.E. 27
Thompson, Major 187
Tipperary 41, 48
Tipperary, Co. 214
Tippett, Major 81, 82
Titanic 44
Tralee 14, 20
Transylvania 43
Trinity College, Dublin 16, 18, 81,
    123, 215, 219, 234
Trinity College Officer Training
    Corps 17, 18, 23, 30
Troy 3, 54, 77, 116, 172
Turk's Head 52
Turkey 1, 5, 27, 38, 40, 41, 43, 48,
    49, 52, 54, 56, 57, 58, 66, 68, 69,
    70, 72, 73, 74, 75, 76, 77, 78, 79,
    80, 81, 83, 85, 86, 87, 88, 89, 90,
    91, 92, 93, 94, 95, 96, 97, 98, 100,
    108–09, 112, 114, 115, 118,
    119–20, 122, 125, 127, 128, 129,
    131, 132, 133, 140, 141, 142, 143,
    145, 146, 147, 151, 152, 153, 154,
    155, 158, 159, 165, 167, 168, 169,
    171, 172, 173, 174, 177, 182, 186,
    187, 191, 196, 202, 212, 216, 228,
    230, 231, 232, 236, 237
Two Tree Hill 153

Tynan, Katherine 187–8, 201
Tynte, Major 122
Tyrone, Co. 123

U Boats 44, 51
Ulster 11, 14, 21, 190, 210, 218, 224,
    228, 235
Ulster Volunteer Force 12, 13, 21,
    233
Ulysses 235
United Kingdom 226
United Nations 232
University Chapel 188

Valentia Island 25
Valletta 47, 48
Vaughey, Ellie 39

W hills 94, 157
War of Independence 209
Waterford 19
Waterloo 8
Waterloo Station 29
Weir, Peter 230
Wellington Barracks 196
Wellington, Duke of 8, 145
Western Front 2, 3, 26, 43, 44, 49,
    50, 87, 114, 159, 201, 224, 227,
    231, 233
Westmeath, Co. 214, 219, 245
Whitechurch 40
Whyte, Bill 122, 221
Whyte, Matthew 46
Wicklow 21, 24
Wicklow, Co. 14, 21, 57, 220
Wilkin, Private 125
Willis, John 15, 203
Willis, Philip 15
Wilson's Hospital School 219
Wiltshire Regiment 144
Windsor Castle 221, 240
Wisely, Lieutenant F.J. 183
Woodbines 50
Woodenbridge 21
Worship, Colonel V. 186

Yeats, W.B. 235
Yorkshire 20, 21, 29
Ypres 3, 200, 201, 231
Yugoslavia 216, 232

Zeus 116